T0336339

Praise for Barbara Jo Brothers and

WELL-BEING
WRIT LARGE

"[Barbara Jo Brothers] is an exquisite writer who captures the essence of Virginia Satir's teachings brilliantly. I think that this work will be a wonderful addition to those wishing to have a deeper understanding of [Satir's] work."

—**Sharon Loeschen**, president of the
Virginia Satir Global Network

"What Barbara Jo Brothers has done with her book is far beyond anyone's work on Virginia Satir to date. Brothers has captured the essence of Satir along with her message and the depth of her process. I am grateful!"

—**Laura Dodson MSW, PhD**, Jungian analyst,
president and founder of the Institute for International Connections

"Satir's ideas can inform psychotherapists, whatever their orientation. Her ideas dovetail beautifully with anyone's clinical work because it comes from the love for the patient and a deep understanding of humans. Her work transcends theory and technique."

—**Carolyn A. Weyand, PhD**, psychologist/psychoanalyst

"MAGNIFICENT—beautifully written, filled with the real, true Virginia Satir. This book will bring back Virginia into the international milieu, which now more than ever before requires her seed principles if this world is going to survive. It offers such a cogent and practical way of seeing her work as well as a luminous portrait of Virginia herself that one is drawn to this master teacher and psychologist as if she were one's finest family member. She becomes the World Aunt and the one who profoundly makes the difference in our very survival as a species."

—**Jean Houston**, scholar, philosopher, teacher,
and researcher in human capacities,
consultant to the United Nations,
UNICEF, and other international agencies

"I can say that [*Well-Being Writ Large*] absolutely held me fast to the end. Barbara Jo Brothers has such an unusual inside view of Virginia Satir and her teachings, and has shared them in a more human than academic way. I sense a dedication to this body of research and personal observation, and her passion to keep these teachings alive and available. *Well-Being Writ Large* should add greatly to the body of available research on the Satir teachings. I applaud Brothers for her dedicated efforts."

—**Sandra Thomas, PhD**, former president of
Converse College, South Carolina

"Brilliant. [Brothers has] such appreciation for the connections and bridges in thought and purpose. Part of what impresses me so much about [*Well-Being Writ Large*] is [Brothers's] generous (and exciting) work of placing Virginia's writings in the company of other great thinkers. It's almost as if they had all just been sitting around a fireplace having a chat together."

—**Judith Bula Wise, PhD**, professor emerita and Satir scholar,
graduate school of Social Work, University of Denver

"In the forty years since her untimely death, the genius and teachings of the 'mother of family therapy,' Virginia Satir, have spread throughout the world, with active training programs on at least three continents. As time passes, the number of professionals who knew and trained with her is rapidly decreasing and it is vital that her essential thoughts and words maintain their freshness and vitality for future workers in the field. As one of her colleagues, and one who early recognized the genius of her teachings, Barbara Jo Brothers, former editor of the *Journal of Couples Therapy*, has been in a unique position to collect, record, compile, and discuss her many writings and teachings. And here it is, the essential teachings of Virginia—in her own words—including her wide-ranging ideas behind her revolutionary seed model of human development. An invaluable resource for any and all persons who want to help families live and communicate more joyfully and effectively."

—**DeWitt "Bud" Baldwin**, MD, professor Emeritus of Psychiatry and Behavioral Sciences, University of Nevada Medical School and adjunct professor of Psychiatry and Behavioral Sciences, Northwestern University Feinburg School of Medicine

"Barbara Jo Brothers, a longtime friend and student of Virginia Satir—world renowned family systems therapist—has captured the 'magic' of this remarkable woman through clear, understandable language and diagrams. Providing recipe and roadmap, Brothers has captured the personhood as well as the thought process of Virginia Satir in this remarkable book of scholarship. There is something for the neophyte as well as the seasoned clinician. *Well-Being Writ Large* serves as clinical guide and companion piece to Virginia's book, *People Making*. A must-read for all family therapists."

—**Wray Pascoe, PhD**, AAMFT clinical fellow

WELL-BEING WRIT LARGE

The Essential Work of
VIRGINIA SATIR

Well-Being Writ Large

The Essential Work of Virginia Satir

BARBARA JO BROTHERS

BEYOND WORDS

Hillsboro, Oregon

BEYOND WORDS

8427 N.E. Cornell Road, Suite 500
Hillsboro, Oregon 97124-9808
503-531-8700 / 503-531-8773 fax
www.beyondword.com

First Beyond Words hardcover edition January 2019

Beyond Words Publishing is an imprint of Simon & Schuster, Inc., and the Beyond Words logo is a registered trademark of Beyond Words Publishing, Inc.

For information about special discounts for bulk purchases, please contact Beyond Words Special Sales at 503-531-8700 or specialsales@beyondword.com.

Managing Editor: Lindsay S. Easterbrooks-Brown
Copyeditor: Kristin Thiel
Proofreader: Michelle Blair
Jacket design: Trish Broersma
Interior design: Devon Smith
Composition: William H. Brunson Typography Services

The text of this book was set in Minion Pro.

Manufactured in the United States of America

10 9 8 7 6 5 4 3 2 1

Library of Congress Cataloging-in-Publication Data

Names: Brothers, Barbara Jo, 1940– author.
Title: Well-being writ large : the essential work of Virginia Satir / Barbara Jo Brothers.
Description: Hillsboro, Oregon : Beyond Words, [2019] | Includes bibliographical references and index.
Identifiers: LCCN 2018025940| ISBN 9781582706337 (hardcover) | ISBN 9781582706993 (eBook)
Subjects: LCSH: Satir, Virginia. | Family therapists—United States—Biography. |
Women psychologists—United States—Biography. | Family psychotherapy—Philosophy.
Classification: LCC RC488.5 .B74 2019 | DDC 616.89/156092 [B] —dc23
LC record available at https://lccn.loc.gov/2018025940

The corporate mission of Beyond Words Publishing, Inc.: *Inspire to Integrity*

These words are dedicated to
Virginia Satir and Sister Fara Impastato,
both radiant beacons:

The quality of mercy is not strained;
it droppeth as the gentle rain from Heaven…

—William Shakespeare,
The Merchant of Venice

Contents

Foreword

by Jean Houston

As a consultant to agencies within the United Nations as well as to related international forums and organizations, I have traveled extensively throughout the world, visiting many countries and cultures as an advisor and trainer in human and social development. My work aims at developing social artists, leaders in many fields who seek an evolutionary model of both personal and social change. I strongly feel that the world that works embraces the understanding of the planet as an ecology, a complex adaptive system in which personal, global, and universal awareness is applied to local concerns.

What was always surprising was that in many of the countries I worked, I would find that Virginia Satir had been there before me, a kind of female Johnny Appleseed sowing her own unique brand of seeds. Indeed, as Barbara Jo Brothers says in this extraordinary book on the work of Virginia, "She wanted to bring attention to the fact that the organic seed model *is* the underlying principle, the natural order of the universe. This principle is that each living entity's natural process is to grow—to unfold the amazing potential packed in tiny bits of life."

Traveling and teaching as many as 352 days a year, Virginia seemed to have touched down everywhere. Once, in an Australian Aboriginal community, I encountered members using her work and words to re-create the power of their culture, restore their self-esteem after two hundred years of denigration, and rediscover the sacrality of their relationships to nature and each other. I recall my meeting with Taiwanese psychologists who were helping to release Chinese families from centuries of repression by incorporating Virginia's methods of truth-telling and appreciation. In cultures globally, I found her vivid presence had diminished cycles of hatred, mended families, and brought people together in teaching–learning communities of peacemakers and pathfinders, outposts of the heart of a borning civilization. She was their mother, their midwife of souls, their guide to the ways and means of creating a world that works.

It may well be that despite present chaos as ancient outworn models have their final catharsis, the world has turned a corner because Virginia has lived.

What you are about to read is a brilliant and luminous presentation of the genius and practices of Virginia and her methods. Barbara, her long-time student, has given us a life work, a potent and profound presentation of the nature of Virginia's unique form of therapy. Virginia's emphasis was always on potential rather than pathology. Barbara shows us the ways in which Virginia created relationships of safety, challenge, and support for others, both as individuals and within families and groups, to move beyond caustic behaviors into new ways of living based on a vision of freedom, fairness, authenticity, and full expression of the hidden genius of the self. Her ultimate method was showing people how to live well in relationship with oneself, one's family, one's community, and the world. She believed the well-lived life to be not only a real possibility but a basic and universal human right. In this, she pioneered the basis for a new conception of humanity.

As Barbara demonstrates, "This ability to perceive and focus on potential rather than pathology set her apart from most of her colleagues. Virginia was never preoccupied with mere problem solving; her focus was on freeing each human being for awareness of living within the context of What Is and for full expression of self."

Virginia pioneered the basis for a whole new civilization as well as a whole new science of human becoming. She was virtually a quantum physicist of human dynamics. She understood that human beings are not encapsulated bags of skin, dragging around a dreary ego. Rather, they are organism environments—"intricate psychobioelectric-chemical-metaphysical-social interrelated systems in interaction with other such systems"—and thus, when allowed to see and be deeply seen, they know themselves as God-stuff encased in biodegradable space-time suits!

Perhaps we are living in the time of speciation, when the next level of evolutionary development emerges. For Virginia, hers was the recognition that humanity and the cosmos are inextricably related; in fact, we do not just live in the Universe but the Universe lives in us. This recognition can shift consciousness in ways that bring humanity toward higher reaches of human possibility. Then we become what we were always intended to be: the possible human who can create a more possible world. As Barbara clearly shows, this constitutes a new development of consciousness.

Clearly, in the psychological world, this requires the need for training therapists in becoming fully human. At a recent meeting of therapists from the world over, I experienced the continuing gratitude that many felt about their training with Virginia. As one told me, "Under her guidance, I became alive not only to my own essence but to the vast potential that resides in all of us. And above all, to her discovery that to heal the family is to heal the world."

Observing Virginia's seminars, one would witness years of trauma and trouble evaporate in hours. People who were in dread of each other were brought up and reintroduced to each other in ways that established a new and higher story between them. Virginia shared with them her gift of deep seeing, evoking the essence of who each was in his or her fullness. When she did this with families or people in relationship, the results were often astonishing, years of trauma and projection falling away in a few hours.

Virginia Satir, the luminous family therapist, "people-maker," and all-around facilitator of self-esteem and awareness would be so pleased with the ways in which Barbara Jo Brothers has studied and presented her work, as you the reader will be too. To meet Virginia within the rich and thoughtful guidance of Barbara is to understand the magnificence of her extraordinary self and the legacy that she has left us.

PREFACE

I have had the distinct privilege of experiencing the unique person of Virginia Satir: to meet, to watch, to listen, to question, to consider, to interview—in essence, to sit at her feet—and ultimately to tell the story of her work. Before I get to her work, allow me to share some of her own words of how she came to it.

I met Virginia in 1968 after having watched her from afar for three years. I participated in two and a half months of residential training, then crossed paths with her numerous times throughout her life. In 1982, I made an opportunity to interview her. I was interested in how she got started, so I asked her how she got from where she began to where she was then. She replied:

> I started out as an educator, teaching, and instinctively I did two things. First, I didn't want to be an armchair expert, and that meant that I wanted to teach a variety of kids. You remember that my earlier wish was to become a children's detective on parents, and that led me into teaching. Second, I wanted to know the kids, so every single night after school, I would go home with a child except when there were teachers' meetings. My kids always did well, and one of the reasons they did well was because I was so close to their families. I saw

all kinds of things going on in the families. Like one episode I remember: A little kid about ten years old came to school one morning and he looked so awful. I said, "What happened to you?" He said, "I was locked out last night. My father was drunk, and I was locked out." That night, I went home with him, and I talked to his father. I wasn't psychiatrically alert at the time so I didn't have any trouble talking to the father. Because I got to know the families so intimately, I saw all these problems. So I thought, there's got to be more I need to learn about all this. That's when I decided to go on for an advanced degree to help me understand about all these problems, and all I knew about was social work. That was in 1936; [in 1937] I started my first summer school at Northwestern University because I wanted answers. In another place, St. Louis, the mother of one little boy told me that I should watch him when he was in shop because he would "get lapses," and he could saw himself right through and not know it. She told me he had been tied to a tree by some older boys when he was five years old and had been sexually molested. After that time, he got these "lapses." I certainly watched him, but I also developed a puppet theater. (I didn't do this because of him but simply to have fun in the classroom.) Through a little series of incidences, this kid, who was very small for his age, became the villain in the puppet play, and he became the savior in the puppet play so many times. After that he lost the "lapses," began growing, and just became a normal little boy. There were a lot of things like this, but I didn't know why they happened. Anyway, I was always looking for information for how things could be better for people. I wanted to understand what was going on. I never went into social work to become a social worker. I went into social work to find information to help me understand about people.

I had seen Virginia interview a family in New Orleans in 1965. Then I saw her interview another family in 1968. There had been a dramatic difference between those two times, and I asked her about what had happened in those three intervening years:

Yes, I got involved with Esalen between 1965 and 1968, and that was when I got into what we called the affective domain, so I was bringing another whole growth dimension into my work. That was the beginning of a lot of new things because at that time I was associating with people like Fritz Perls, Ida Rolf, Jim Simkin, and all kinds of people in relation to that. It was also the time when I did work in Cleveland at the Gestalt Institute and all kinds of places. So I was integrating a whole lot more things, plus learning about an area that I had not known anything about: the whole affective domain. So what was happening, I'm sure, is that I knew a lot more, I had done lots of things with families, I had opened up entirely new possibilities for people, and that still continues. If you saw me treat today, I'm sure you'd see the same general things, but the whole way in which I manage things is different.

I commented that she seemed a lot freer, expanded. She agreed:

Yes, I think that's true, and I think that continues. If you had seen me work with a family the other day, I think you would have seen me even more so, but now I have plugged in the whole spiritual thing. I have eight levels of things I look and work at now. I've learned a lot more about systems. I keep on learning more. I know a lot more now about integration of right brain–left brain learning, all the things about how we take in things, and all the channeling and stuff that Richard Bandler and John Grinder extracted from my work, with my permission at the beginning—the psycholinguistics part that was going on in relation to that. I have been learning a lot more. I'm sure that I grew in my feeling of comfort about what I'm doing. Just remember: I was the only woman for years with mostly [male] physicians. I have seen more families than anybody else practicing in the field. And I know that. Which I never thought about, but I had.

My final question was, "What do you feel has been your major contribution to the field of psychotherapy?"

I was thinking about that yesterday. I think the main things—there are two—are hope and that the therapist needs to be a person, a whole, full person in carrying it on. Those are the two main things. Third, of course, I can make it light, because people often comment on my sense of humor, so it doesn't have to be so tragic. My hunch is that those are the three most important things. The ideas and the ways that I choreograph stuff excite people, and they see new possibilities. That's based, of course, on the idea that as long as something remains in an abstract form, it doesn't have any life; when I make body pictures and things of that sort, then it comes to life.

When I asked Virginia, "How shall we bring this to a close?" Virginia's response was to ask me how I felt about what was going on between us during the interview. (So typical of her . . . Why was I surprised again to feel that shift back out of the head?) To stop and ask how I felt was an invitation for interaction, for the human kind of completion that is so characteristic of Virginia and her work. The importance of allowing for the natural flow of communication and the attendant importance of expression of self . . . the therapist needs to be a person, the educator needs to be a person, the interviewer and interviewee are both persons—this is her basic theme. I believe this humanization of all aspects of interpersonal interaction is Virginia's richest contribution to psychotherapy: the one-two-three steps toward the visibility of the human beings before whom we sit, the learnable/teachable components of the route toward my seeing, hearing, feeling who you are, and, as an integral part of that process, my showing me to you.

Thank you, Virginia.[1]

Virginia Satir for the Twenty-First Century

Today, I still believe that Virginia Satir's work shows her understanding that all life is relational and the Universe is a network of interconnected systems. Knowing that no individual functions or even exists in solitude is the awareness that took her the step beyond earlier great thinkers such as Sigmund Freud and Carl Jung. Their focus was wholly on the inherently limited and unrealistic concept of individual dynamics.

Virginia's work writ large is this: a vision and blueprint for world peace.

Describing herself as a combination of Johnny Appleseed and Paul Revere, she frankly said that her primary goal was changing consciousness on a massive scale. Shifting the consciousness of enough people—reaching critical mass—would liberate the world from narrow, unrealistic thinking, delivering humankind from the familiar bloody threat and reward model under which we all suffer.

This book examines the ingredients Virginia put forth and elucidates the steps she took and taught to move humanity down the path toward wholeness. It builds on her own books, *The New Peoplemaking* and *The Satir Model*, showing the framework underneath.

Virginia developed a shorthand caption for the design of this movement toward the "wholing" of humanity: "peace within, peace between, peace among." In "peace," by no means did she mean passivity. For Virginia, peace is a dynamic, ever active dance toward the embrace of reality coupled with profound respect for the uniqueness of each specific person.

A comprehensive definition of peace as far more than simply the absence of war is not unique to Virginia. Jacob Needleman, professor of philosophy, said:

> Something infinitely more honorable than war, infinitely more active and requiring a higher level of courage and sacrifice, and which shows . . . the real essence of . . . ideals of what it means to be human beings and to care for each other. This is peace on the field of life in all its vibrancy. (Needleman, 2002, 215)

Virginia did more than define. She was quite clear on this concept and came up with specific training exercises to expand the humanity aspect of a person's quest for her or his specific being in the world. As Virginia so often said, "to care for each other" is a "teachable/learnable skill." Virginia not only understood peace as an active process, she addressed herself to the nuts and bolts of bringing that process into being within family systems. She taught the ways and means.

The purpose of this book is to track those ways and means—Virginia's discovery about how "peace within" an individual relates to "peace between" two individuals and may generate "peace among" an entire community. The phrases appear on a postcard made from a photograph taken of Virginia toward the end of her seminar in Russia in 1988, just months before her death. The seminar contained the elements of becoming more fully human, as did all of her seminars. In this important location, she had taught the process of peace within, leading to peace between, leading to peace among, in a group of American and Russian psychotherapists. It poignantly symbolizes the last stop in her own journey in creating "peace among."

Peace within depends upon valuing the self; peace between depends on acknowledging the worth of the other; peace among is an aggregate of people respecting selves and others. Effective communication and its relationship to self-worth can move from one person to that person's family and out to the wider community.

Virginia saw her basic task as generating a worldwide shift in consciousness toward a more realistic assessment of the worth of self and others. Amplifying respect to this magnitude could have enormous positive consequences for humanity—for all living things.

Basic to the work is Virginia's acceptance of the seed—or growth—model as the fundamental charter of the Universe. One does not so much learn how "to use" the seed/growth model as one learns how to stay out of its way. The model is awareness of process: constantly active reality. What this means is so obvious, yet tragic numbers of parents, educators, and community leaders miss acting accordingly. Honoring the seed model means observing the nature of a living being, seeing what it needs to thrive, removing obstacles from its growth path, and adding nurturing ingredients to the mix.

Virginia's awareness and conscious use of the seed/growth model emerged, at least to some extent, from her understanding of how quantum theory and modern physics relate to human nature. She quite consciously designed her work and training in such a way as to accommodate and reflect modern science's increasingly more accurate picture of our world. In her careful crafting of communication, she taught the appropriate use of language as a means of reflecting the basic principles of the cosmos (see chapter 11). Steering students and family members away from the toxic habit of labels, she kept the focus on the dynamics of interaction. Just as the universe is not a vast set of adjacent, separate boxes floating in space, neither are specific human beings. Modern physics tells us this truth about the universe. Virginia created a therapeutic mode that reflects the latter. That innovation, based on that comprehensive premise of cosmic relatedness, was her step beyond Freud and Jung.

Virginia's genius lay in large part in her understanding of the importance of observation as key to the process of understanding. Her childhood on a Wisconsin farm brought her into proximity with the nature of growing things. She never forgot that experience: living things grow with fierce persistence no matter how deviously, according to the inner life process contained within the seed that thrust that entity into existence. This is the fact that guided Virginia's discovery: the deliberate use of the powerful yet delicate, inner-changing freeing process that follows the trail of the burgeoning seed.

In essence, Virginia discovered a process of collaboration with the fundamental charter of the universe. As she made the discovery, she developed methods of teaching people how to board the same train of thought, followed by germane action. Virginia not only learned how to view therapy "outside the box"—she *opened* the box.

Growth is a constant state. Unless a living thing is outright killed, the path charted at whatever point life first activates, from cell and seed, continues within a given entity. Growth persists—blindly, mindlessly, sometimes even at the price of its host's life. Growth, in one form or another, is a given.

With her deep reverence for the Life Process, Virginia developed ways to move with that flow, to make truly *conscious* the drift of human consciousness. She found that fighting the current is counterproductive and squanders or perverts energy that is pushing toward growth. Rather than looking at eliminating symptoms, she looked at freeing the energy bound in those symptoms.

Virginia believed she was but "re-minding" her students and clients: everything is process; everything is in the process, not the content. Shift the process, and our world shifts with it.

Chapter Note

1. Excerpt from "Virginia Satir: Past to Present," written from an interview with Virginia Satir by Barbara Jo Brothers. This was published in Voices: *The Art and Science of Psychotherapy*, volume 18, number 4; Winter 1983 issue: *Steps Toward A History of American Psychotherapy*.

1

FOUNDATION:
LIFE EQUALS GROWTH

The life force, there is no end and no beginning; it is just there. If we were to think of it as an ongoing river, every once in a while something comes together like a fountain—which is one of us—takes that life force and makes all kinds of splashes.

—**Virginia Satir**, 1982

Virginia Satir often stated that we are *all* part of a vast, universal system in which the Force of Life provides energy for growth. This is an all-encompassing system; nobody steps outside this circle.

From that fact, Virginia took the next reasonable step and examined the means of aligning with the power of the permeating energy field. She looked at the elemental patterns that sustain life in all living things and made extensive clinical observations of those patterns as they manifest in humans. She observed that growth results not from rewarding and punishing but from nurturing and removing obstacles from the path of the growing entity.

From this understanding, Virginia developed her framework: *the seed model*. As the founding mother of family therapy, Virginia both used and taught this basic seed model as the most effective means to engender constructive change in family systems and in all other human systems as well. Throughout her training, she pointed out the dysfunctionality inherent in the antithesis—the domination/submission model—on which most human systems are based. Virginia saw the domination/submission model as simplistically and artificially imposed on systems, interfering with their more basic and natural growth process. Part of her mission was to start movement toward a societal shift in consciousness—worldwide—for people to be aware of the importance of distinguishing between these two models (see chapter 13).

It was not Virginia's intent to come forth with a new model, call it "the seed model," and set about to create techniques accordingly. She never developed a technique simply for the purpose of inventing a new technique. Her intent was much broader. She wanted to bring attention to the fact that the organic seed model *is* the underlying principle, the natural order of the universe. This principle is that each living entity's natural process is to grow—to unfold the amazing potential packed in tiny bits of life, the unseen atoms and molecules whirling within the being's structure—and ineluctably stretch outward to its goal.

Virginia's work was to generate awareness and facilitate shifts of consciousness to accommodate this natural fact. She saw human beings as shining stars within the structure of creation. Virginia wanted to help sustain that light in each person, for each separate shining augments the light of the whole. She did not *invent* this seed model; she discovered its relevance to specific persons and systems. She set about revealing its ubiquitous, undergirding presence.

Working steadily, for decades, all around the world, she was also a one-woman research lab, gathering information about human interactions from many different cultures. Virginia's work included live demonstrations of Family Reconstruction (see chapter 4) with volunteers from her usually large audiences. She wanted to make clear the basic similarities among human beings regardless of ethnic origin. She was also deeply invested in the empowerment of persons, teaching the relationship between self-esteem and communication as the major route to that end. People empowered with the understanding of their own unique personhood have no need to continue the domination/submission model. Their power would be allowed to emerge from within themselves; there would be no need to demonstrate personal power by imposing it externally to control others. They would be free to follow the organic flow of their own personal form of growth and development.

From her work within thousands of different family contexts from Caracas to Hong Kong as well as all over the North American continent, Virginia made pivotal observations about the basic nature and components of growth. She designed her work from that base. Her enormous success wherever and with whomever she worked validated her observations. Application of those principles gets results: the seed model is the framework for life.

In an interview with Sheldon Kramer in January 1988, Virginia discussed her lifelong habit of working from clinical observations rather than from theory:

> I was somebody who never wanted to settle for being an armchair expert. I was sick to death of people who talked about people without knowing. I was addicted to the facts about people, so I gave myself permission—in fact, a requirement—that I spoke from experience. And when experience did not match the theories, I turned off the theory. That was something inside of me that's followed me all the time. Most people think theory first and make the experience match the theory and they throw out their experience . . . I watched the experience first

and I've found that people criticize me for it, since people take the theory first. And I wasn't like that. (Kramer, 1995, 161–162)

Virginia was immensely practical. Rather than create complex theoretical models from simple basics, she distilled complex concepts into simple statements. Every concept and statement came from keen observations of multiple subtle and complex gestures and interactions. Aware of the depth of what she was uncovering in those observations, she asked of people: "Please do not confuse simplicity with superficiality. Please do not. My work and what I do is . . . deep . . . However, every bit of it is based on simplicity . . . It's simple and powerful in a good way" (Satir, 1983b, 611).

For just one example, Virginia based some of her communication training exercises on the work of Alfred Korzybski (1933). His work with language was based on the discoveries made regarding quantum physics and how they relate to misuses in modern language (see chapter 2). Her work took into account the fundamental principles of the universe, laced here and there with Taoist philosophy, was mindfully spiritual, and always solidly grounded in careful observation of the behavior of specific human beings in interaction within systems.

The goal of this book is to elucidate the profundity packed densely within Virginia's simplicity. Her work was based on the very workings of life itself, the energy that propels the universe—both simple and complex as a single living cell. Witnessing this paradox is to keep a pecan for months—even years. Plant it and you get a tree. Eventually, more pecans emerge. With enough time, you get a grove—all from the life or growth energy, somehow loaded into a lone pecan, pushing forth from within each one. A "simple" pecan—but who knows how the pecan contains a forest within its small shell? This latent power, unquestioned by everybody, is also not *explained* by anybody.

This mystery was not lost on Virginia. She often spoke, in wonder, about the potential packed into tiny cells. She understood the implications of the seed and how creation of a nurturing environment unleashes the force of the growth lying within. This model was her foundation as she worked with those "seeds" of potential flourishing: human beings.

World leaders, by and large, are ignorant of the implications of this power. Virginia sought to rectify this ignorance through teaching as far and as widely as possible.

Virginia made clear her credo, the alignment of her work with the living force in all growing things:

> The life force, there is no end and no beginning; it is just there. If we were to think of it as an ongoing river, every once in a while something comes together like a fountain—which is [each] one of us—takes that life force and makes all kinds of splashes. Because we were born little, we will splash in accordance to what we were taught, not in terms of how we could splash in many different ways. So here are the underpinnings: we activate the life force, we codirect how things are going to happen; we do not create ourselves. Now there is a very great difference from having a picture of "how you should be" and cutting off or hiding that which does not fit. Totally different approach. So you can see that anything about child-rearing that is based on this [seed model concept of inherent natural growth] is going to lead to a totally different result than when based on this [threat/reward approach]. (Satir, 1994, 6–7)

The "different result" toward which the understanding leads is the perception of the unique nature and potential of each person and the acknowledgment of what is going on in a given moment of time. Tremendous power is available within the process of recognizing and acknowledging *What Is*, the here-and-now reality of a given current context (see chapter 7). Virginia drew our attention to the profound implications of each of us fully attending to *what is* and each of us being as packed with inner resources as that pecan that holds a forest within its small walls.

Virginia's *awareness* of those inner resources, the concept of "person-hood" and its attending ramifications, was among her richest and most important contributions to the field of mental health. She fashioned her meditative centering exercises to provide one venue for "drawing attention to your resources." In the centering exercise (see Appendix A, page 297) with which she opened and closed all training sessions, Virginia spelled out access to "going deep inside to that treasure which you call your 'self'—which you know by your name" (Satir, 1983b, 151). This concept of inner resources as treasure is by no means self-evident. Few people reach adulthood with a clear picture of the value of their own unique inner core or the value of time spent becoming familiar with that reality. Her centering exercise provides a simple practice for supportive self-validation. It was one of her routes toward engaging the whole person in her seminars and later in the student's work as a therapist.

Being selfishly "self-centered" and being centered within one's self are two very different processes. Would that every teacher and preacher, as well as every parent, might know the difference. Ignorance of the importance of self-appreciation within a context of appropriate humility is worldwide. Self-valuing and accurate self-evaluation are often denigrated because of our tendency to confuse those with narcissistic self-absorption. Virginia was the champion of the higher self, which she firmly believed exists in every human being.

This ability to perceive and focus on potential rather than pathology set her apart from most of her colleagues. Virginia was never preoccupied with mere problem solving; her focus was on freeing each human being for awareness of living within the context of What Is and for full expression of self. She wrote:

To reawaken the freedom to look, the freedom to touch, and the freedom to listen is a vital part of what restores the human being's ability to function. When you placed yourselves in a position where you could make contact and talk freely, those two things began to restore something that was being destroyed. If you did nothing more when you have a family together than make it possible for them to really look at each other, touch each other, and listen to each other, you would have already swung the pendulum in the direction of a new start.

The meaning behind this may not be as profound to you as it is to me, but it seems basic. You can talk about all the treatment theories you like, but if you are not able to free people to contact each other, what good are theories? (Satir, 1975, 103)

Virginia did not deal in theories; she dealt with persons and their processes. She paid close attention to the nature of human interactions. In succeeding chapters, I elaborate on the significance of awareness concerning the essential uniqueness of each human being, as well as on differentiating constructive and destructive communication styles.

Different as she was from her colleagues, particularly in her earlier days, the last thing Virginia wanted was to be considered some kind of never-to-be-replicated genius anomaly in the psychotherapy world. She devoted her life to teaching what she had discovered and began a systematic training process toward that end. As she said:

It will be nice on my tombstone if they say, "Oh, Virginia was wonderful!" and everybody goes, "Yeah, Virginia was wonderful!" That's not enough for me. I want something that says: "*What Virginia did was not such a miracle. What it was is that she danced to a different drummer and she looked for different lenses.*" And, all of that is teachable. (Satir, 1987a, tape 6)

Notice, Virginia said she *danced* to a different drummer. One does not envision her marching along in any straight lines; no, Virginia came dancing through the mental health field, tossing flowers of wisdom. Even her choice of language lifts us out of the lock-step, linear way of perception. Choice of words was by no means accidental; congruent communication was always Virginia's goal.

She was seriously concerned that people understand her work as neither magic nor miracle. She had freed herself to listen and look for *what is*. What she wanted most was to be able to share her discoveries:

> One of the things that I want to do is to demonstrate that everything I do is teachable. Maybe not in the usual ways, but it is teachable. It has now been developed over and over again . . . What I pioneered so many years ago, over fifty years ago now, was freakish at that time. At this point in time, it's beginning to be mainstream. (Satir, 1987a, tape 6)

Virginia's seed model for psychotherapy is a comprehensive model for living well in relationship with oneself, one's family, one's community, and the world community. She believed the well-lived life to be not only a real possibility but a basic and universal human right.

She had discovered key universal principles in her fifty years of professional experience and she was deeply committed to public education regarding those principles. She believed it made no more sense for mental health professionals "to keep such information to themselves as mathematicians [keeping] . . . the multiplication tables to themselves" (Starr, 1991, 5).

Virginia did not use a psychoanalytic or a medical model. *Growth* was her model. Witnessing irrepressible growth from within the potency inherent in the living being brought Virginia to observe that what was often labeled pathology was simply growth gone crooked, rooted in the organic need for completion common to all living organisms. Not interested in creating another assortment of boxes with which to categorize the emotional ailments of people, not interested in tricky techniques, Virginia always made straight for the heart, looking soul-deep to find the unique person within. Her intent was to free that specificity within for full and congruent expression in the world. She often used the term "manifestation of life" when she spoke about people. She was deeply respectful of each human being, however humble or "limited."

She explained how the principle of growth applies to human behavior, how much apparent "dysfunctional" behavior is simply the thwarted growth process pushing toward completion:

> Low self worth follows the principle of growth, which says, "I want to complete myself, I want to complete myself." And that is what is going on inside of all of us, all the time: that direction toward growth. However the direction toward growth may be only to fill in a hole we feel we have.
>
> So . . . incongruent ways of communication [see chapter 6] are all forms of holes: blaming, placating, super-reasonableness, irrelevance, are all forms of holes in our own self-worth. *The nature of growth is to try to fill something up . . .*
>
> Inside of us is the push to try to grow, to try to fill in what we don't have. Growth is powerful. It will grow crooked. It will grow in all kinds of ways. The problem is not just to be concerned with growth, because that is going to go on—it is the direction of it and what we do with it.
>
> How many times, how *many times*, have I heard, I got married and I thought it was going to be Nirvana. I was going to get a child and all my problems would be taken care of. In other words, I look at you and I feel my own hole and I see you as a filler of my hole. I have a child and now, you, the child, fill my hole.

If you take my statistics, which are not necessarily exact, but are a pretty good guide, 50% of people will say yes, no matter what they feel, 30% will say no, no matter what they feel, 15% will try to inundate you with their knowledge, and 4½% will be irrelevant. That only leaves a half a percent . . . [who] will be whole and feeling their self worth. With very few exceptions, that means we all came into the world [through] people who had holes in them. And [who] used us to fill those holes. Then, of course, we learned how to be incomplete so we go around and get other people to fill our holes. I am saying this now so you can look at a condition in human beings. It is not to be judged, neither pitied, but understood. The world is only coming around to the fact that we can be whole people from the beginning.

So, if you can now—lovingly and I would really like you to do this lovingly—think about your holes, only this time you are not going to try to get other people to stuff them full. (Brothers, 1990b, 13; Satir, 1986d, tape 18; Brothers 1990, 13)*

Thus, the *push toward wholeness* is the operative dynamic in what is often seen and described as pathology. Virginia was concerned with wholeness. She understood that human beings are not linear events that occur in sequential, discreet segments. Instead, they are intensely intricate psychobioelectric-chemical-metaphysical-social interrelated systems in interaction with other such systems. Everything goes on at once and goes on all the time.

She carefully showed how behavior of each person in a group or family stemmed from that interior selfhood often cramped while yearning for release, how the resultant cramped behavior could disrupt the "system." She showed how the internal self longed not to be truncated

---

* Transcribed excerpt from a lecture given by Virginia in the Sixth Process Community Meeting.

and could dare to act congruently once affirmed—made aware of her or his power to do so.

Virginia's work was explicitly multidimensional, designed in response to her understanding that people are not one dimensional. She used an intriguing metaphor to illustrate this:

> I believe that people were meant to be round not flat . . . And that we have been surrounded for thousands of years by things that have asked us to be flat [see chapter 10]. So it is natural for sickness to be with flatness and health to be with roundness, if you follow my metaphor . . . I will be doing everything I can to respect whatever flatness I find, because that is a place that many people begin—and go towards roundness. (Satir, 1999, 5)*

The awareness of this multidimensional nature, the "roundness" of people, is a major reason Virginia put much more energy into live demonstrations—videotaped and audiotaped—than into writing books. The venue of the book was far too limiting. So far, nobody has found a way to write a holographic book. We are limited by the single-file march of the word across the page. Virginia sought to engage the whole person in training and learning events.

Virginia's own books are deceptively simple. This is because she was, quite literally, as interested in being understood by the average four-year-old as by scholars and therapists. This present book unfolds and examines the complexity behind that simplicity. She was far more interested in drawing forth the *actuality* of personhood in her seminar participants than in creating academic definitions. Never trying to

---

* Transcribed excerpt from a lecture given in Virginia's First Process Community Meeting in 1981.

impress, she was always trying to inform. She described her writing style and intended audience:

> I write in a humanistic style. We have developed an academic hierarchy. If the language is not academic, it means that the concepts are not profound.
>
> In college, I had a professor, Dr. Thorn, who said that when you wrote, if a four-year-old could not understand it, you probably did not understand it yourself. What I took him to mean was that when thoughts were clear, they could be expressed in simple language.
>
> I still feel that way. I have heard and read much in my lifetime from which it was hard to distill meaning, yet the words sounded very profound. Language can become a barrier as well as behavior.
>
> I am more interested in getting my meaning across than appearing academic. You, the reader, can translate into your particular language to make it more comfortable for you. (Satir, 1983a, 133)*

Over her lifetime, Virginia beautifully integrated an extraordinary amount of the "hard to distill." A colleague of Gregory Bateson and familiar with the work of Korzybski, she was very purposeful in her use of language, carefully constructing it to serve to clarify concepts in the training for personhood.

In this book, I take Virginia's lead in using conversational style rather than a formal, scholarly presentation. In the following pages, I explore this "third energy"—to which she refers in her centering exercises—the nature of relatedness, the concept of wholeness, and the process by which a person may become her or his own decision maker, which Virginia denominates as "one's *third birth*" (see chapter 5). We continue to con-

---

* Virginia Satir, Third Birth Notes, April 11, 1983, from her personal notes for her intended next book.

sider the motivating force of self-worth feelings and the importance of centering the self. We look at "patterns that connect" as well as "patterns that *dis*-connect"—and how those communication patterns relate to self-worth questions and personhood. We address the physical implications of incongruent communication.

Exploring the contrasting benefit of the organic seed model and the often terrible limitations of the domination/submission, threat/reward model, we look at Virginia's definitions of spirituality and how she applied her seed model to the possibility for world peace.

Finally, Virginia expressed a clear distaste for being called "Satir." Therefore, throughout this book, she will be known as "Virginia."

As this book went to publication (seventeen years after September 11, 2001), ever more cataclysmal events have occurred. Each new world-rattling, tragic terrorist attack is a reminder of the fragility of life and the importance of the healing nature of the seed model. Each new attack on anybody's shores illuminates the profound consequences in allowing the threat/reward model to dominate world affairs.

2

CHANGING CONSCIOUSNESS

All my work and writings are toward this one aim: becoming more fully human . . . [I am always looking for] means by which the wonderful resources in human beings can go beyond the old imposed idea about what should happen . . . I make no apologies for moving into totally different ways and I hope to move [in] those ways on [to] a mass level.

—**Virginia Satir**, 1986

Virginia Brought a Chalice

Virginia did not fit the form of the usual family therapist. Her span was far larger. Her intention was to facilitate—if not initiate—a major societal shift in thinking and attitude. This shift in consciousness would include the following understandings:

1. Humanity and the cosmos are inextricably interrelated.
2. Each person holds a unique spot in the overall field.
3. Recognition of the fact of uniqueness can shift consciousness of self-worth.

4. Congruence in communication is vital to self-worth and functional relationships; shifts toward congruence can, in themselves, change consciousness.

5. Add these four concepts above into the consciousness of just 6 percent of the world's population and humanity could be nudged into a mindset that would support the flourishing of our species.

"I hope to move those ways on [to] a mass level," Virginia has said—that is, she *consciously intended to effect change in the human race as a whole*. By "moving into totally different ways," she was bringing the chalice of reconciliation, cooperation, and partnership. Her intent was to replace the centuries-old strife-ridden competitive model based on who's the biggest guy on the block with a radically different one, based not on overpowering but on *em*powering. Virginia was interested in releasing a floodgate of new energy that could sweep all of humanity toward the higher reaches of its possibility. Her ability to accomplish this, on a family-by-family basis, was obvious. Why not bring the gift to all humanity!

Virginia understood the relationship between world peace and training human beings for enhancement of their own humanity. As wars rage and conflict grows around the world, it is ever more urgent that we understand what *does* work in the facilitation of human bonding and make that knowledge available to greater populations. Therapists have access to information about what makes families connect and thrive, what enables groups to resolve differences without killing each other, how to teach children discipline without beating them. We must find ways to get that information out to the rest of society; the current wars could be the prelude to the finale. The emerging specter of large-scale terrorist action dramatically intensifies the possibility. We could be running out of time.

In an interview with Sheldon Starr in 1985, when asked about training family therapists, Virginia spoke to the larger picture: the training of the human being for *being* human. If therapists are to be change agents, their own eyes need first to be cleared of the mists of the inhuman rules that most of us learn in early childhood. This paves the way for a larger shift of consciousness—bringing the information from the therapy world into the lay world. Virginia understood this:

> I equate the evolving, healthy person with a beautifully made and finely tuned instrument. Our instrument is finely made. We need to learn how to tune it better. That means developing a philosophy and an approach that are centered in human value and use the power of the seed which is based on growth and cooperation with others. (Satir, 1985)

Philosopher with Sleeves Rolled Up

Virginia was a philosopher with sleeves rolled up and apron tied on. She created living demonstrations of philosophies very old and very new; she designed processes and exercises that made experiential Lao Tzu's (1944, 1965, 1985, 1988) *Tao*, Pierre Teilhard de Chardin's (1963) ultra-human, Mahatma Gandhi's (1957) *ahimsa* [truth-force], Gregory Bateson's (1979) "pattern that connects," and theoretical physicist David Bohm's (1994) concept of coherence in speech paralleling the power in coherence of light, which forms the laser beam. Alfred Korzybski's (1933) concepts flow through her work. With the exception of Bateson's and Korzybski's work and, to some extent, Taoism, Virginia's work cannot be said to have been directly influenced by these thinkers. Nonetheless, her work embodies their principles. If they were the theorists, Virginia supplied a masterly laboratory experience. The pattern that connects, the flow of the Tao, Gandhi's truth-force, and Teilhard's ultra-human are all fundamental aspects of reality encompassed by Virginia's seed model. The model features the power of coherent speech achieved through congruence.

Healing and harmony go together. Self-esteem is the gatekeeper of congruence—which is the charioteer of harmony (see chapter 11). Congruence holds healing energy. Communication is the package congruence comes wrapped in, making possible the harmonic convergence—in the now—of body, mind, feelings, facial expression, and verbal expressions. Virginia considered healing energy—freed through congruent communication—to be a spiritual experience.

By "harmony and congruence" Virginia did *not* mean lack of conflict or affect; both are encompassed and part of that dynamic process. Not only did she consider this to be true, she lived the reality in her work.

The human being is said to be the meeting place of the energy of the earth and the energy of the heavens (invisible reality). Virginia illustrated and provided an experience of this in a centering exercise done with triads, for the specific purpose of demonstrating, to her group of trainees, how centered selves form a connected energy with each other. This freshly connected energy is another property unto itself—much more than the sum of the parts. Virginia spoke, beginning a centering meditation:

And now let yourself again come in touch with being a child of the universe . . . of feeling the sense of life force that is in all that is around you: the plants, the animals, the people, the grasses, the sky, the trees.

And as these two energies meet, the energies of inspiration and the energy of groundedness, creating still a *third energy* [italics mine]: the *energy of connectedness to other beings*, human beings. (Satir, 1983b, 102)

New Paradigm

Virginia represented a new species of therapist. She hoped to help the entire profession make an evolutionary leap and thus spoke of the need for a "new way . . . a development of consciousness" (Starr, 1992b, 9).

By that, she meant Kuhn's "paradigm shift":

The term paradigm is used in two different senses. On the one hand, it stands for the entire constellations of beliefs, values, techniques, and so on shared by the members of a given community. On the other, it denotes one sort of element in that constellation, the concrete puzzle-solutions which, employed as models or examples, can replace explicit rules as a basis for the solution of the remaining puzzles. (Kuhn, 1962, 175)

Big changes follow paradigm shifts:

[We] must first note briefly how the emergence of a paradigm affects the structure of the group that practices the field. When, in the development of a natural science, an individual or group first produces a synthesis able to attract most of the next generation's practitioners, the older schools gradually disappear. (Kuhn, 1962, 18–19)

The profundity, the seriousness of Virginia's intention, the tireless generosity of her work—which continued literally until her death—is perhaps best understood in the light of the reflections others made on the meaning of "paradigm shift."

Rupert Sheldrake, renowned British biochemist, himself trying to illustrate a new paradigm, discussed Kuhn's concept of paradigm:

Kuhn argues that normal science is a cumulative and progressive activity that consists of solving puzzles within the context of shared paradigm; but that scientific revolutions, which are extraordinary and relatively infrequent, involve the establishment of a new paradigm or framework. Typically, this does not, at least at first, make sense to practitioners brought up within the old paradigm; period of controversy ensues, which ends only when existing professionals have either been converted to the new paradigm or have died off and been replaced by a new generation familiar with it. (Sheldrake, 1988, 265–266)

In *The Passion of the Western Mind*, Richard Tarnas, professor of philosophy and psychology at the California Institute for Integral Studies in San Francisco, wrote:

The pursuit of knowledge always takes place within a given paradigm, within a conceptual matrix—a womb that provides an intellectually nourishing structure, that fosters growth and increasing complexity and sophistication—until gradually that structure is experienced as constricting, and finally a crisis is reached. Then some inspired Promethean genius comes along and is graced with an inner breakthrough to a new vision that gives the scientific mind a new sense of being cognitively connected—reconnected—to the world: an intellectual revolution occurs, and a new paradigm is born. (Tarnas, 1991, 438)

Virginia Satir was that Promethean genius.

Her work represents this kind of paradigm shift in two ways: one, her awareness of the need for training therapists in becoming fully human, which includes her recognition of worth and uniqueness in all people; two, her expansion of the use of therapeutic principles in family therapy for application to the entire "family" of humankind. The shift *toward* valuing the uniqueness of every person and *from* the hierarchical paradigm to the organic paradigm, would have an enormous effect on the way the world does its business, as well as on the way individual families operate. The widespread understanding of the way these principles can be applied, worldwide, could ripple around the planet in the greatest paradigm shift ever.

That new paradigm brought uneasiness to the family therapy community in the early seventies when the discipline was still trying to form an identity. Virginia described a new, more encompassing border where one had so recently been set. Even as family therapy was evolving, Virginia was pulling it along into its expanded version—all the lesser ones of us struggling to keep up. "We have just succeeded in getting all the *family* members into the office, Virginia, what do you mean the *world*?!" There were those who thought she had diverged from the discipline of psychotherapy with families; what she had really done was expand the definition. Said Bunny Duhl, a few weeks after Virginia's death, to the American Association of Marriage and Family Therapy in New Orleans: "Some have accused Virginia of 'deserting the field . . .' I would reframe that. The field Virginia helped create could not contain her. She was bigger than us all" (Duhl, 1988).

Like Gandhi and others, Virginia was about paradigm shifting. These leaders envisioned literal changes in the world as results of their work. Part of the reason Virginia did not take the time to write the books we now wish were written is because she had dedicated herself to *doing* the needed work. Each person centered in the awareness of her or his own worth was another force for removing the pain of toxic and debilitating emotional hunger from the world. It was as if we were all candles and a certain number of us must first be lit in order for there to be sufficient light to see the Whole. Virginia was busily bringing light into the room—indeed the whole house. She was not going to take the time to *write* about lighting rooms.

"By knowing how to heal the family, I know how to heal the world," Virginia said (Laign, 1988, 20). The dynamics in the family system reflect those in the world community; the basic principles are the same. She had identified and was demonstrating a paradigm far better suited to the needs of human beings—and all living beings—than the vicious hierarchical model. Her stated goal was to deliver every single person she encountered from their prison of self-doubt and old learnings. Virginia's goals were hardly modest ones. She seriously intended to make changes in the way the *world* works. She did not, in any way, see this as an unreasonable challenge; geniuses do not. Giving humans a leg up in the evolutionary climb was as much a part of her agenda as it was a part of the visions of Gandhi, Teilhard, and ancient mystics.

Virginia was worried by the limitations of peace movements mobilized around the concept that the absence of war equals peace. She knew that far more was involved in making peace: one had to know how to make authentic connection, how to join with each other's energies, and how to move into cooperation on broad scales.

She understood that our culture is largely unaware of the function of the seed model. Nevertheless, we are designed by and for it, body and soul. Competition, with its inherent threats of failures and rewards, implies domination and submission: being "less good" and "a loser." All this is inseparable from the hierarchical model, which ineluctably squelches self-esteem and, with it, creativity. This squelching via hierarchy not only occurs on the lower rungs in organizations where people are discounted but also on the upper rungs where people become isolated, cut off from authenticity, alone.

Virginia pointed out the problem with life in this mold: "we always have to worry about the threats and rewards." This worry is the "biggest anxiety of the world" (Satir, 1987a) and is the major feature in international relations, national relations, inner cities, and among all human systems wherever one looks. Behind threat is fear, which usually provokes capitulation, which never works because there is always more fear following. People get stuck in a cycle that does not change. In addition to the life-diverting factors in the competitive, hierarchical model, Virginia described the "other poison in our world": we have somehow managed to work it out so that people feel like they are not as good as that one, should be better, et cetera (Satir, 1987a). She was referring to the ubiquitous and fruitless damaging human habit of trying to compare the self to some external standard. Each person is a unique entity, making comparison impossible. Too few people are aware of that fact—uniqueness—and its potentially freeing implications. Instead, they engage in sterile, deadly comparisons—equally unaware of the futility and destructiveness of their often exhausting efforts.

Putting self-esteem at the heart of her training was Virginia's response to unlocking humanity from this omnipresent torture chamber. Virginia described herself as a variation of Paul Revere and Johnny Appleseed. Teaching to her trainees the importance of awareness of intrinsic worth and leading them to this awareness was a concrete way of fostering the seed model in the world: this was her call to action. Her seeds were wide-awake persons, through whom the life force could flow freely, arousing creativity—life's business.

The Founding Time with the Mother of Family Therapy

The full range of Virginia's philosophy of treatment might not be easily understood in all psychotherapy circles. From the earlier days of family therapy, she was always on the edges of newness, doing what she could to tug it into being and toward wholeness. This is what she did with every pair and group of units, tug their ragged edges toward each other to make the new unity that she, with her expanded vision, could see. With that gift of being able to sense the Greater Pattern, she pulled us all toward that potential unity visible to her. Most people, psychotherapists included, have been imbued with the idea that threats and rewards are useful in some, if not all, circumstances. The concept of an organic growth model that undergirds and allows rather than threatens and forces is a radical departure from the dreary "if you don'ts." The step from nuclear or extended family to family of humanity was where the therapist given to linear thinking and development of technique could lose sight of Virginia. Watching her knit together a family was one thing; following her great strides toward the edges of the bigger picture was another. Virginia's eye was always on the whole picture.

In the earlier part of the twentieth century, Freud discovered the unconscious, an enormous contribution to understanding humankind. Discovery of the unconscious meant awareness that there is more to the self than meets the eye—even one's own eye in terms of one's own self. However, Freud left us with the impression that our depths are murky pools of unbridled passions and destructive urges: a small baby is a dangerous creature, who, like a young horse, must be broken and trained. The young human child, thought to be utterly without regard for others, was considered a creature in need of being humanized and civilized. The unconscious, labeled "id," teemed with violent impulses and malevolent instincts, with sexual energy and aggression being featured items.

Virginia didn't think so. She completed her own classical psychoanalysis with an analyst of good reputation and found the process wanting. She wrapped her own vibrant brain around the concepts and decided a self was a bright and shining possibility—not a demonic driven force. Early in her teaching career, in the early 1960s, Virginia flatly said, "I do not postulate sex as the basic drive of man. From what I have observed, the sex drive is continually subordinated to and used for the purpose of enhancing self-esteem and defending against threats to self-esteem" (Satir, 1967a, 55). Neither preoccupied with pathology nor restrained by Freud's drive theory, she linked dysfunction with self-esteem. She believed all negative behavior could be explained by the basic drive for self-valuing. The human creature has a compelling need to feel good about herself or himself, with the equally compelling tendency to look to the other as measure. Virginia wrote:

It was as though I saw through to the inner core of each being, seeing the shining light of the spirit trapped in a thick black cylinder of limitation and self-rejection. My effort was to enable the person to see what I saw; then, together, we could turn the dark cylinder into a large, lighted screen and build new possibilities. (Satir, 1988, 340)

She witnessed the darkness Freud saw, but, in her view, the darkness was the trap and not the essential person. With this view, the change process would be a partnership rather than a battle of wills. The spirit of the human being was not simply ridden with destructive impulses. A baby was not a small monster but a little chest of jewels. Nurturing, respect for uniqueness, and human rather than inhuman rules could help the small human develop his or her unfolding personhood.

Virginia often said that nobody grows from the point of feeling bad about themselves. It is self-esteem that governs behavior and self-appreciation produces self-esteem. Virginia made a sharp distinction between behavioral description and identity. Her prescription for dealing with "bad" behavior (behavior born of low self-esteem) as opposed to "bad people" made note of the inverse relationship between appreciation of self and depreciation of others.

Virginia knew that the person of the therapist is a key factor in the therapy process. Now, it is established fact that observation changes behavior. Light in the scientist's laboratory dances merrily around in particle form until the physicist peers directly at it—then it turns into a wave, like a child doing tricks for a parent. Having whirled around a while, waves may then revert to particle (Capra, 1983, 67–69; Zukav, 1979, 93, 112). Similarly, the therapist's presence in a room with people seeking help will affect those people. *For good or for ill, the therapist brings herself, her energy, her own personhood, to the therapy situation.*

Virginia used this universal system principle with great consciousness. It was part of her objection to the "blank screen" policy; she knew her very presence was having an impact on the people in the therapy room with her. Her very view of the true essence of the human being with whom she was in contact did, in fact, bring about a change of behavior in the person. She saw who was really under there, and, by God, that person began to emerge before our very eyes.

During my own training periods with Virginia, I saw these changes in people with whom she worked. I would arrive at a workshop and size up the other participants, noting whose company I wanted to keep and whose I did not. By day three, invariably the obnoxious people had lost their abrasive qualities and turned into people who no longer annoyed me. By the same time, the dull and boring ones had all begun to sparkle.* Virginia clearly had discovered the ingredients for making harmony among people by showing their essential selves to each other.

How did she do it? That is the subject of this book.

Years ago, I attended a mega-meeting sponsored by the Philadelphia Child Guidance Clinic. It was 1972, and the luminaries were all illuminating.† They and Virginia were all on the panel; I sat in the audience. With the fresh eyes of the novice, I was immediately struck with the absurdity of the competitive element: each was arguing to prove his way the best. This was so curious to me because everybody could see, from the video tapes each produced, that all were effective. Since these were the leaders in the field at the time, I could not understand why they were not looking for common elements of the success of which each was producing evidence, rather than struggling for hegemony.

Years later, I see that whole event as a prime example of what Rianne Eisler (1987) discussed in *The Chalice and the Blade*, the difference between societies that feature competition and those that feature part-

---

* These were objective changes that we could all see in each other, not just a shift in my own attitude.

† Some configuration of those same men who were the hosts—were, two years later, dueling in Venezuela (Pittman, 1988).

nership. Caught up in our blade culture, the men on the panel had to play out their competitiveness.

They could not see the chalice that Virginia brought. They were fighting to defend their own points of view. Virginia, meanwhile, had isolated a set of universal patterns and longed to bring the gift of her discovery to the family of humankind. This true partnering was what she brought to us in that chalice[1] and what I had seen missing between the leaders of the new field.

Virginia's observations about the correspondence among self-esteem, communication, and relationships also explain the dynamic of competition in the blade culture, which features domination and submission. On the one hand, given low self-esteem, I hack away at you, thinking I will make myself look better if I make you look bad. On the other hand, awareness of my own uniqueness removes my misguided perceived need to compare myself to you. There *is* no comparison possible to uniqueness. The person who truly appreciates his or her own uniqueness has no need to either dominate or submit and is free to follow the cooperative partnership model about which Eisler wrote—and Virginia worked to bring about in groups and families.

Always on the cutting edge, Virginia started the first training program in family therapy at the Mental Research Institute (MRI) in Palo Alto, California. She was part of the institute's founding group, which included Jay Haley, Don Jackson, and Gregory Bateson;[2] again, she was the only woman.* For years, Virginia was the only woman in the nonpsychoanalytic psychotherapy world that she was helping to shape.

Virginia was glad to be part of MRI and appreciated the knowledge gleaned, albeit from intense focus on only one family. However, she needed to move on, and did. Thus, her work with thousands of families in

---

* There were other leading women therapists—such as Karen Horney and Anna Freud—but they were all psychoanalysts and not part of the separate discipline of family therapy.

contrasting places among various cultures revealed to her certain patterns of communication that she found replicated in any group and that she recognized as universal in the broadest sense.

She found just five distinctive patterns; everything people did with each other was a variation of one of the five (see chapter 6). Once one knows what to look for, the five patterns are easily recognizable even by small children. Moreover, Virginia emphasized that they were all *processes*, not entities or identities. Once there is awareness about their form and the relationship between these five patterns and self-esteem, there is potential for radical change toward wholeness.

Four of these patterns, what Virginia described in other places as the stress ballet (1991), serve to disconnect one human being from another. That overall effect of disconnection was the reason Virginia found it imperative to elucidate these patterns. She knew well that the human race is in a position to permanently disconnect. That was why she roved the world; it was her belief that awareness is the difference-making factor. The person aware of the five patterns and the patterns' relationship to self-esteem and self-esteem questions is in a position to make different choices. Such a person need not be trapped in that ballet, which steps away from the Life Force—a dance which can even lead one prematurely off life's stage.

Convinced there are no evil people, Virginia was passionately devoted to showing how the "evil"—the destructiveness—lay, instead, in the *process* between people. This conviction was a major force in her success as a therapist and contributed greatly toward her drawing forth the essential personhood in the other—essence rises to the surface in a person as cream rises up through milk. The soul, however battered and broken, would flutter forth and shimmer, bathed in the presence of Virginia's own soul. Once a person had this moment of truth, there was no going back; that person would carry, forever, this glimpse into her or his own potential.

"All" Virginia had done was to beam in on the person's uniqueness.

Thus, it is easy to see that, for Virginia, manipulating people into "mentally healthy" behavior was the antithesis of her work. Heart and soul components are vital factors and, by definition, not calculated performances by the therapist upon the patient. She had experienced the pain of seeing the heart and soul removed from her work by those individuals who reduced it to sets of techniques and manipulations. *Without* the heart and soul, Virginia's work, done as if by marionette, ceases to be the luminous, wholing process she could bring into being. When NLP[3] was still a concept, she had welcomed codification of her work. When she saw the reality, the end product, she was filled with horror. She said she prayed that people with hearts and souls would put those human qualities back in NLP again (Brothers, 1983, 54). It is essential to understand that what Virginia did with families had much more to do with *who* she was in relation to *who* they were than with any *what* that she did. "Becoming more fully human"—her own caption for her work—simply cannot be done without heart and soul. Techniques that focus on "the problem" rather than the personhood of self and other were the antithesis of her work.

Thus, psychiatric diagnoses made Virginia uncomfortable. She called such labeling insulting and self-defeating. She never found people able to grow from a point of feeling bad about themselves. Insulting them at the outset would, therefore, be counterproductive. It also limits one's own vision, allowing stereotype to replace the person. It was her experience that people grow from a point of feeling good about themselves. For Virginia, this is not a cotton-candy, bubble-headed, nice-nice thing, nor is it narcissism. She defined a narcissist as someone who thinks the world revolves around oneself. In contrast, the true lover of self is a person who is able to be the center of his or her own world: to be a choice-maker in relation to one's own destiny. To be in touch with one's entelechy is a different thing from being focused solely on one's own needs with no awareness of the needs of the other. Awareness of one's own essential self—one's uniqueness—frees creative energy. In contrast, constant attempts to measure up are very draining. The "shoulds" fall away when comparisons are dropped, leaving a space for *what is* and what may yet be.

The motivating force behind humanity is the need to be valued by self and others—the need to be able to think of the self as worthy no matter the other's reaction, the need not just to be loved, but to be considered loveable and to consider oneself loveable. For Virginia, this was not simply an academic exercise in philosophic thinking. She knew the fate of the world hangs on it. Awareness of this could provide both the means and incentive to check the entropy process: the falling out of focus and random dissolution that occurs in systems. The patterns that disconnect, left unchecked, would sever us all, not only from each other, but from Life itself. Simply stated, nobody is going to blow up the world if they value themselves and the rest of humanity.

Virginia worked knee deep in psychological blood because of her belief in the disconnecting power of those four patterns of incongruent communication and her belief in the healing power of the congruent pattern. That belief took her to Europe, to Israel, to Russia, to Central America . . . and into the heart of nearly every human being she met.

The chalice borne by Virginia Satir was her blueprint for moving humanity back into the basic functional design carried within the Life Force.

Chapter Notes

1. In March of 1988, about six months before Virginia's death in September, she led a seminar in Miami. I had not seen her work in an extended workshop since my most recent monthlong training,

in 1974. I had a sudden urge to watch her work again; how was she currently presenting her material?

This was months before her cancer was diagnosed. Although she mentioned some "indigestion," neither of us were conscious that anything was drastically amiss.

The night after the seminar, I had the following dream:

A friend and I were seated on some bleachers overlooking a kind of bay. (In real life, this friend was in recovery from cancer. Also in real life, Virginia had met this person with me a few years previously.) Virginia climbed up the bleachers and approached us. Somewhat wistfully, she asked if she might sit with us. I replied, "Of course, Virginia, you are always welcome to be with me wherever I am."

The scene shifted to the water's edge, and Virginia was moving out into the water on a barge-like vessel. The vessel stopped, returned to shore. Virginia got off and came to me, handing me a green plastic cup—making the point that she had come back specifically to be sure to give it to me. The cup was large and substantial—one of those heavy plastic kinds—but a disposable one, nonetheless. Just a plastic cup.

Then she returned to the barge and pushed off from the shore. I stood on shore puzzled, looking at the cup, wondering why she would have made a special trip back to hand me such an unpretentious object.

Make of that dream what you will. To me, it suggests that one or both of us did know, on some level, about the undiagnosed cancer. At any rate, as she sailed away, I was left with a "chalice"—utterly modern but green, symbolizing life—as an apt metaphor for Virginia's work.

2. Gregory Bateson was an eminent thinker, anthropologist, and natural scientist. He first coined the term the "pattern that connects."

Virginia said of him: "Gregory Bateson probably contributed more to my understanding of human communication than anyone else" (Satir, 1986b, 279).

3. Neurolinguistic programming is a technique developed by Richard Bandler and John Grinder in the mid-1970s and based on the work of Virginia Satir, Milton Erickson, and other prominent therapists.

3

MAKING CONNECTIONS: THIRD ENERGY

As these two energies mingle together, the third energy they create is the energy of connectedness with another human being.

—**Virginia Satir**, 1983

In a time when mutually advantageous human connections may be more important than they have been at any other time in history, we begin our examination of Virginia's seed model. We start by focusing first on human *connection* partly because, on the physical level, that is the point from which each specific person began: two human beings—parents—making physiological connection. Life is activated. The point of authentic *emotional* connection activates a less tangible, but no less real, property. An incorporeal power comes into being as a result of two human beings in congruent interaction. Congruence is, for Virginia Satir, the fitting together of one's intentions, feelings, words, and gestures, all in harmony. Then we have a congruent communication—

two people who, at that moment, are each in touch with her or his entire being.

Mutual deep understanding creates its own form of energy. Virginia referenced this phenomenon as "a third energy" and noted how this phenomenon is related to recognition of self-worth within two people in dialogue.

She alluded to this phenomenon while using one of her tools for bringing her trainees toward internal congruence: meditation-like exercises to focus and center energy within the self (see Appendix A). In 1982 in one of her centering exercises, Virginia described the grounding energy of the earth, the inspirational energy of the heavens, and referenced this other kind of energy that emerges between persons in congruence: "a third energy, the energy of your connectedness with the other person . . . comes as we [each] recognize our worth[s]" (Brothers, 1991a, 11–12).

This illustrated one of Virginia's penetrating insights: she identified and named an ethereal but real human process, difficult to define but easy to recognize when experienced. This examination of the elements and consequences of human interaction, on a person-specific basis, was one of Virginia's major contributions and a demonstrative dynamic in the seed model. She was able to show such universal principles at work in person-specific experiences.

All interaction inherently includes communication. It is not just that we cannot "not communicate"—communication literally forms who we become as we progress from our cradles to our graves. The *way* we communicate with each other shapes our personalities. The history we make in our interaction with our parents remains to guide us, for good or for ill, throughout our lives. Verbal and nonverbal communication between us and our parents thread our forming psyches. Some studies show that the influence of information coming from the outside world may even begin while we are still in the womb. Styles of communication affect our bodies as well as our psyches—and affect the bodies of family members and partners, throughout our lives, even affecting the length of those lives.

This effect may be either adverse or advantageous, and—once we have been given the information to understand—the *choice* of how we communicate is ours. This focus on communication, per se, was one of Virginia's unique contributions to the mental health field and, potentially, to those who are engaged with human systems in any way. It is a major key to understanding human behavior. Communication is the means by which a growth model can replace the time-worn threat/reward model.

Virginia's choice was the "[road] less traveled by"*—not trod by most of her contemporaries at the time. Virginia's choice was a well-informed decision. Forking off from the road of psychoanalytic and individual therapy, her choice came from the massive volume of clinical observation of hundreds—likelier thousands—of families. She had witnessed, on several continents, how families work and how they do not work. Her path provided a wide-angle view of virtually every sort of human system, as she moved around the world for decades, observing and teaching. Her focus was on the processes within these human systems. She paused briefly, very early in her career, to learn psychoanalytic theory. Then she was soon out on that road "less traveled by," looking and learning—and creating a more evolved form of psychotherapy.

As she observed the human systems in which she worked, Virginia witnessed and understood the healing effects of straight, clear communication as well as the destructive effects of inadequate, distorted communication. Using herself as both model and vehicle, her focus would be on what works rather than on what does not.

---

* "Two roads diverged in a wood, and I— / I took the one less traveled by, / And that has made all the difference." From "The Road Not Taken" by Robert Frost, published 1916 in the collection *Mountain Interval*.

Virginia did not immerse herself in examining and categorizing the nuances of the results of incongruent communication. Instead, she would lead patients into experiences of congruence, teaching them how to "get there themselves" later, when they were on their own. Virginia's way of dealing with "pathology" was the seed model, not the medical model: simply remove obstacles to growth and growth follows naturally. Congruent communication would serve, as fertilizer does on fields, to maintain the emotional growth in persons. Virginia's view was that "pathology" is a feature of the *process*, not the person. The focus must be on righting that process and allowing the growth principle to resume an undistorted course.

Virginia described the "third energy" that emerges between two people who manage, at a given moment, to communicate with each other in a full, straightforward, clear manner. It was this rich grid within which she worked, making the way for the flow of clear exchange. Two individuals would then be able to arrive at the nurturing point of mutual understanding. *Understanding.* Agreement was not the goal; understanding—effective communication—was the point.

It is important to note that arriving at such a point is not necessarily a simple process. This apparently rudimentary description of transaction is not formula but guideline. Virginia would often spend hours helping a family or pair arrive at such a place. It is also important to note that a point of mutual understanding may not necessarily be pleasant. (Simply feeling good was, by no means, the point.) One may not like what one discovers. Nevertheless, generally speaking, mutual understanding generates solid connections that do feel better, subjectively, than do tenuous ones. Anger, clearly exchanged with respect for mutual humanity, does not produce the toxic feeling that accompanies blaming. Instead, it may serve to energize productive exploration for meaning as well as expression of feeling.

The apparent "magic" in Virginia's work was her ability to make rapid, deep, and authentic connection with virtually *any* person from any culture, country, or age group. Being in her presence was like enjoying a warm spring morning on some sweet hillside from one of the all's-right-with-the-world days of one's childhood. Like being bathed in sunlight and dried with warm and gentle breezes.

She could then lead almost any two people into a place of similar abundant flow of satisfying connection with each other. (There were occasional exceptions, but they were very rare.) This kind of connecting came from a carefully honed skill and her conviction that human beings are each unique and highly valuable points in the vast net of Being-ness. Out of this reverence for Life, Virginia mindfully attended to each representative thereof. That representative might only be a small form slumped in some institution with just enough intellectual functioning to be able to look around the room. From Virginia, she or he got the same degree of respect she accorded heads of state.[1] The *same*.

Preparing to Connect: Grounding

Understanding the power that comes with mutual respect and mutual understanding, Virginia designed her "meditations" to help bring the person into internal balance before she or he entered into interaction with another. In her earlier days, Virginia called these "meditations" "centering exercises." Later, she added the Taoist concept and language of the person "bringing together the energies of the heavens and of earth" (Bynner, 1944; Chen, 1969; Mitchell, 1988) and other guided-imagery phrases. These exercises were used to quiet the mind and to focus one's attention on the here and now while also reminding the self of one's own inner resources. This was preparation for the day's work—and might also be preparation for any day's work. It was also an exercise in achieving inner peace within the self, the beginning point for world peace.

The following is a centering process, drawn from her third month-long Process Community Seminar (1983). In this context, she began to introduce the third energy concept: human connection generates a kind of energy at the point of contact between two grounded people. She packed important ideas into the experience through which she led the participants. This exercise's purpose: *to help build a context conducive to making connections* between people, which she considered essential for both the learning and growth process. Notice that she began with very grounding instructions:

Let the tension go out on an outgoing breath . . . and let yourself further become aware that you are safe and secure in your chair, and feel your body, your feet on the ground and your bottom on the chair, your back pressing against the back, giving you that solid support.

And let yourself further become aware that your feet, resting on the floor, are not only supported by the floor, but by the energy that comes from the center of the universe, coming up through your feet and legs and into your body, being your source of groundedness . . . This energy is forever available for people through the day, all day long, all of the time that you live and breathe on this planet . . . It is only for your awareness to be in touch [that is required], and you take advantage of the energy. Energy of groundedness that comes from the center of the earth.

Let yourself become aware of the energy from the heavens, as it moves down through the top of your head into your face and neck, arms and chest, meeting the energy of groundedness . . . That energy from the heavens, the energy of inspiration, of sensing, of imagination, the place where all the real imaging is grounded. And as the energy of intuition, [of] inspiration, of sensing, meets the energy of groundedness, it forms still a third energy . . . [Also] the energy of intuition, imagination, and sensing is forever there. It waits only for you to acknowledge access to it.

And as these two energies mingle together, the third energy they create is the energy of connectedness with another human being, the energy that flows out through your arms and skin and eyes, facial expression, to other persons, creating the bonding, the joy, the possibilities of building with other people . . . I'd just like you to become aware that you have energies like a three-legged stool, energies from this connectedness, your intuition . . . Energies which create a *balance* of yourself. (Satir, 1983b, 1–2)

With this passage, Virginia was helping her audience to come to the preliminary self-awareness necessary to make connections with the richness which rewards the work of making connections. She was opening their inner doors.

Like sunrise and the break of day, this third energy born of *connectedness* can seem to be so ordinary an occurrence that we do not stop and take conscious note of its magnificence. Virginia sought to bring persons to take that conscious note, which makes all the difference. She sorted out the components that make that connectedness possible, presenting that third energy as a dynamic living force. In the excerpt from another centering exercise, from the Second Process Community Meeting, 1982, given in the next section, we see a superb example of that sorting out in which she gently uncovered and nurtured the living flame of that energy wherever she found it.

Virginia was much more than simply a very warm human being; she was the keeper of the flame of human possibility.

The Connection Experience: Generating Third Energy

The reader must be cautioned that any excerpts from her taped lectures, demonstrations, or exercises are taken out of a context in which

Virginia was carefully laying groundwork for a whole month of subsequent training.

"It is not about content," Virginia used to say. "It is all about *process*." Precisely because Virginia spoke of process—"processively"—it is extremely difficult to convey the depth, yet everyday practicality, of Virginia's system in the single dimension of the written word. However, this very depth and practicality—coupled with the terrible need of our time for parity, for unity, for congruence—makes the attempt even more compelling now than when she taught it herself.

Virginia began the demonstration with an internal centering exercise as preparation.

Virginia spoke:

Let your eyes gently close—and as your eyes close, again, I'd like you to be in touch with the miracle you just performed: you just sent a thought message, and your eyelids just closed. You didn't scold them, you didn't reward them, you just sent a message—"I need you to be closed"—and your eyelids just closed. Let yourself be in touch with the possibility that all the rest of your body can be on those intimate terms with you. All you need to know how to do is to give the message. There is a fantastic implication in that comment. I'd like you to just be in touch with it.

Let yourself be aware of your breathing, and perhaps each time you are in this position, putting special attention on your breathing, you can allow that breath to move even more fully through your body. And maybe it will lay the groundwork for you after this seminar to do the same when you begin something: to collect your energy and to choose your focus. Before you start something, allow yourself to punctuate the closure of [what came before], then do [this kind of centering process] again.

I do it many times a day. It is almost like the periods in sentences when I read; every sentence ends with a period or a question mark or whatever. We need that [punctuation] to keep ourselves balanced.

When you can and when it feels comfortable, let your eyes gently open. (Satir, 1982)

Virginia had visited her own core and knew that there is far less to fear from making this inward journey than from avoiding it. She was sharing a kind of experience that had been useful to her. She did not consider the preceding exercise to be hypnosis. She did recognize that she was using a form that would engage all levels of the participant, conscious and unconscious, right brain and left brain.

Examination of the Connecting Process

In a lecture beginning another one of her monthlong seminars, in 1982, Virginia announced her intent to aim both at the intellect and at the "gut" as she taught, emphasizing, "You and anybody you treat just belong to the same human race . . . and have exactly the same things to deal with. The problem is never, in my opinion, that the things are different to deal with" (Satir, 1982).

The difference is in the way of coping. So, aware of the hazard of hubris among professionals, she continued:

And I would like to make a very strong statement: I believe that whatever it is I see is going to be the totality of my world—whatever I see. Whatever you see is the totality of *your* world, what you pay attention to is the totality of your world. It is not the totality of *the* world.

What I am trying to do for myself and others is to expand the totality of what I see.

... With therapists and parents and many people who are in guiding positions in the world ... [who] look at all of the things that aren't right ... [the] highly developed skill to look at the things that aren't right ... almost always when I ask people to talk about themselves, they will tell me things that aren't right ... Then I have to pull out all the things that *are* right ... that they haven't noticed. And I think that happened because, when we were little, our parents got the most trouble from the things that weren't right. They wanted to make it better, so there were more words about things that weren't right, more nos, more criticism. And they took the rest for granted. (Satir, 1982)

This lecture would be followed by a demonstration about congruent communication. As preparation, Virginia gave a thoughtful definition about how communication is a window wider than words!

The simplest meaning: it is an interaction between two people that is designed to carry information and meaning : ...

The sources of the information can only come between two people from two places: the sources are person A and person B ... you are the source of your own information and meaning. Very important to remember that ... where do you get your information? [There are three sources] (1) factual—a chair has four legs is a factual piece—(2) emotional (3) other people information ... Factual. The meaning of four legs...The association to the fact that there are four legs on each chair is different for everybody. The fact is always subject to the interpretation and the fantasy, which is where the real meaning takes place ... [for each speaker].

After we develop speech, there are always two messages going on—always. There is the verbal message, and there is ... the affective ... Every message—it doesn't matter what it is ... a cough ... a series of words—because [that message] is going on in a live body, it always has another message. (Satir, 1982)

She also made the point that we are always saying more than we may think we are saying—through verbal messages, nonverbal messages, messages the body gives to the self. What we say and what we feel are both communicated even when they point in opposite directions.

Virginia followed this with a meticulously led demonstration of the principles in congruent communication by guiding the interaction between two volunteers:

VIRGINIA: Sam, have you ever met Louise before? You have some kind of idea about her.
    [Louise], have you ever met Sam before?
LOUISE: "Yes."
VIRGINIA: [The affirmative answer] does not mean that one met the other and that the other met the other. Please do not think that is true. (Satir, 1982)[2]

Virginia's very first act was to remind the pair—who had said yes, they had met before—that this notion then is a common fallacy. They had not really met at all. She immediately began to lead the pair toward expression of internal experience—the route by which they might truly meet (Satir, 1982, 3).

Virginia led the demonstrating pair into bringing their senses into awareness, introducing the concept of observation—looking as well as listening—into the interactional process. Pointing out to them that they would ordinarily be the ones to pick the subject, Virginia moved immediately into the steps toward congruence: asking that each share with one another here-and-now internal feelings. She requested the participant audience to begin observation—that they should look as well as listen.

Simply through directing attention toward eliciting comments on visual observation of physical movements, Virginia showed how people immediately begin to draw conclusions about what they see.

Next, Virginia led the training group to make a distinction between describing what is observed to making interpretation from observation. By this means, she was addressing the importance of being aware that what we see can be mistaken for "total reality," a point she made later in the lecture.

She continued to lead the pair, as well as the participant audience, in learning to separate the conclusions drawn from the description of what was observed.

She stopped the pair to point out words that are suggestive of interpretation rather than description:

> [Peter, the participant, observed]: "I saw Sam caress his legs as he expressed his feelings."
>
> VIRGINIA: You saw him move—well, I don't know if it was caressing or not—that is already a conclusion. But, anyway, you saw him move his hand on his legs. One of the things I hope you will be able to do is to become really precise in how you talk about what you see. That is a conclusion. There is nothing wrong with that as long as [you are aware] it is your conclusion: I saw him move his hand down his leg, and, for me, that was caressing his leg. All right, so that was more physical movement. (Satir, 1982)

Virginia moved on with the demonstration pair to highlight the importance of the fact that we are always "transmitting messages" through our nonverbal behavior.

We are out there all the time and only partially aware of the messages we are giving. Everybody else can see more than we ourselves see. Now once you get that truly in your mind and truly in your consciousness, you never again will say to anybody when they give you a piece of information about how you are looking, pacing, or whatever without thinking, "A thank-you" instead of, "A criticism." (Satir, 1982)

Virginia has addressed one of the factors essential in the revolutionary nature of her psychotherapy: interpretation is always based on limited views. Although some forms of psychotherapy rely heavily on interpretation, seen in this way, it is clear how "interpretation" has the capacity to be outright destructive.

Virginia emphasized the importance of remembering that "interpretations" always issue from the experiences of the interpreter:

If I can get this really clear to you, you will have something to last you all your life: *Anybody's interpretation about another person represents their own experience and what they do with it.* That doesn't make it right or wrong, it represents something. And because it does, that is how each of us can be a resource to the other. Now, first, Louise didn't know that she did that [with her hand and mouth], which is giving out messages to people. Then when she first hears that she did that, her body is very good at accepting the fact that—when [giving feedback] . . . is done in a nonjudgmental, loving atmosphere—then she can accept it. She gets an interpretation over here that can be a gift to her. It is Peter's interpretation, but it could be a gift to her. In therapeutics, one of the things that happens is therapists could be seen to behave as though he or she knows what is going on by [drawing conclusions from] those signals. That is really witchcraft. (Satir, 1982)

Indirectly, Virginia began to make the point of the importance of the ability to comment on behavior. Giving family members and trainees permission to comment on what they observe and experience is critical for communication to be congruent. She described this process as if it were giving a gift to the other party in the interaction. Throughout the process, she checked with each partner about their internal experience. This continual flow of "checking in" is an essential aspect of the process of building congruence.

Having carefully engendered the necessary nurturing context for congruence to emerge, Virginia could safely switch back in midstream and make a point about receiving messages that could be perceived as hurtful. Ever mindful of the importance of protecting delicate self-esteem, she carefully inserted this experience well into the demonstration. She purposely waited until she had guided the pair far enough into congruent interaction for them to have begun to understand.

> Now, just for the moment, I am going to do this another way—maybe I can use you, Peter—Peter looked and saw that [hand go over the mouth]. He says to himself, "That woman is withholding." And then he looks at her. He just looks at her. Just for fun, I would like you to put your hand over your mouth like that. You are just thinking, you don't even say anything about it. You just look at her with those eyes, just look at her. That is also an interaction, and maybe in our growing up, we had more things like that than we ever did about what was said. (Satir, 1982)

There is a "secret" here. Virginia pointed out how it is the process that makes all the difference: "What is so great is it could be labeled that what Peter saw was something negative. So how could Louise love something negative? *The content, that was not the important thing. It was that they were able to share it*" (Satir, 1982).

Virginia led the pair through the process of offering feedback without judgement, specifying that they were working on the level of accuracy of perception. After taking the pair and the group through a carefully constructed process, which essentially felt good to all concerned, she paused to address observation of the self-worth level first by leading Peter to nonverbally demonstrate an action that could be interpreted as criticism. She carefully bracketed that illustration so that the flow of congruence would continue. Her care here is important. She was scrupulously building a context suitable for maximum learning as well as personal psycho-emotional growth. As she said often, "Nobody ever grows from feeling bad about themselves" (Satir, 1968).

Virginia summarized:

> Now I would like you to use this as a model for all the layers that go into the communicating. At each level, something could happen that could make Peter's heart freeze, could make her [Louise] back off. What I want to demonstrate to you: we all have in our hands the capacity to use our communication for our health, our growth, our intimacy. And that is what I would like you to learn, when you leave here at the end of this seminar. That you know that [capacity for use of communication] so well and it is such an art for you . . . And when a hug comes after that, what is it that we are hugging? *We are hugging the person, but we are hugging the human spirit that has made a connection.* (Satir, 1996b, 1–10)

When Virginia mentioned "human spirit," she was referencing that space of third energy that opens when real connection is made between two persons. There was no mindless sentimentality in what Virginia was doing—her every move was filled with intent to introduce and/or maintain authenticity in each specific human interaction.

Principles in Connecting

Therapist's Use of Self

Virginia has led the volunteers in a demonstration serving as an illustration in both the process of building bridges and the therapist's use of self—bedrock to her philosophy of treatment and training.

In her long years of experience throughout the world, Virginia observed and codified fundamental principles in human interaction. She understood that congruence—which she drew out in the demonstration—is the route toward building solid emotional bridges between two people in an interaction. The major thrust of Virginia's training always carried an emphasis on bringing the therapists' own behavior into awareness. With such awareness would come the possibility of making the choice for congruence. If we think of the therapist's use of herself or himself as the major instrument of change in the therapy process, it is easy to see how work must begin with the therapist before that person starts to work with anyone else. Of course, fear and self-doubt are powerful forces that will block congruence in therapists as well as in patients. The therapist is as vulnerable to self-esteem issues as is the patient.

Demonstrating Essence Meeting Essence

Virginia would lead family members as well as volunteer participants through a step-by-step process that resulted in each arriving at the essence of the other—to the point of "hugging the human spirit that has made a connection" (Satir, 1982). In these examples of Virginia's sequential progressive guiding, it is important to note that Virginia did not use any "techniques," trance or other. She used, instead, meticulously gathered information that she shared, in comprehensible segments, with the interacting pair. What she was doing was using the very essence of herself to connect with the essence of the other. Use of the self of the therapist to contact the deep self of the patient is a sharing process, not an act that one person performs on another.

Preparation: Centering

As we have seen, Virginia would begin her work with a centering exercise to bring the participants into balance: to collect energy and to choose their focus. This centering process could be used by the participants, on their own, in the future. While it might contain some of the elements of self-hypnosis, this centering process was not simply a trick to bypass the conscious into the unconscious. It was a method for affirming the sacredness of the human spirit in each specific person and of bringing that human being into interior and exterior balance and harmony. In Virginia's experience, this movement toward balance and harmony was all part of the congruence process necessary for effective therapy and life.

Not "Technique"

Virginia's goal was never to covertly influence participants and/or patients but to help all her trainees become their own very conscious choice-makers. This instruction for centering or meditation—for drawing inward—becoming aware of the relatedness of consciousness to physical response, then focusing on one's breathing, was what Virginia would call a "vehicle" rather than a technique. Choice of words was important to Virginia. The word "technique" is defined by *The American College Dictionary* as "a method of performance." Dramatic as she may have been in her presentation, "performance" was not her major goal, and performance was not what she intended to teach. Studied and static performance was the exact opposite of what she was about. Relatedness, human connection, and the means toward authenticity was what she intended to teach. This kind of goal precludes the inherent manipulation in using a technique: therapy is not something performed *on* a family, couple, or individual; it is a process geared toward increasing their range of choice of behavior.

Teaching Skills—Not Treating Pathology

After bringing the group into focus, Virginia would show the pair how to use real communication as a learnable skill—which reflects exploration of level-one congruence (see chapter 10)—that is, "being in touch with our feelings, accepting them, acknowledging them to others, and dealing with them" (Satir et al., 1991, 79–80). The result of the carefully constructed sequence is heightened intimacy. The bridge is built between the two, not by focus on the problem of building a bridge and certainly not through focus on what is wrong between the two or by covert hypnotic suggestion. The bridge materializes naturally as a result of the combination of respect, truth, careful observations, awareness, and shared information. This natural, building emergence is the way the seed model works.

Virginia clearly explained that she does not find an emphasis on pathology to be useful. What is important to her is the clearing away of the obstacles between the two persons. She pointed out that "information" is far broader than the surface level of the literal and the factual. Information includes the affective messages that pass back and forth between two people, sometimes conscious, often not. We are sentient beings, and we respond to each other's words on psycho-emotional-physiological levels. Feelings ripple through the human body generating and being generated by a variety of chemical and electrical reactions. We shuffle, cough, and redden in response to our contexts. These changes in color and motion are visible signals that communicate to the other. Consciously or unconsciously, we respond to these bodily communications in each other. Virginia believed it essential that her therapist-trainees be conscious of *all* these levels of information.

The Communication Sequence

In her demonstrations, Virginia put a zoom lens on a communication sequence and guided the pair through steps to arrive at congruence. It was Virginia's intent to train her therapist-participants to be aware of what they saw and heard—that which was being visually and auditorially transmitted—and to be aware of the difference between description and interpretation. Much of Virginia's genius was her ability to take the obvious and mine gold nuggets useful for therapeutic purposes. For example, of course we all go around drawing conclusions—it is a necessary part of mammalian life to do so. Yet, the drawn conclusion is always subjective, always filtered through the lens of the concluder. Thus, it is quite possible for the conclusion to have nothing whatever to do with the person whose behavior has provided the stimulus and to have much to do with the glasses through which the witness watches.

Virginia pursued all her points with mindful gentleness: self-esteem is key to growth. She would defeat her purpose if any of her efforts resulted in an unreconciled diminishment of self-worth. Modeling this awareness, she would lead the volunteers, progressively, through a process where verbal feedback may be experienced as a source of enlightenment rather than criticism. As she did so, she would explicitly demonstrate the way to reach into the self-worth level: "Peter can say to Louise, 'How did you feel about my doing that?'" The mere respectful inquiry about the feelings of the other in the course of an interaction is a suggestion that the feelings of the other are important to the inquirer. Respectful attention on the part of one party promotes feelings of self-worth in both parties.

The ability to engender, maintain, experience, model, and teach this style of communicating was a crucial factor in Virginia's concept of good psychotherapy. The content, and certainly the search for "what's wrong with . . ." were of negligible importance in most cases and downright destructive in some. Her goal was to teach therapists the relationship between awareness, self-worth, communication, and coping. To paraphrase an axiom, she was not particularly concerned with the size and species of the fish caught; she wanted therapists in her training to learn how to fish—the art and science of fishing.

Truth Is Healing

Truth, wrapped in soul-deep respect, is the core ingredient of coming into the full presence of another human being. Honoring the full and *true* personhood of the person with whom she was working would afford Virginia the opportunity to eventually "hug the human spirit that has made a connection" (Satir, 1996b, 10).

Chapter Notes

1. In looking through her letters in the University of California, Santa Barbara library, I noted that she had not bothered to answer a letter from Karl Menninger but had carefully responded to a fifteen-year-old girl with whose family she had worked.

2. A full transcript of this demonstration is in the transcript of Virginia's second Process Community Meeting, available in the Satir Collection in the Davidson Library at the University of California, Santa Barbara.

4

FULL AND CENTERED SELVES

Remember, we are the stars of our own show . . . seeing ourselves as the center of our own life and seeing ourselves as the cocreators . . . between ourselves and whatever name we call where we get our life from.

—**Virginia Satir**, 1983

Self-Worth > Communication

Self-esteem was the cornerstone of Virginia's work. *All* dysfunctional patterns of communication are born out of individuals' desperate attempts to maintain a sense of their own worth—the rules learned in their family system guiding which style of communication they will choose. All the violence done to one another in speech and deed represents desperate attempts to maintain an internal sense of valuing of self, with the best information individuals bring from what they learned in their particular families of origin.

Virginia made clear that the incongruent, dysfunctional responses are always born out of misguided attempts to protect the delicacy and vulnerability of the self. She knew that those twisted in the patterns that disconnect are not there by conscious choice. Nobody gets up in the morning and says, "Let's see how I can mistreat my child today." These responses are there because the parents are doing the best they can, given the information they have. They are there because of old learnings, learned within their families of origin, where nobody knew the correlation among self-esteem, communication, and relationships. All such abusive situations and relationships are born out of low self-esteem and corollary attempts, on the part of the parenting person, to lessen to a tolerable point that terrible feeling of being without worth or value.

Virginia saw no difference in this pattern between the microcosm nuclear/extended family and the greater family of humankind. The antidote to the toxin is the same. The dictatorial parent and the tyrannical political leader have the same format. Self-worth of the specific person must be the point of intervention. Self-worth and congruent communication are hinged like door and frame. They combine to make possible authentic connection between human beings.

She also knew that congruent communication is a teachable, learnable *skill*. She could teach it to small children; it is not a matter of intellect. It is a matter of heart and spirit, mindfully focused. In order for the skill to be taught and learned, *feelings* must be engaged. The person who is "becoming more fully human" will not arrive without going inside to get in touch with emotion. This is the reason Virginia taught most of her work through role-playing and body choreography. She knew it was necessary to include visceral images with every concept.

Because of its apparent simplicity coupled with its *unfamiliarity*, the fact that congruent communication is of enormous importance can be tragically missed. Virginia used to say that congruent communication goes on between people about 5 percent of the time; 95 percent is consumed with the much more familiar four patterns of incongruence: blaming, placating, being super-reasonable, and being irrelevant.

The ability to clearly state one's feelings and beliefs is necessary for congruent communication. "Just say what you feel or believe" may be simple but may not be equally easy. The "doing" can be stopped by the dam of your own internal rules, releasing the barriers of self-doubt— the self-worth dialogue.

Congruent communication is like a running river. If it is authentic, it is the very Flow of Life. It flows between the banks of rules we construct about what is permitted to be said to whom and under what circumstances.

Now, Virginia was aware, long before body therapies were fashionable, that the human being is a multi-flowing, biocomputing, spiritual, sensate entity. In the late sixties and early seventies when I first made her acquaintance and entered training with her, it was that lack of recognition of the whole, breathing bodied person that was one of the major errors in the world of psychotherapy. The world has caught up with her to some extent in that there is now an intellectual consensus that bodies are more than just structures to carry patients into the consulting room and that they cannot be separated from feelings. *All* aspects of this chemistry-and-electricity-of-the-moving-parts-of-a-person is part of that *flow* of communication.

Here is where the linear, left-brain—in her term, super-reasonable—therapists parted company with her. Virginia saw humanity as part of a Whole, not as a collection of individuals to be divided up into categories. It is the whole field—and the field as a whole—that makes the difference. Does one get to know a rose by pulling apart a bud?

Because of this broader perspective, Virginia was not interested in merely eliminating symptoms or solving problems; she was interested in reconnecting human beings with their own core, their own reality, their essence. Thus connected, they could use their own resources first for coping, then for collaborating to make all things new.

Interconnectedness

Being able to have each person stand in their own little puddle and connect.

—**Virginia Satir,** *1986*

There are intrinsic linkages among identity, autonomy, and interconnecting intimacy. Persons who know themselves, who are able to function as separate persons in the world, who have an abiding sense of self-worth are in a better position to make authentic, and therefore intimate, connections with other persons.

Virginia's philosophy correlates intimacy—the connecting of one self with the other—with the ability to value and nurture the self. Virginia viewed our *selves* as our greatest resource; therefore, she focused her work under the heading "becoming more fully human" (Satir, 1986a, tape 5). The development of the self and the skill of human connecting are inextricably related. All the training and treatment she provided reflected this basic tenet.

Virginia's picture of the self was that of treasure, an unmeasured resource available for harvest. Her meditations reflect her attitude:

And now also let yourself come in touch with your resources, go to that place deep inside where you keep the treasure that is called by your name.

And as you reach this very sacred place deep within . . . (Satir, 1989, 19)

How very different is such a beginning point from one that presumes our innermost depths are roaring volcanoes, mindless bestial forces that must be tamed. If I hold both my essential self and yours as a cornucopia of possibilities, how much easier it is to move toward the supportive valuing of my self or your self, prerequisite to autonomy and intimacy. It is here that Virginia took the step beyond Freud. Freud had discovered the unconscious—Virginia went beyond to what she saw in the self's core, and discovered the immense power in high self-esteem and in authentic interaction between such awake human beings.

Because Virginia understood the inescapable connectedness of everything, she saw with passionate clarity the relationship of congruent communication to the development of the self and sought indefatigably to promote this congruence. Thus, Virginia's awareness of the real connectedness of all the unique citizens of our planet led her toward her concept of celebration and connection when two people meet. With her distinctive slant, Virginia used an active rather than a static image. Instead of John Donne's somewhat stationary "land" ("no man is an island"*), she saw life as a river that goes on all the time, with us each popping up at various points, like "individual fountains," as "manifestations of life" (Brothers, 1992a, 11). Virginia made Donne's point, but within her frame, the bell does not only toll, it also *peals* for thee. She wrote: "Before I ever go into the process of meeting this being . . . In my mind, I am preparing myself for a celebration, because to meet another human being is a celebration. Magic. Many of us do it and we don't even notice the celebration" (Satir, 1987a, tape 2).

Thus, if anyone's death diminishes me, then every splash of new life—any child's birth—also *increases* me. Virginia's behavior with her fellow human beings certainly reflected her belief that this is so. She

---

* "No man is an island, entire of itself . . ." From "Meditation XVII" by John Donne, published 1624 in *Devotions Upon Emergent Occasions*.

joined profound respect for uniqueness with an equal awareness of a fact so fundamental as to be obscured by its very familiarity: there is no such thing as an "individual"!

Think about it; one could hardly find a more artificial concept than that of "individual" human. Like it or not, start to finish, human beings cannot and do not exist except in relation to other human beings. Whether you were gestated in a womb or a test tube, two other people were first required to produce and donate the special cells to make the third person a possibility. And, once born, the human requires human-handed care. A human infant born on a beach does not crawl to the sea for survival as does the infant turtle. Human contact is both physically and emotionally essential. Moreover, as we develop, we soak up attitudes and ideas around us so that long before we ever reach adulthood, our inner recesses are virtual choirs of internal dialogues. Even the hermit alone with his or her thoughts carries with her or him the voices of those who raised and influenced him or her in childhood. Our species simply does not exist except in relation to each other. For this reason, a theory that speaks only to "individual dynamics" is always going to provide only a partial picture of integration and the means to get there. It is here that Virginia took a step beyond both Freud, who mistook those inner choirs for instinctual drives, and Jung, whose emphasis was on the individual. Individual dynamics just do not occur in a vacuum. Whatever given Jungian complex a person may be presenting will always be in some form of dialogue. Autonomy and individuation are, of course, necessary for the integration of personality, but it is not possible to be a human being who functions in *complete independence* of other people.

It may be that the human being is not unlike the atom, once supposed to be "the place where the buck stops" in the search for basic units. Modern physics, plumbing those depths, continues to find more mystery rather than less. The contents of the atom are no more definable than is the human spirit; the tiny "pieces" dance around like willful children when spied on, managing to exist as a "piece" and as motion all at some-kind-of-wonderful once. Perhaps it is the same with the core of the individual human being; the very essence of the human being may also be so relational there can be no looking at it in static form. Nothing in our universe seems to exist in solitude or static form; all of matter is a whirl of pulsing electrons (Capra, 1983, 67–69; Korzybski, 1933; Zukav 1979, 60–61, 93, 112). Since interrelatedness is a necessary given, to tend to the *style* and *quality* of that relatedness makes excellent sense.

Thus, *interconnected autonomy* is living the dream of *us* as opposed to being dragged through *yours* or being mired in a single-minded pursuit of *mine*. That is the task of constructive, as opposed to corrosive, human connecting. According to Virginia, getting into the constructive as opposed to the corrosive is, in the first stage, much like what they tell you as your plane is taking off: "Place the gold cup over your own nose and mouth first . . ." She, too, literally suggests that attention to one's own intake of oxygen be the first order of business as soon as potential conflict seems to be imminent, the "gold cup" being an excellent metaphor bearing breath, which sustains life:

> Now when I am in the face of someone who is putting me down, who is yelling at me and so on, and my body twists up, that's a natural physiological reaction . . . is a signal that says, "Hey, there is a little bit of emergency around." Because when our body is tied up for any reason the relationship of the oxygen in our breath and in our body to the flow of adrenalin is such that the adrenalin cuts off the nurturing of the oxygen. And if we keep that into any length of time, our body has to react to that, becoming tight when it doesn't need to be any more. Those are the secondary reactions. This is what is the link between your stress, which is also a reaction to your communication, and your health.

Now what choices do I have? The first one is to *breathe*, because I want to take care of number one first and put myself in a relaxed position. The second one then is . . . once I do that, I can sense the other person and then I can call up all the choices that I have, that I know, about how I can respond at that moment in time. (Brothers 1990b, 3–4; Satir, 1983b, 68–69)

The above is a recipe for assumption of a constructive attendance to self necessary to health-enhancing interaction. Not a narcissistic spinning about—"What can I get out of this?" "What is in it for me?" "What do I need to flee from?"—but a *preparation* of the self to be ready and able to receive the other.

Intra-connectedness and Autonomy

The existence of genuine autonomy presumes adequate self-nurturing, inextricably interwoven with intimacy. Authentic versions of one are not possible without the other. Virginia said of nurturing: "that nurturing is being in contact, loving, valuing, being able *to have each person stand in their own little puddle and connect*" (Brothers, 1990c, 4; Satir, 1986a, tape 18).

The "standing in the own little puddle" assumes the self who is aware of the ability to make choices about moving toward or moving away from the other. This kind of standing suggests an ability to ask for help yet not take no to be a definition of the self. "People never knew how to nurture themselves," Virginia said. "We have yet to have a society which knew how to do it" (Brothers 1990b, 11; Satir 1986a, tape 18). If I ask and am told no, I can receive that response as communication about where the *other person* stands in a moment in time, rather than presume it means I am not worth that person's time. I must first believe I am a person of worth, Virginia said in one meditating/centering exercise, directing a person to the "treasure which you call your 'self'—which you know by your name" (Satir, 1983b, 151). In another such exercise, she said:

> Notice your ability to see and hear and touch and taste and smell. To feel and to think and to move and to speak, and above all to *choose*. To choose out of all that you have at this moment that which fits you well, and to notice that which you haven't used for a long time in your psychological quanta—bless it and let it go. You have no longer any use for it. Then give yourself permission to add to yourself, to develop, to create, that which you need but you yet do not have, and to know that can go on for the rest of your life; letting go of that which no longer fits, honoring that which fits well, and giving yourself permission to create that which you want and need. (Satir, 1989, 19–20)

The ability to make that choice is what enables the "standing in one's own little puddle." Virginia drew attention to the "I" as executor, to "ego" in Freud's sense of the word, directing the known "I" to join hands with the less evident, depth reaches of "I" (the higher self in Jung's concept) as support for autonomy through affirmation of identity.

The maintenance of intimacy requires a certain level of autonomy—possible only through adequate self-care—on the part of both parties. Autonomy requires a certain level of intimacy—possible only through adequate care of and for the other—to guarantee each continued ability to function well independently.

Autonomy Versus Pseudo-Autonomy

There exists in our culture[1] a great confusion about what constitutes autonomy, what can be considered "independence." In the clinical examples throughout chapters 6 and 8, we see the adverse consequences of exaggerated, pseudo-independence in which the person does not permit themselves the nurturing gained in appropriate interdependence with another human being (Brothers, 1987a). Autonomy, or independence, are often equated with what is, in fact, simply the *denial of feeling*. "Mature" behavior is thought, in our culture as well as in many others, to be reflected in tightly controlled affect. Open expression of feeling is considered "childish" as opposed to "adult."

Virginia described four different forms of behavior (described fully in chapter 6) resulting from the person's inability to be congruent in expression of inner experience. The stance that she described as "super-reasonable" is the kind of behavior a person displays when defending against an inner feeling of being devalued; the person does this by cutting herself or himself off from feelings. Virginia wrote:

> [Those who are being] super-reasonable are the most difficult to [work with] because they're so congruent for this society, and the [emotional] starvation that goes on with the super-reasonable is terrible. And so many men have defenses that fall in that category.[2] (Satir, 1983, 89)

It is this dysfunctional, incongruent communication stance that is too often mistakenly valued in our own culture as "mature," "adult," or "independent."

Authentic Autonomy

Proper self-care is a necessary component of real autonomy and an antidote to the poisonous effects of pseudo-independence, which makes no provision for the more natural flow of feeling. Behaving as if one's feelings do not matter may place tremendous stress on one's physical being as well as one's emotional/psychological being. Unimpeded development of soul and psyche and expression of one's "inner-ness" are very closely related. Blocking one blocks the other. Appropriate appreciation *of* the self *by* the self clears the way for healing self-expression—so that autonomy becomes a reflection of the ability to make choices rather than a rigid standing alone against prevailing winds. *Autonomy is a fluid ability to make choices* in the moment *about response to the other.* This is very different from the frozen quality of the person who has cut herself or himself off from feelings because of not wanting to be censured for "immaturity," thereby continuing the downward spiral of the already low self-worth. It is the difference between a static preprogrammed response and a dynamic organic response.

Virginia's model for therapy was to bring each human being she trained or treated into the fullest version of self, with full celebration of that self's "particularness," including consistent and abiding "forgiveness" of that self for shortcomings, real or imagined, along with a sense of responsibility *to* self *for* self.

Virginia used her metaphor of holes in need of filling to describe the attitude of loving gentleness with which one should consider one's needs and one's body, pointing out that it is neither necessary nor advisable "to try to get other people to stuff them full" (Satir, 1986a, tape 18).

This responsibly loving attitude toward self is the basic ingredient of self-worth. The celebrational attitude toward the self's many-faceted, multihued uniqueness weakens the power of the Grand Inquisitor that keeps the human race perpetually haunted by rules of what one *ought* to be and do. Virginia explained: "If we have been used to a self-concept that says this is how we 'ought to be,' it is not going to be very easy for us to think of ourselves as unique" (Satir, 1986a, tape 12).

Identity, free of inhuman rules, can rest comfortably on awareness of uniqueness. Autonomy depends on identity and vice versa. Authentic intimacy requires the presence of two "selves" who are each willing to give themselves permission to assume the center position in their own world (as distinguished from believing the world revolves around them).

Mutual Congruence

Intimacy is a mutual sharing of inner experience in a spirit of mutual respect, free of those inhuman rules that say, "Don't feel," "Don't express anger," "Don't show fear," "Don't cry," and "Be this way; don't be *that* way." Intimacy presumes the courage to allow a transparency between two selves with the hope of being valued rather than judged, "guarded" only by the inner conviction of the worth of self, all feelings included. Intimacy presupposes a congruent telling of one's inner truth—all parts of organism-as-system speaking a single message.

Virginia would have us understand there is an unequivocal relationship between the path toward "wholing," becoming more fully human, and *what is real*. It is in the interplay between real selves that whole selves are more and more born. It is in acknowledging the value and needs of the self as one approaches and shares with another self doing the same thing that wholeness comes about. Reality meeting reality equals "wholing"; only congruence allows for this meeting of reality. One does not become *whole* except in intimacy, but one must first begin to be real—congruent—for intimacy, true intimacy, to be possible.

Beyond Freud and Jung

Much of Virginia's contribution to the mental health world lay in her understanding of the relevance regarding thinking of self-worth in the context of *whole systems*. This thinking was one of the results of her extensive clinical observations: the inherent power in *inter*personal systems. This systems-aware, self-worth-aware thinking accounts for how Virginia's work and ideas can be seen to stretch beyond that of Freud and Jung. The work of both men was focused primarily on the *intra*personal. Virginia saw the importance of the *inter*personal, the action shared between two selves. People could not be removed from the context of relatedness, and that very relatedness is, itself, formative.

One of Jung's greatest gifts to psychological thought was his thorough respect for the contents of the great pool of the unconscious. If Freud gets the major credit for having discovered the unconscious, Jung advances the discovery by shining a more favorable light on its contents. Jung can be credited with putting the capital in "Self," believing that the realm of the unconscious contains information to be trusted and explored in contrast to Freud's picture of a wilderness, raging with roving instincts and drives that one would not like to meet at night in a dark alley.

Jung saw the depths of the Self opening out toward ever deepening Mystery, connected to a greater intangible network: the collective unconscious. Virginia, who would often refer to the specific human being before her as "wonderful manifestation of life," was in accord with Jung about the collective flow in which we manifest our separateness. Virginia extended Jung's idea about the collective nature of our being to include not only our individual places in that great network of existence but also the literal *way* we connect with others.

Jung's work can be easily integrated with the Satir Model. Laura Dodson, Jungian analyst and close associate of Virginia, ably demonstrated this fact in her national and international training workshops. Dodson commented on the relationship between Virginia's work and that of Jung:

> Virginia spoke in a language of symbols and images. In an extroverted manner, she used the symbolic language of the unconscious— pictures, images, and metaphors—to help people integrate unconscious material into ego functioning. This was work that Carl Jung had done in an introverted way. While he worked with symbols from dreams, imagination, and cultural myths, she created external images in the form of family structures and psychodramas. As with

Jung, her belief in the innate wisdom of all persons awakened the inner healer in those with whom she worked.

At the same time she worked profoundly with the unconscious, she was infinitely more practical than Carl Jung in her awareness of everyday issues. She taught in a systematic, simple, earthy way, drawing examples from things that everyone had experienced . . .

She practiced a rare combination of education, depth psychology, self psychology, object relations work, systems psychology, reality therapy, and hypnotic suggestion. In the last fifteen years of her career, she entered more deeply into transpersonal psychology . . . Her family systems work then took leaps toward viewing the universe as an interrelated system and toward transforming whole cultures. (Dodson, 2000, 111)

Virginia believed that each person's appreciation for her or his own inner richness was prerequisite to her or his personal growth. She valued Freud's contribution to understanding our respective inner worlds, even while she recognized the limitations of psychoanalytic theory.[3]

Virginia was interviewed in 1982 as a leading maker of history in the mental health field. As part of that interview, she was asked about her own personal therapy, Virginia responded that she had gone through a full analysis—and, in spite of having had a good analyst from an analytic point of view, found it wanting.

The physicians told me, "This is not a physical problem; it's a psychological problem." So the only thing I knew to do, being in a city and in work that was so psychiatrically oriented, was to get psychoanalyzed; so that's what I did. It helped the physical things, but it didn't really remove the basic things behind them. (Brothers, 1983, 49–50)

Virginia's reaction to this disappointing experience was "There's gotta be more than this." She began, therefore, to invent it, and thus Virginia began her part in the inventive creation of a new mode of psychotherapy: including the whole family in simultaneous treatment. She called this *conjoint family therapy.*

While she created this new modality partially as a result of the experimental attitude that characterized all her work, she was also on a conscious quest to improve on psychoanalysis, which was the only kind of therapy in practice then. She had found it wanting. Her own analysis had failed to help her identify or address vital issues, and she was disillusioned about the derogatory attitude inherent in the analytic mode. These were motivating factors for her creation of her own, specific, comprehensive, growth-based model.

Inventing family therapy meant venturing into the whole system from which a person emerges. By asking the entire family to attend sessions, Virginia could observe the greater context and intervene in any aspect of it. She could watch (rather than just hear about) the family dynamics: how the behavior of one family member affected the rest. All in all, through working with the entire family, she found herself able to promote the emerging personhood of parent and child alike.

Her insights into what would be therapeutically useful were by no means always the result of a series of happy accidents, as she would sometimes present it. They were the product of her relentless search for knowledge—for salient information on human behavior—and of her remarkable genius for synthesis.

Much of Virginia's earliest work took place in Chicago. By 1951 she had seen her first family. "In Chicago, everything was, of course, completely psychoanalytic . . ." but, she said, "I knew the psychoanalytic method wasn't going to work so I was from scratch . . . and so that's kind of how that all started. And then it just evolved from there" (Brothers, 1983, 50).

She went on to point out that, of course, nobody is ever completely "from scratch" because everybody is always influenced to some extent by previous experiences. Case in point: Virginia did not throw out Freud's work wholesale. She took it and built on it or discarded aspects of it, such as remaining aloof from patients. In all her days, as Virginia noted, she never stopped being in a learning mode for what would be helpful to human beings.

Virginia observed that she actually breached many psychoanalytic principles, for example, seeing the client's family. In those heavily psychoanalytic days, this was considered a serious breach of good therapy. This "transgression," now well-known as an important therapeutic modality, was the beginning of her work with families. Today, of course, the mental health field actively prescribes what was once forbidden—after the pioneering work done by Virginia Satir, Murray Bowen, and Don Jackson.

It was this willingness to depart from the norm that paved the way for Virginia's brilliant insights into the critical relationship between self-esteem and communication. With two or more clients in the consulting room, the therapist can observe interaction as well as participate. Virginia's work thus assumed that all human experience is relational. Any psychological theory explaining the human animal must take into account the intense interactional factor. Virginia, whose mind was never limited by practices currently in vogue, understood this. To sum up: Virginia's substantial contribution to the invention of family therapy was born of her personal experience with the shortcomings of the only theory in town at the time. And, rather than negating Freud's work, she extended it, adding what had been missing.

In "The Use of the Self of the Therapist" (1987b), Virginia recognized that Freud's main thesis was "human beings carry the seeds of their construction as well as their destruction," pointing out that "this was a radical idea that eventually initiated a revolutionary breakthrough in mental health practice" (Satir, 1987b, 18). While giving Freud full credit (as was characteristic of her), she made the point that he opened his practice a hundred years ago:

> I would like to think the advent of another *new* [italics mine] century will bring with it another change of consciousness about ourselves— one that places a high value on humanness. The therapist who makes self an essential factor in the therapeutic process is a herald of that new consciousness. (Satir, 1987b, 17)

Keenly aware that our entire universe is made of interacting systems, Virginia saw the self as indivisible from our greater context. Her respect for the self was based on her awareness of the uniqueness of each person, as well as the kinship we share with each other—our oneness, one with the other. Central to Virginia's model is the concept that we cannot become whole persons without attention to our interaction. The goal and the evidence of psychic growth are congruence and wholeness. Internal integration—a resolution between our "old learnings" bequeathed us by our parents and new information brought "by looking at the past with new eyes"—is both affected and reflected by congruence in communication. This awareness makes possible access to the riches of the self.

The therapist does not "do therapy" on clients; the therapist is an integral part of the therapy process.

Major Vehicle

One of Virginia's major vehicles for leading participants into wholeness and personhood was Family Reconstruction. This process is fully described in *The Satir Model* (1991) and in *Family Reconstruction: Long Day's Journey into Light* (1986) by William Nerin. Family Reconstruction is Virginia's form for the psychotherapy process. Participants take roles of the family of origin, often going back several generations, recreating important scenes to make clear the genesis of whatever erroneous old learnings had been planted. Stances, described in the "stress ballet," are used to form living pictures of the "star's"[4] history.

At the last annual Avanta Process Community Meeting that she led (June 1987, Mt. Crested Butte, Colorado), Virginia summarized the way in which she developed her method for exploring the family backgrounds of her clients and trainees:

> The universe is orderly. We as human beings operate that way, too. We cannot always see the order of our humanness, mostly because we do not look or we do not look with open eyes.
>
> To find that order was important to me. I knew it was there somewhere. For me, the basis of that order is the Life Force. I also found that things follow certain things and that everything has a consequence, and in that sense, everything has a price and also a reward. And so I began to look at things in that frame.
>
> I began to see the universal in the specific of each individual's pain. I saw the pain connected to the loyalty to parents. That in itself was not new. Freud knew that. I started to follow the relationship between what people learned in their families and their behavior.
>
> During the early days I ran weekend marathons where I saw people try to free themselves from their negative experiences in ways that did not seem to be helpful.
>
> Nevertheless, I started to put things together, such as:
>
> 1. Parents were not natural enemies of children, as psychoanalysis had led us to believe.
> 2. People were doing the best they could. Why then would things turn out so bad for their children?
> 3. People carry the constructs of their families within them.

4. People were dealing with their constructs, not with the actual father or mother. It was the interpretation of their experience that needed changing.

5. Next I learned about traumatic incidents. It was not the traumatic incident that caused people's pain. It was the way people reacted to the traumatic event. It was the way people coped. I saw people experiencing identical events and being affected very differently.

6. I found the problem is not the problem, but that the coping or lack of coping became the problem. I would look for ways of taking these constructs from within and externalizing them.

7. Externalizing the internal process led me to role-playing. When I added the context to the process, I started having people play the parts of mother, father, siblings, and significant others within the three generations of the family of origin. The content became the context [that is, the story provides the setting or container within which the Guide facilitates the changes and transformations expressed by the star's goal].

8. Then I equated this with a theater. I developed a dramatic form, which included fun and humor, and allowed us access to the brain's right hemisphere.

9. I also found that role players knew what to say even with very limited information. I realized the universality of the process and the ability of role-players to tune in to the process with very limited data.

10. I found this process to be multilevel, spiritual, and very powerful. By now the approach is well developed and is known as Family Reconstruction.

11. Parents are children grown up, and they do the best they know how. (Satir, et al., 1991, 221–223)

As we bring this chapter to its close with Virginia's own words, she has given us a bare, reflective, simply-worded account of her life's journey of selfless immersion in human experiences that brought her to the discovery of a life-necessary truth for all. Congruent communication between unique selves, mutually aware and respectful of this uniqueness in their own selves and other selves, makes possible sustaining interconnectedness. Without this quality of interconnection, we live prematurely shortened, shriveled lives. Virginia discovered, heralded, and modeled this truth and invented the means by which others could make it concrete in their own lives. This truth would deliver us from a destiny of leading "second class" lives (Satir, 1986a).

Chapter Notes

1. The mention throughout this book of "our culture," "America," or "American culture" refers to the dominant culture of the United States of America. While it is important to recognize that the Americas are made of many cultures and that the United States itself is also made of many cultures, there are certain characteristics associated mostly with "American" culture. Although Mexicans and Canadians are also North Americans, their cultures differ from that of the United States.

2. Virginia certainly did not intend to imply that this style of response is limited to men. This kind of response is by no means linked to gender but does represent the current North American culture's endorsed version of appropriate responding—an extension of the "boys don't cry" mentality. It is also a particular "occupational health hazard" of the intellectually gifted of both sexes.

3. In her first Process Community Meeting in 1981, Virginia gave some background about the development of psychotherapy and stated her position on Freud:

> The only treatment, a theory of treatment, was the psychoanalytic one. To some degree there was Jung and Adlerian, but for the most part it was psychoanalytic, which meant it was the wrong thing. Now, I want to make a public statement: I have nothing against Freud. In fact, I enjoy him, and if he were here today, he would probably be at this meeting because he was that kind of person. But he was frozen [by] posterity in such a way that rigid people who followed him made something different of the whole psychoanalytic thing. That doesn't mean that there weren't others to do differently. But this was a theory and a treatment of people that took a long time. (Satir, 1981, 66)

4. Virginia referred to the leader of a family reconstruct as "guide" instead of "therapist" and to the participant as "star" instead of "patient" or "client." This was part of reinforcing self-esteem but also reflected Virginia's view of psychotherapy largely as an educational process.

5

PERSONHOOD: ESSENTIAL CORE

It was as though I saw through to the inner core of each being, seeing the shining light of the spirit trapped in a thick black cylinder of limitation and self-rejection. My effort was to enable the person to see what I saw; then, together, we could turn the dark cylinder into a large, lighted screen and build new possibilities.

—Virginia Satir, 1988

What Is Personhood?

"Personhood" is not one of Webster's words. In the dictionary, one finds only the definitions of "person," "the actual self or individual personality of a human being," and the suffix "-hood," "denoting state, condition, character, nature, et cetera." Nonetheless, "personhood" has slipped into modern usage.* No doubt, this is because we have come to see that we need such a term—which is a hopeful sign. Perhaps it represents a small evolutionary step. Virginia Satir invested the word with a more profound

---

* See the references (page 324), under Walters, James W. *What Is a Person?* (1997).

meaning than Webster's definition would suggest. Were our society to continue to articulate serious questions about "the nature of the actual self," there could be profound changes in social policies as well as styles in psychotherapy. Virginia commented on these shifts toward a different consciousness on the part of culture:

> What started as a radical idea 100 years ago has become part of a recognized psychology predicated upon the belief that human beings have capacity for their own growth and healing . . . As we approach the 21st century, we know a great deal about how the body and brain work and how we learn . . . We have also created the biggest monster of all time—the nuclear bomb. We still haven't learned to accept a positive way of dealing with conflict.
>
> Amid these changes is the growing conviction that human beings must evolve a new consciousness that places a high value on being human, that leads toward cooperation, that enables positive conflict resolution and that recognizes our spiritual foundations. Can we accept as a given that the self of the therapist is an essential factor in the therapeutic process? If this turns out to be true, it will alter our way of teaching therapists as well as treating patients. (Satir, 1987b, 24–25)

Virginia worked with her students as *persons*, not teaching them techniques but leading them to search their own depths for authenticity and to learn how to recognize constructive styles of interaction within a pair and how to distinguish what builds walls from what builds bridges.

Understanding that the therapist is a part of the system in any given family therapy context, she worked on helping each student therapist become a fine instrument. "Use of self" meant developing enough self-awareness and self-worth awareness to be able to communicate therapeutically with self and the other.

Common sense dictates that the therapist and the patient must inevitably impact one another as human beings. This involvement of the therapist's "self," or "personhood," occurs regardless of, and in addition to, the treatment philosophy or the approach. Techniques and approaches are tools. They come out differently in different hands . . . The whole therapeutic process must be aimed at opening up the healing potential within the patient or the client. Nothing really changes until that healing potential is opened. *The way is through the meeting of the deepest self of the therapist with the deepest self of the person, patient or client* [italics mine]. When this occurs, it creates a context of vulnerability—of openness to change. (Satir & Baldwin, 1983, 19–25)

Therapists must attend first to putting their "own house in order" to be trusted with those of their clients. The very self of the therapist is, in fact, the first and foremost tool.

Third Birth—Becoming Our Own Decision Makers

Had Virginia lived long enough to write her next book, to be titled *Third Birth*, we would have seen a more explicit definition of the word "personhood." In her personal notes (1977), Virginia addressed herself to the point at which we assume personhood:

When does it happen that you and I become a person? I think it happens when we become our own decision makers—having our *third birth*.

This is the time when we recognize clearly that we are the center of our own universe, and accept all the responsibility, privilege, and risk that goes with it.

Most of us grew up to believe that our center was outside our-selves, represented by another person, a degree, money, or position. As such we had to use our precious energy to own and control the things outside of ourselves—leaving very little energy to keep our-selves in any kind of harmonious balance.

I think we have four births . . .

The first birth is when egg and sperm meet.

The second is when we pop out of the womb.

The third is when we become our own decision maker.

The fourth is when we join all consciousness.

As I see it, each succeeding birth literally depends upon the one before. Each birth takes place within an entirely different context. Each has its own timing and tasks.

Man cannot create life. He activates it. The life force is carried in all of us.[1]

. . . The third birth is that time when you feel your self to be your own decision maker—to take charge of your own life. Or in other words, when *you* take your life in your own hands—to love, to protect, to guide, to nurture yourself in terms of your own nature.

It is the time when you act, owning your action and assuming full responsibility for the outcomes of your actions.

It is the time when dependence means an awareness of, and negotiation for, the things you cannot do for yourself. That time when independence no longer means something in relation to the outside, but means acting in full autonomy out of your own integrated core.

It means the time when you are clearly familiar with your bound-aries as distinct from someone else's, and when relationship means the meeting of two wholes rather than two holes.*

---

* Virginia Satir, personal note, February 25, 1977.

Virginia was a splendid midwife to the "third birth" as she guided her clients and trainees toward awareness of their ability to be in charge of their own lives. It would seem that most of us spend long periods in "proximate personhood" (Walters, 1997, 63), having the capacity long before the actuality. It was Virginia's goal to lead as many as possible into their "third birth" and thus on to full personhood.

Watching her work, one could begin to see how she used the essence of her self to affect whatever other "self" is part of the working context.[2] One might say one becomes a "person"—or comes to one's own personhood—when that "shining light of spirit," that inmost core or essence, awakens to the various elements of self and actively takes hold of integrating those elements. Virginia's definition of "self"—differing from her definition of "person"—is that of a system: "I believe that each human manifestation is a pattern of interaction among eight variables."* This multivariable definition of self expands the view of person, which Virginia defined as a unique manifestation of Life.

Self Mandala

Knowing that a visual image would be useful to show the dynamic nature and complexities of such a pattern, Virginia called this configuration the Self Mandala. She noted the first part that each "I" has a body, one's "temple or house." Although this physical aspect is a principal part, it is not the full person. Each "I" has a brain, its second part, that we suppose houses our mental or intellectual part. Each "I" also has, third, an emotional part, representing our feelings. A fourth part is the sensual—data received and transmitted through eyes, ears, skin, nose, and mouth. None of those parts can be sustained without the fifth part, nutrition, the food we eat. Virginia pointed out that the sixth part of an

---

* Virginia Satir, Third Birth Notes, April 7, 1980.

The Universal Human Resources

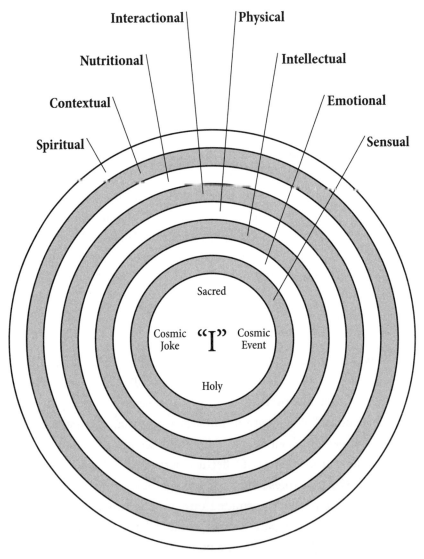

*Satir, 1983b, 258, Process Community, Crested Butte, Colorado

"I" is the interactional part, our social part and link to others, suggesting that, perhaps, it could be called our "I-thou" part. Virginia noted the seventh part, the context in which we live, including air, temperature, sound, light, places, time, and physical environment. The eighth and final ring of the concentric circle is the spiritual part, our life force.

Aware that we are far more than simply a sum of our parts, Virginia referenced that mysterious spiritual aspect:

> We can buy all the chemical ingredients at a drug store that make up a human body, but so far no one has been able to put them together in such a way that a real human being emerges. Robots, yes, but human beings, no.[†]

It is necessary to understand the relationship among *all* eight parts to understand a given person and their motivations, Virginia explained:

> One part may be manifest more than another. When I seek to under-stand any dilemma or manifestation, I look at all these aspects and discover how each is perceived, understood [within our current body of knowledge about human behavior], and how the interplay is understood.[‡]

Virginia's point: a human being is a one-of-a-kind *system*, all parts in simultaneous and continual interplay. No one aspect of the eight can, realistically, be considered in isolation—even though people behave all the time as if that were possible.

Every human being is essentially an ongoing process.

---

† Virginia Satir, Third Birth Notes, April 7, 1980.
‡ Virginia Satir, Third Birth Notes, circa April 1980.

Processes Are Pervasive

Indeed, as I began this book, I almost did precisely that. There was a strong pull to emphasize and highlight a single element—the importance of self-worth to the individual—until I realized that to do so would falsify the very multidimensional reality I wished to present as accurately as I could.

Single units are an illusion.

The atom—once thought to be the basic, elemental unit of matter—is not a unit at all but a little ball of whirling processes; so are we, the human system. The "basic unit of matter" does not appear to be matter at all. Scientists, squinting into their instruments, do not see an ultimate small "object"—they see a *process*. Trying to look at what they thought of as a particle, they witnessed it become a wave. Not static. Not "I'm a particle; now I'm a wave." No, a dancing little process, shifting back and forth between wave and particle. To make matters more complicated, the dance was observed to be influenced by the fact that it was being observed (Wolfson, 2000, tape 18; Zukav, 1979, 112). That means this micro, pulsing process enters yet *another* process—a state of interaction with the beholding scientist. Even in the tiniest world of essential matter, the process is influenced by the presence of the observing scientists. So it seems that the basic unit at any level of reality is never a wholly isolated individual but is somehow a relational-relating process. "Individual" is an illusion; interacting system seems, instead, to be basic reality.[3]

Likewise is this true of the human being. Virginia wanted to make clear the true meaning of "person of the therapist." To do this, she spent time pointing out that each individual person is a system unto themselves—and, therefore, in continual process. In Virginia's words:

What I have found is that *every experience has a dance to it.* That is what I call *process* . . . there is no such thing as being able to stand still.

Even if we stand still our blood runs inside . . . Movement is always going on all over the planet, 24 hours a day and has since the beginning of time. (Satir, 1981, 25)[4]

Virginia understood that the person of the therapist was an integral part of the therapy process. She said:

There are three parts. The essential nature of the variables [as they relate to] to each other to accomplish the outcome; the order and sequence which is developed; the series of transactions among the parts. All the parts have an action, a reaction, and an interaction. When you apply that to a therapeutic situation, when you are dealing with an individual, for example, and you are the therapist, there is an action, a reaction, and an interaction going on. The sad part is, there for a long time, nobody ever thought the therapist had any part in that; it was only the patient. But the fact of the matter is this [interaction] is going on all the time. (Brothers, 1990b, 12)

Virginia referenced that period in which no thought was given to the systemic nature of any human interaction. In any system, all parts act and react with each other. The personhood of a specific therapist influences the action, reaction, interaction pattern in the process between him/her and the patient. The concept of the therapist as "blank screen" has no validity when taking into account the principles of systems.

Virginia held human beings in deep reverence. She honored, to her last breath, the human capacity to change, to grow, to surmount obstacles, to live. She was touched with deep compassion by the failure of so many to choose change, to remain "boxed in" by inertia and fear—a "dark cylinder" filled with hidden, unused potencies instead of daring to become the "star," a "shining light" (Satir, 1988a, 341), free, engaged in the dance of life and released from the exhausting pace of the stress ballet.

She understood the profound implications of our uniqueness, our inherent connectedness, our power to implement life-giving or life-destroying processes. This view of the facts of human reality filled her mind, shaped her work, moved her to dare dreams of unity and peace for the human race—and are prerequisite for those who would like to become therapists in the footsteps of Virginia. She also noted the ground swell of increasing awareness portending a cultural shift in perspective:

> The world is changing here . . . giving out some new possibilities. So now we have the beginnings of another view of how we can look at people . . . We saw Abe Maslow talking and Rollo May talking about that the definition of a relationship is one of equality. Now that sounds peculiar to people, because how can everybody be equal? You know, some are tall, some are short. What that really means is that our navels are equal in the sense that we all came the same way. So, this had to do with value and worth, that people are of value. And they equaled each other in value and manifestation of life force. If we really believe what we are told on the theological level, that we are made in the image or likeness of the Creator, then how can we be unequal? We can put it in any terms we want. So we began to say *person equals person because they have navels and because they are manifestations of life force.*
>
> This was so new, this important discovery, and at first it brought dismay. How could I, a four-year-old, feel equal to my mother, a 44-year-old? How could I, a 45-year-old, feel equal to my mother who is 70 years old? How could I, a student feel equal to my professor? [Not] because you have all the same amounts of knowledge or the same age but because you are a manifestation of life force . . .
>
> Now this was discovery, and there were lots of discoveries in relation to that. Now, as far as the definition of a person was concerned, what we knew was that a person was unique . . . Every person is a combination of sameness and of differentness to every other person.

So it is not that if you love me we will be the same and if you did not love me, you will be different, but the genuine, basic nature of the human being is a combination of sameness and differentness.

That meant then, that there were no duplicates of people. And it also meant something else: think about [a] fingerprint. (Satir in Brothers, 1999, 2–3)

Six years later, Virginia spoke to equality of value again, adding the implications for therapists. At the start of the following quote, she had just finished talking about the changes that came after World War II, the human potential movement, the feminist movement:

Each person is of value. Whether that person is four weeks old or 84, the equality of value [as being the same], began to assert itself . . . to be of value . . . What we had been doing was to say, "Well, if you're four years old, be seen and not heard. If you are black and uneducated and 24, you're not worth very much." We had put all categories of human beings in a "worth" basket and we had said "this is worthy, this is not worthy." [So this] was a whole new thing; we are at the edge of that now, we are not by any means or manner finished. I still get people saying, "You mean everyone is equal?" "How can that be when this one doesn't have this education and that one doesn't do this or that?" I say, "It is the *equality of value.*" Now, *the minute you get into value, you know you are getting into a life force. You are getting into the value of life . . .*

"'*Me*' Will Always Be There"

This is a new concept we have, relationships based on equality of value which means we have to separate *role* from *identity*. Your role is simply a definition of function. It's not your identity. We have to do the separation.

Let me give you a little example . . . I go to places and maybe meet someone who says he is a doctor. I ask, "Are you doing it now? If you are, don't send me a bill!" The point of it all is that we have become role conscious and so the identity has been squashed underneath the role . . .

. . . You in the helping professions, I think, have suffered from the idea that you should have a certain role. One day I decided that I had no role except what I did in a moment in time which was a function of something. A function: when I'm through mothering, I'm not mother anymore. Why do I need to be a mother when I'm not one. And, if I'm not in a particular relationship, I'm not; that's a function. *But, I carry myself with me all the time.* If you are with me in a treatment context, you'll be meeting me. And, we will work out the role, *but* me *will always be there* [italics mine]. My humanness is what is going to be the model. (Satir, 1987a, tape 3)

Virginia was again referring to the importance of awareness of one's own uniqueness. The essence of self, that "shining core" tragically unrecognized and muted by fear, has far more relevance than any role.

Inner Shining: Essence

Virginia's concepts seem similar to Jean Houston's (1987, 1990) thoughts on essence. Both expressed unequivocal respect for the inner core of a person and both intend facilitation of the expression of that core. A paragraph from a lecture by Jean Houston can help us grasp more deeply Virginia's "Me":

Essence, What is essence? What do we mean by essence? Essence is not a place. It is not a time. It is not an insight. It is not a state of mind. It is an actual presence. It is a given to your nature. It is the deepest part of your nature. Some call it soul. It does not come with education. Matter of fact, I'm not sure it even comes with living. It may be a given. It may be the universe potentiated in you. The Oneness living in you. It is beyond symbols, and therefore it is not archetype nor angel. It is neither wise old woman nor wise old man or divine child. These are symbols that merely point the way to essence: "that a way is essence." It has been referred to in a number of traditions as the Diamond Body. (Houston, 1990, tape unknown)

Houston's words reflected Virginia's "shining star," the core of personhood Virginia worked to free. This "core," this essence, is the basis of uniqueness, the inner power which must bring harmony into the systems of the self.

Archetypes Inform, but Do Not Equal Essence

These symbols, these archetypes, these flash bridges to essence give liberating information about the nature of one's existence and even at deeper levels, the nature of reality itself. But they do not give the living embodied experience of essence.

. . . And I'm going to suggest that becoming Christ/Buddha/ Krishna, you're ultimately boring God. Because there are plenty of Christs and Buddhas and Krishnas about but there's only one you. (Houston, 1990, tape unknown)

As a poet* put it:

---

* My father, Robert Lee Brothers, 1908–1979.

"Sunday . . . The Bells Say . . . "

Guitars are mute in Mexico,
The bulls at peace in Spain,
Around the world the people go
In pleasure and in pain.

They give one day to Deity
And keep six for their own;
How odd a thing it is to be
A worshipper alone.

No need to kneel, we only nod,
An informality
Between The One and Only God
And the one and only me.
(Brothers, R. L., 1998, 93)

While Virginia saw hiding behind "role" as a feature of the darkness that often obscures the "star," Houston saw "personality" in the Greek sense of "persona" as "mask" and as used in Greek drama. She saw that living "under" this mask dries up essence—just as clinging to role at the expense of essence obscures and shrouds in a black cylinder the shining of the "core."

Houston characterized personality versus essence:

Personality develops in the loss of essence to fill the resulting void and replace the painful deficiencies. Personality is the absence of essence. It is the statement of that loss. Covered by layers of personality, essence gets lost somewhere in the unconscious. Then what happens is as you live out of personality, awareness contracts . . . I am talking about physical awareness—what you see, what you hear, the way you are able to be . . . It contracts to local diminished identity. Perceptions and conceptions contract. You get stupid! You get boring! And your personality gets more and more boring until you cannot bear to live with each other. (Houston, 1990, tape unknown)

Houston and Virginia were on the same track here. This "contraction" that Houston attributed to the substitution of the depth of "essence" with the shallowness of "personality" is the point at which we could see Virginia's stress ballet (described in chapter 6) enter the picture—the four incongruent stances (described in chapter 6) would begin. Self-doubt, undisciplined by commitment to congruence, can push the unaware person into a defensive mode. Anxiety increases because, as we will see in the next chapter, incongruence only deflects and does not serve to effectively defend the delicate inner self. As psychological discomfort mounts, awareness, perception, and conceptions do contract and are not available to us. Virginia's training demonstrated how awareness and appreciation of one's uniqueness—one's essence—facilitates free use of senses. Perception expands accordingly, which is one major reason Virginia knew training in awareness of self is important for those practicing psychotherapy. Training in awareness of self would produce more perceptive psychotherapists.

Houston was reflecting on the same reality to which Virginia referred. Incongruent behavior—which always minimizes or dismisses personhood—is a static and, therefore, limiting response. Congruence, which both facilitates and issues from awareness of essence, is the dynamic response, opening to the full and authentic spectrum of possibilities (see chapter 6).

What Virginia was saying about "role" was similar to Houston's warning about orienting oneself around personality in that both are sidetracks leading away from authenticity. What Virginia meant by "identity" was analogous to what Houston meant by essence: "the minute you get into value, you know you are getting into a *life force*. You are getting into the value of life" (Satir, 1987a, 1-6). Virginia was equating awareness and true identity with valuing essence of the self. Like Houston, Virginia also pointed to this awareness of value as a spiritual experience.

The central element in Virginia's work: she constructed a method for allowing people to meet essence to essence, a way to facilitate the emergence of essence. It is between people because *everything* is between people. People live within an interactional context, not as sealed off individuals. Interaction on the essence level, between the awakened core, the "star" within each, is a deepening process for both persons.

Essence calls forth essence. Essential selves, in relation to each other, reinforce the essential nature of both.

Such an event's communication of core with core is the culmination of congruent communication and illuminates Virginia's observations about the implications of congruence in human behavior.

Houston described people who "live out of essence," citing well known "saints" who have learned how to live within the context of essence, or "the highest part of self," most of the time. She pointed out that such people tend to come from a point of "radical empathy"—that healing often takes place in their presence. *"When we align thought with the highest part of self,"* we *"experience authentic power"* (Houston, 1998, tape 1).[5]

This description parallels Virginia's observations about the implications of congruence in human behavior, the operative term being "alignment"—alignment of thought and self. If one dusts away the self-doubt, one has access to the riches of one's inner resources. Self-doubt would always stand between me and the highest part of myself. This is where Virginia's concept of the relationship between self-esteem and communication applies. The enhanced power in congruent communication gives one access to more of one's energy. Holding back feelings and trying to present a front (perhaps the function of what Houston called "personality") drains energy, diverts energy. That is a reason for there being power in authenticity. In her years of clinical observation, Virginia witnessed the power in alignment of speech and thought with the core of the self. She demonstrated this effect in her own demeanor and called it forth in patients and trainees. And was Virginia not a great healer—an expression of the radical empathy to which Houston refers?

The "I Am" self and the "congruent" self seem to be the same self. That was why Virginia referred to the congruent meeting of two human beings as a spiritual experience.

Implications for Treatment

Virginia's view of personhood as being a dynamic *process* greatly influenced how she dealt with the very first step in treatment—diagnosis. She saw the folly in using "frozen" patterns to designate a client: "what we have been used to doing [in use of the DSM IV] is freezing something and calling it our analysis [or diagnosis] instead of seeing that this moves" (Satir, 1981, 68–72).

Virginia made a critically important point. She was commenting on the fact that mental health professionals, in making a diagnosis from the DSM-IV, are, in essence, "freeze-framing" an interaction. Even a description of a system must take into account the system is always in process—is an ever-shifting field of response and counter response. This is one reason Virginia did not find diagnosis, in the ordinary sense, particularly useful. She was much more interested in understanding the interactional patterns of a given family system, at the same time, recognizing that what she saw in one moment would be different in the next moment.

Therefore, usual diagnostic procedures—which focus on labeling a person without taking into consideration interactional factors or context—are a hindrance, not a help.

During a lecture, a member of the audience asked Virginia to share her views on "psychotic people." Here is Virginia's response:

Let me just say, first of all, that if you would allow me I would like you to restate something. And I will give you the words and see if you feel all right about it. I heard you talk about psychotic people.

Would you change that to people who have, at moments in time, psychotic manifestations? Would you say that and see what happens to your throat?

[Participant repeats question using the suggested statement.]

How did that feel when you said that?

"Foreign."

Okay, because it is new, because we have been so used to glibly applying labels. Go in hospitals, "go down to that paranoid," "go down to that back injury," "Go down to so and so.

Remember all those words that come out of your mouth reinforce something.

Now, say it again and see if you have hope.

[Participant repeats the question.]

How did that feel to you when you said that?

"Different."

Of course it does, because what it does is leave the personhood intact and puts your mind on the condition. And when you do that, you are not going to give any feedback to people [that they are merely a] category. And so you are freeing the life of that self-worth, in your own mind, to exist, to become your colleague and support to help with the behavior that comes out. The principles [of the relationship of self-worth to use of language] are exactly the same. (Satir, 1981a, 189)

Virginia recognized the critical importance of honoring every given human being—her or his personhood; all of reality is an interlinking net of shining selves, some simply more aware of that fact than others. In her passionate desire to help each self be more aware of her or his value, she had jotted down in her personal notes a kind of first-aid remedy for assaulted selfhood. It is a brief declaration written toward the end of her career. Being her own words, these few sentences seem to shape both a fitting mantra and appropriate coda for this chapter:

Only One Thought Away
Positive self worth is only one thought and one action away.
I am of positive worth because I am a person.
I am of positive worth because I am a manifestation of life.
That, we all are.
When we believe that, the struggle then becomes only the creation of a form to express it.
Any change creates both a problem and suggests a solution.
Any change can be a crisis.
Any crisis offers up possibilities:
Try to stay where you are,
Retreat to a "safer" place or *venture into new territory*. (Satir, circa 1986, personal notes)

Chapter Notes

1. Appearing to agree with Virginia, leading physician-bioethist Tristram Engelhardt, PhD, MD, said:

In general secular bioethics, one will not be interested in when human life begins, unless one is attempting to determine when the human species evolved. Life, it would appear, is an unbroken

continuum some four billion years old, and human life a phenomenon some two million years or more old. In general secular morality,
one is, or should be, concerned with determining when in human
ontogeny humans become persons. (Engelhardt, 1996, 140)

2. Anybody with a serious interest in understanding Virginia's work must
view several different videotaped sessions in which she is working with
families and seminar trainees. There is no way to access the breadth of
her work through reading only.

3. For readers who take issue with this view of atomic activity, and with
a layman's apology to readers who are physicists, this topic relates to
Werner Heisenberg's Uncertainty Principle as understood by Niels
Bohr—as opposed to that of Albert Einstein:

In essence, Bohr argued that the *entire phenomenon* in which
the measurement (or any other quantum measurement, for that
matter) takes place cannot be further analyzed into, for example, the observed particle A, the incident electron, the microscope
and the plate at which the spot Q appears. Rather the *form* of
the experimental conditions and the *content* of the experimental
results are a *whole* which is not further analyzable in any way at all.
In the case of the microscope, this limit to analysis can be clearly
seen, for the *meaning* of the results depends upon the way in which
the spot *Q* and the particle *A* are linked together. But according to the laws of quantum theory, this involves a single quantum
process which is not only indivisible but also unpredictable and
uncontrollable.

. . . Many physicists, if asked whether the electron exists in some
fundamental sense, would answer in the affirmative. However Bohr
himself had emphasized that there is no meaning in talking about the

existence of the electron except as an aspect of the unanalyzable pattern of phenomena in which its observation takes place. This state of affairs has led to the observation that physicists come to praise Bohr and decry Einstein (because of the latter's refusal to accept the full implications of this feature of the quantum theory) but that they actually think like Einstein while tacitly ignoring Bohr's teaching. (Bohm, 2000, 81)

Bohm decried the communication failure between the two:

A deeper analysis of this whole question shows that what was really at issue was the different notions of order involved. Bohr and Einstein both held to subtly different ideas of what the order of physics, and of nature, should be and this led to an essential break in their dialogue, a break which is reflected in the distance that lies between relativity and the quantum theory even today. In particular, Bohr believed that the order of movement of a particle would admit ambiguity while Einstein felt that such a possibility was too absurd to contemplate. The source of this failure in communication between the two giants of modern physics therefore lay in their incompatible notions of order. (Bohm, 2000, 104)

Bohm seemed to support Virginia's position that all of life is process, an indivisible whole. At no point can a "pause button" be pressed to stop the action and to view any one particle independently.

4. Always directing her lectures holistically, Virginia was working for simultaneous right and left brain incorporation of the presented material. When the developers of Neurolinquistic Programming studied her working, they could see her covering all the modes through which people process information. In this example, she was speaking—the

auditory mode; she was writing on the board—the visual mode; and she threw in a gesture—the kinetic mode.

5. Alignment, congruence, and coherence seem to be universal principles that can be seen to have important effects on human behavior. For example, theoretical physicist David Bohm elaborated on the importance of the alignment of thought in creating "coherence" (Bohm, 1996, 14).

6

THE PATTERNS THAT
DISCONNECT: INCONGRUENCE

*Now what do human beings do when they feel deprived and limited?
That has something to do with the life-force. And what does the life-
force do? Life-force cannot be killed, it has to be reformed . . . It can be
reformed into very negative behavior, into gruesome kinds of physical
anomalies and difficulties, into hatreds . . . the amount of energy that
goes into a hatred . . . is a very big one. It's displaced energy from someone who feels deprived and knows no other way to go. So what we begin
to find here then are all the defenses we use and all the rationalizations
we use for that defense.*

*Human beings cannot live with fear, they have to do some-
thing about it.*

—**Virginia Satir**, 1983

The Patterns That Disconnect

Perhaps one of Virginia Satir's most important contributions to the world
is what she observed on patterns of communication and the implications
this knowledge contains for healing communities as well as families.
Those implications range from pivotal insights into emotional factors
in the etiology of cancer to serviceable explanations of the behavior of
a terrorist.

Along with the crucial importance of self-esteem to human flourishing, Virginia understood the profound importance of teaching how basic
is communication to healing humankind. Indeed, there could hardly be

more critical information about human dynamics from a purely practical point of view. Virginia focused her great and deep compassion there.

The five universal behaviors that manifest when a person is under the often daily stress of the presentation of their own self-worth questions are four styles of incongruent communication: placation, blaming, being super-reasonable, being irrelevant—and the rare fifth, *being congruent.** These five patterns of communication are not just a set of ways a given pair of human beings *may* employ in their behavior on a given day. Virginia Satir found them to be *the* ways that people interact with each other. *All* people. Everywhere.

Developing Definitions of Incongruence

Never a fan of the sixties trend of "losing one's head," she was working steadily to understand what she was witnessing in human behavior.[1] Virginia was not only seeking to understand human behavior. She was also working tirelessly toward expressing her discoveries in a simple, but lucid, way, using language that was sufficiently pictorial to accurately define the behavior.

In 1964, Virginia had defined congruent and incongruent communication:

> The messages I have listed in this chapter have all been relatively congruent within the context; they have jibed with each other.

> a. A congruent communication is one where two or more messages are sent via different levels but none of these messages seriously contradicts any other. For example, the husband says, "The dog is

---

* When intention, action, body, and language concur—"run together."

on the couch," in an irritable tone, in a context which tells the wife that he is irritated and why he is irritated.

b. An incongruent communication is one where two or more messages, sent via different levels, seriously do contradict each other. One level of communication is context itself. For example, the husband says, in a delighted tone, that the dog is on the couch, but from the context the wife knows that he hates dogs; whether they are on couches or anywhere else.

. . . "Incongruent" refers to a discrepancy between the report and the command aspects of a message . . .

Simple contradictory communication is where two or more messages are sent in a sequence via the same communication level and oppose each other

a. Perhaps A says the following:
  "Come here. . . . No, go away."
  "I love you. . . . No, I hate you."
  "I'm happy. . . . No, I'm sad."
  "My wife is tall. . . . No, my wife is short."
b. Perhaps A does the following:
  Pushes B away. Pulls B back.
  —Buys a ticket to the movie, but doesn't go see it.
  —Puts his coat on, then takes it off.

But such simple contradictions cannot occur without some accompanying metacommunication, since one cannot *not* communicate.

a. Although the self-contradictions listed above are relatively clear, they are also accompanied by smiles or frowns or tone of voice, and in a context.

b. When contradictions occur between different levels of communication, they become *incongruent*. (Satir, 1967a, 82)

In 1980, Virginia jotted down the following thoughts—personal notes made regarding the ingredients of incongruent communication. She was exploring, in her own mind, the obstacles to assuming full personhood and wholeness. She was thinking in terms of balance and harmony as she mused on the problems raised by the patterns which disconnect family members—and members of the human family—from each other.[2]

The lacks, errors, distortions, and denials that develop when there is inharmony or disharmony show up in the individual coping and decision-making ability.

Those who have been seduced into doing all the adjusting to other people make decisions on the basis of the other person, no matter what they want. They feel guilty most of the time.

Those that are angrily required to fit in with other people become blamers and are seeking revenge.

Those that are required to fit in with things, be "objective," become super-reasonable.

Those that can never predict anything become irrelevant. It is only the balance between
what the child is,
what the context is, and
what the people are
done by fitting all parts equally, does that human being come out harmoniously.

If a person is placating, he/she is hiding wishes.

If a person is blaming, he/she is hiding intimacy.

If a person is being super-reasonable, he/she is hiding both.

If a person is being irrelevant, that person is hiding everything. *

In effect, the person who speaks *in*congruently "hides" her or his real internal experience. Those who are placating or being super-reasonable are hiding what they truly want. Those who are blaming or being super-reasonable are blocking intimacy in their attempts at self-protection.

"What the context is" simply represents actual reality. When Virginia said, "What the child is, what the context is," she was referring to the difficult to define, ever-changing, flowing here-and-now—this specific child at this point in time and place. Virginia observed that sanity lies in the ability to congruently comment on *what is.* Wholeness lies in the ability to communicate on what *is*—as opposed to what a person might *pretend* in his/her misguided attempt to protect her/his fragile feelings of self-worth. Context must always be considered as a part of the assessment process in any human situation.[3]

Further, selves are relational and, like it or not, we are all connected. Keenly aware that our entire universe is one vast system made of interacting systems, Virginia was also quite cognizant of the self as *indivisible* from our overarching context.

Virginia was holding in view the "greater context" and her respect for each self based on her awareness of the uniqueness of each person; immense as is the world's population, each person is a *unique* dot on the map. Along with this fact is the fact of the kinship we share with each other—our oneness, one with the other. We cannot become whole persons without attention to our styles of interaction with the others, as well as becoming aware that each of us is a singular original version.

Virginia often observed that very few of us learned, growing up in our families, about this relationship between wholeness and communication. Internal integration is a resolution between our "old learnings"

---

* Virginia Satir, personal notes, April 7, 1980.

bequeathed us by our parents and new information: wholly new and that enlightenment brought "by looking at the past with new eyes." It is both affected and reflected by congruence in communication. This awareness—via the view from those "new eyes"—makes possible access to the riches of the self.

Virginia's work made clear the goal of personal growth as well as the evidence and means of growth: congruence and wholeness. Evidence and means are part of a process which, itself, is a system at work. Virginia cited Bertalanffy's (1971) systems theory:

> Any system consists of several individual parts. Each part is essential and related to each other part to attain a certain outcome; each acts as a stimulus to other parts. The system has an order and a sequence which is determined through the actions, reactions, and interactions among the parts. This constant interplay governs how the system manifests itself. A system has life only now, when its component parts are present.
>
> Sounds confusing? It isn't really. You put yeast, flour, water, and sugar together to make bread. The bread isn't like any one of its ingredients, yet it contains them all . . .
>
> All human life is part of a system. (Satir, 1988a, 130-31)

Virginia's way of using concepts from systems theory together with her information on the central nature of human communication is broader than both Freud and Jung, who focused primarily only on internal individual dynamics. In contrast, Virginia looked both outward and inward and all around and wrote:

> In any given human being at any point in time, there is a dynamic interplay among all eight levels [of the self]. [See image The Universal Human Resources, page 80] It would be as if there were a formula of

A (Body) + B (Brain) + C (Emotion) + D (Sense) + E (Interactions) + F (Nutrition) + G (Context) + H (Soul) = S (Self). All parts do add up to a self, although the self is more than the sum of the parts. Still, each part can be studied separately . . . The truth remains that each of us is a system. While we can talk about each part separately, they function together just like any system. Just like a family. (Satir, 1986b, 287)

Virginia added to the concept of integration of the self in two ways essential to her teaching. She recognized that human beings are *relational* and that our communication styles affect ourselves and others so profoundly that we cannot talk about wholeness (a more serviceable term than "mental health") without talking about communication patterns. She also recognized that we cannot talk about wholeness without taking into account our physical being. Congruent and incongruent communication patterns produce physical manifestations in both the speaker and the listener. Being able to consciously tune into physical sensations and feelings is prerequisite to integration.

The Four Stances of Incongruent Communication

Once one is made aware of what to look for, the incongruent patterns, can be recognized clearly and easily.

It is vital to understand what incongruent behavior looks, sounds, and feels like: Virginia's four categories of incongruent responses that an individual is very likely to make when self-esteem issues arise. That knowledge can guide one toward the health—even life— givingness of congruent behavior. The individual who is *aware* of the following patterns may choose to respond congruently to the stress involved in questions of self-worth, and, for example, may simply say, "I don't feel so good about myself right now; let me check out with you what you really meant when you said _____. I had the feeling you were questioning my competence (integrity, value, worth, whatever) just then. Is that true?" That is an example of congruence.

The following are the four styles of incongruence:

Placating

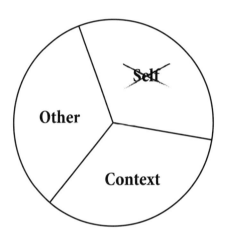

Self is crossed out; at the farthest extreme, self is eliminated.

I don't count; I agree with you no matter what I think or feel; no matter the circumstances.

Behaving as if my feelings do not count—only you and yours count. I agree with whatever you say. In placating, I behave as if my feelings and my essential self do not matter. Self is neglected.

Half of us sell ourselves out. When the question comes up—are we adequate, valued, cared about?—we "cave in" and say, "No, no, I am not. I am not important. But you are. You are what matters, I don't. No. I don't. But please love me for acquiescing like this. Please say I can stay here with you. Please don't throw me out."

Blaming

Other is crossed out; at the farthest extreme, other is eliminated.

You don't count; I disagree with you no matter what I think or how I feel; no matter the circumstances.

Behaving as if your feelings do not count—only mine count. Whatever it is you have to say, I do not agree. In blaming, I behave as if your feelings and your essential self do not matter. The other is neglected.

A somewhat smaller number of people do not cross themselves out. Instead they say, "Who cares? F— you, I don't give a d— what you say. I know the answers and you are lucky to have me around. My feelings and what I want count; you, and who you are, are not all that important."

And it works for a moment or two. I feel a sense of power while that goes on. Then I begin to get lonely up here at the top, very lonely, lost in my own "wealth of information and authority." Strength becomes the iron gate between us instead of the bridge across.

Being Super-Reasonable

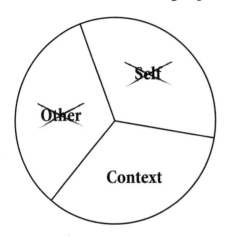

Self and other are crossed out; at the farthest extreme, we are all eliminated with the "goal" taking the place of the human beings involved.

Behaving as if feelings do not count, only the context counts. I behave like a robot and drain my face and voice of all emotion, no matter what I think or feel inside.

I dry my feelings up. With those feelings go all my juices, because there is a gland for every feeling and a juice for every gland. I begin to die of the physiological consequences of the drying. The deadliness also escalates externally because I am free to commit any atrocity in the name of my particular "god" or cause.

But isn't there a more expedient way? Can't we forget about our own feelings for the sake of this goal? What about the task? What about getting the job done? All those feelings are so inefficient. How quickly it would all go if we did not have to attend to them. Feelings have to be set aside now so we can just get this done, accomplished. Isn't this what we are here for anyway. This task? This goal?

Being super-reasonable—what many otherwise very intelligent people mistake for "objectivity" and "mature adult behavior"—is behavior in which neither our feelings nor our essential selves matter. Even our bodies do not matter; only the task—the goal—matters. *Persons* are neglected. It is a position that locks away a person's feelings, which signals humanity seriously in danger at that moment.

Being Irrelevant

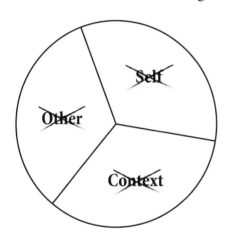

Self, and other, *and* context are crossed out; reality slips away. Nothing counts. My behavior is to distract at every moment—to get the attention off myself; perhaps, then, nobody will notice my "worthlessness."

And the ultimate price of that response is insanity.

Nothing counts, not you, me, or the context. Distracting behavior is to get the attention off myself; perhaps, then, nobody will notice my "worthlessness."

Those engaging in this stance say, "Ah, but perhaps nothing really matters. I don't, you don't, it doesn't. Nothing. Perhaps if we just tried to forget it. Or change it into something else. Or tell a joke. Distract us from the subject. Do anything, but please don't think about how we feel or who we are. I might be able to bear it if we just pretend like nothing is there and nobody notices me. If we ignore it, maybe it will go away. Let us prevent any verbal acknowledgment."

Being irrelevant: in which nothing matters, neither our feelings and essential selves nor even our context. All reality is neglected. The ultimate expression of this response is insanity.

The Stress Ballet: Shifting Through the Four Styles

Virginia used the term "stress ballet" to describe the motions through which a given dyad would go, shifting among the four incongruent communication styles in response to stress. A person might start out with placation and, rise to her/his feet, so to speak, and launch into blaming, then resort to the robot-like stance of super-reasonable behavior or irrelevant behavior—then change again. Changes would often be in response to the dyad partner's given stance. Virginia called such a series of interchanges the "stress ballet": each stance is so uncomfortable that people usually shift from one to the other because of the discomfort.

The Inner Dialogue: Self-Worth Questions

The inner dialogues that accompany all these outer manifestations hold the key for change. The four static, incongruent stances are all—often desperate—attempts at maintaining self-esteem.

The blame game is characteristically simplistic and a knee-jerk way to try to feel better about one's self. We are all familiar with the following:

Blamer
Outer dialogue: "You are awful; look what you caused!"
Inner dialogue: "Now if I can convince us both of that, I won't
   have to feel so bad."

Placator

Outer dialogue: "You are right. Of course I caused it. How can you put up with such a chronic klutz like me?"

Inner dialogue: "Even if I didn't do it, I probably did something else wrong that hasn't been discovered yet. Maybe if I prostrate myself in sufficient abjection, I will obtain some sense of forgiveness."

This is a scene between blamer and placator where each person's self-esteem issues are behind the inner dialogue remaining inner and not becoming explicit. The incongruence between the actual feelings and what is verbally expressed prevails. In effect, it is as if the blamer curses the placator and the placator accepts the curse.

A somewhat more malevolent scene exists when none of the above, not even the outer dialogue, is verbalized at all. No dialogue and no attempt at resolution means no intimacy, leaving an estrangement that becomes a pit available to receive emotional debris in which physical illness as well as emotional pain may begin to generate.

Moving from the blaming/placating configuration to the super-reasonable: unexpressed *feelings* are the scourge of the psychological sophisticate. First owning and admitting, internally, to feelings is prerequisite to their expression. There are those who think of themselves as wanting to "remain rational" because we think our intellect is our major tool. We have read psychology and been to seminars and self-help groups—we know enough not to openly blame the other; we have grown enough not to openly blame ourselves. So what is left to do with this bad feeling I still have in relation to you, my colleague, to you, my friend? I cannot angrily say, "See what you caused"; I am not supposed to be judgmental. I cannot piteously say, "See what I caused"; *intellectually* I know I am supposed to be responsible for valuing myself. How very difficult it is for us to say what we may actually be experiencing *internally*:

"I still feel bad about what went on between us. I feel puzzled about what to do even with my own feelings, let alone yours. Still, is there not some way we can work together to solve what continues to lie between us?"

Placating and Blaming

As all of the four styles of incongruent communication require a partner for implementation, blaming and placating are interrelated. Very often, those whose unenlightened favored choice is placation team up with those who most frequently choose to blame. People who feel that they are so unworthy that they deserve abuse are drawn to those who will accommodate them, and vice versa.

Placators often spread themselves out obsequiously, practically holding out engraved invitations to another to walk on them. It can be a real challenge to pull such a person to his or her feet and find a way to empower her or him. (A social worker acquaintance was once heard to say, "I believe if I was ever going to beat up anybody, it would be a battered wife.") Unconsciously, such people fuel their own abuse.

People who are placating often feel they really cannot live without the other. The issues feel like life-and-death matters. The unexpressed inner dialogue of the placator is "I'm afraid I won't live unless you allow me to be with you." They are willing to give their very selves away in a kind of devil's bargain for insured survival. Carried far enough, the placating stance can result in suicide. When one, whose history includes much placation, begins not-yet-skilled attempts to replace placation with congruence, that person often will pass through blaming en route. Often mistaken as achievement of goal of self assertion, *this is actually only another step in the stress ballet.* It is a step, however, *toward* congruence—the person who has begun to blame has at least begun to stand up for self.

The blamer's deep, inner dialogue is "I might not look so bad if I can make this person look worse." The desperation is somewhat more obvious in the person who chooses to placate and please others than in the aggression of the blaming person. One only needs to look beneath the surface. The feeling of vulnerability is there, nonetheless. A very great loneliness can accompany the kind of power one feels by virtue of dominance. The person who chooses blaming to mitigate his or her lack of sense of self-worth has chosen a method that will break down at that loneliness point. One will find oneself looking around and thinking, "If I am so wonderful, why am I standing here alone?" The loudness of the tyrant and his or her need for love have a direct correlation. Rather than reach out for the emotional connection at such a point, he or she will, instead, escalate the blaming. Bellowing is a measure of the depth of the need and of the bellower's sense of emptiness.

Some years ago, there was a long period of far too much celebration of "expression of anger" among therapists and heirs of the human potential movement and not enough emphasis on "Then what?"[4] There is a temporary catharsis in expressing anger. However, unless the other person present is able, through some glint of wisdom or greatness of spirit, to accept the anger without feeling in some way diminished by it, this cathartic relief is short-lived, the reason being that our connection with one another is being eroded, if not severed, in such a process. The person who obediently expresses the anger—without the information that such expression is only one step in a larger process—may not take the next step of openly talking about the deep disappointment, which lies beneath most anger.

Suppose in my anger I say to you, "Get outta my face!"—and you do. Then I am left there alone, my having told you off being my only comfort. I may then nurture my rage in an attempt to generate *some* kind of warmth, because I am left here with only myself to generate energy.

In order for there to be a coming back together again, one of us must say, on some level, or in some way, "But we are both intrinsically valuable people. I care how you feel. Please tell me how this experience has been for you." Obscuring this potential process by pretending to oneself that the anger is "not important" also provides no route for resolution. In that scene, I bury my guilt and then avoid contact with you in order not to be called back to the site of the burial and "scene of the crime." I avoid contact with myself—with my own insides—to elude the pain of the feeling.

It was Virginia's observation that about half the people she encountered would, when under emotional stress, sell themselves out to please the other person; the immediate response would be "My own opinion—ideas, wants, needs—cannot possibly be as important as yours are." This response can range from sickeningly sweet, patronizing "agreement" all the way to the extreme of the continuum—suicide. The next most common response is to blame the other to gain a sense of importance at the expense of the other. The outer message is "You are not worth it, and I am!" The inner fear is "How am I measuring up?" Although this stance bears the seeds of self-care, its alienating nature mitigates against connection with the other. Carry this behavior far enough and you would be going beyond disagreeableness and on to homicide.

Many therapists think they have created therapeutic triumphs by facilitating the "expression of hostility." Unfortunately, that is only part of the journey. The expression of anger that contains condescension rather than respect is a very alienating activity. The "superior" person, bent on proving the "inferiority" of another, does not win friends in the long run.

Such a person may be very convincing and may even influence great masses of people. The aura of a point of power is seductive in a sea of people longing to be led. For every Hitler, Stalin, Osama bin Laden, Jim Jones, Jerry Falwell, and Reverend Moon, there are their followings—hundreds who feel great comfort in not doing their own thinking.[5] Being able to manipulate is very different from being able to engage in real communion with others. Welding power without respect for the worth of others, without interest in helping them maintain self-esteem, leaves a great emptiness in the "power" person and great vulnerability in those manipulated.

It seems that the placating-blaming pattern Virginia discovered in all human communication, in every culture she visited, stretches back five thousand years. It accounts for the "dysfunctionality" described by Rianne Eisler (1987) as the "blade" culture. The extreme end of the blaming continuum includes violence. For example, if a group decides the best way to take care of their feelings of inadequacy is to grab a sword, jump on a horse, and streak out across the steppes, lopping off heads, and if the heads' previous owners had a matching sense of not being worth much, obviously, those who hid in the bushes and watched will conclude they are better off siding with the guys with the swords. It may not be terribly attractive, but it is going to last longer. It is not hard to trace that way of thinking straight to Hiroshima. Anger may beget a sense of power. A sense of power goes a long way toward helping a person feel worthwhile. The problem is that power, when based on who can kill whom more quickly, really does not "win friends and influence people" on the person-specific level. The sword wielder is not likely to attract cuddling until or unless she or he at least lays down the sword. Thus, the consequence may be very great loneliness along with the kind of power one feels by virtue of dominance—or the lack of feeling when the stress ballet moves to super-reasonable behavior.

In the stress ballet, a person may move into another stance in response to the inner pressure of feeling inadequate. The person seeking a feeling of power from simple dominance might, instead, shut off feeling. The Stalins and Hitlers persuade their followers to disconnect from their own humanity—to suppress their own feelings and to respond robotically to orders.

Under stress, people move from one incongruent response to another; all behavior is always in process.

Awareness of one's own uniqueness obviates any need to compare oneself to another. By definition, no comparison is possible in complete uniqueness. Self-worth questions are behind all scoreboard keeping. The person who truly appreciates his or her own uniqueness needs neither to dominate nor submit and is free to engage in cooperative partnership.

What Virginia would have us remember is that perpetrators of abuse as well as those who are abused all come from trying to protect their very delicate, often badly battered, inner selves.

Being Super-Reasonable

Taking a special place among scores of others in recent history, Osama bin Laden and his followers provided a consummate example of the most extreme results of the super-reasonable stance.

In the now infamous September 11 tragedy, those terrorists who crashed themselves into the buildings and into our lives were not the sort of men who would be arrested in barroom brawls or issued tickets for road rage. These men were so self-contained that they could live among us all for years, blending well into our own (preattack) task-oriented culture. These were men who could put their context, their task, before any human concern. They serve as beacon-light examples of discounting their own humanity as well as that of the three thousand or so people they slaughtered: "Look, this is how you prove lives and the feelings of all you leave behind do not matter." This was no impulse-driven act of hatred. This was a cold, deliberate act of men who had so frozen their own hearts and souls that nothing in their lives remained except their goal. Relentlessly, like so many robots, they marched toward their own destruction and that of several thousand human beings who happened to stand in their path. Only their context counted—human beings did not.

Can anything on the face of this earth be more chilling and more dangerous than a man locked into this kind of response to his own insides?

Virginia's description of this super-reasonable, robot-like response was this:

> The third thing we can do is to make believe that only "it" exists . . . What we do with this is make it super-reasonable which means that everything becomes an "it." We cross out me and we cross out you. That's why so-called organizations that are "sophisticated" don't bother with people's feelings. Not at all. They must deal in long words. I no longer get impressed with long words . . .
>
> . . . We move into another whole level which is far harder to bring out, because it looks like it is so congruent with society and that is super-reasonable which is the flip side of irrelevancy.
>
> Irrelevancy is the flip side of super-reasonableness. We are into another ball game. Every time I present this, I know what difficulty there is, because this part here is *so congruent with the society* and people don't see that it is an incongruent thing, how they are discounting themselves.
>
> All of these add up to something missing, some important thing is missing. We do not live in this world alone so "me" and "you" are very important. We cannot live in this world without connecting with the context, because the context has power and it has information for us. (Satir, 1987a, tape 5)

When Virginia said, "It looks like it is so congruent with society," she is making the point that the American culture equates super-reasonable behavior with mental health, calling it "objectivity."

Thus, for example, the hapless Timothy McVeigh, Oklahoma City bomber, our own homegrown terrorist, may be the monster our own culture created, a product of the mentality we endorsed. He was sent into the army for the first Gulf War, where his natural inclinations received technical training and social reinforcement: "Here is how you squeeze all mercy out of your heart and *serve the cause* without being distracted by feelings for your fellow human." (The war may also have been part of the breeding ground for the World Trade Center terrorists.[6]) The McVeighs of the world, the Nazi death camps of the past, and the World Trade Center hijack bombers represent the destructive extreme of super-reasonable behavior. Nationality, religion, or ethnic background are not the operative factor—response to inner dialogue and choice of communication stance is.

We should never have executed McVeigh; we should have kept him around and studied him. The world desperately needs to understand and address this toxic process—soon. McVeigh and the terrorists represent the extreme end of the super-reasonable continuum.

Closer to the middle of the continuum, the super-reasonable style of responses is a real occupational hazard for the intelligent person. The inner dialogue of the individual who engages in this type of communication may be "This task is more important than how either of us feels. I will devote myself to it, and then maybe I won't feel so worthless." People who choose to respond to inner feelings of inadequacy by leaning toward the cerebral can be more difficult both to spot and to address in terms of therapy and general soul-growing. One is bright enough to know one *ought* to feel worthwhile; one is bright enough to know that it's "not nice" to treat others badly. It can be a serious temptation to just squash the troubling feelings. So the person with high intelligence escapes into cerebration and out of passion. This is life with the life sucked out of it. One major problem with this route is that it is terribly *boring* as well as dangerous.

In the feelingless response, the context becomes more important than the human beings involved. Many people in our culture equate this with an "adult" or "mature" response and do not understand the serious danger also posed by chronic use of this response, to the *physical aspect* of the self. In Virginia's homespun words, "there is a gland for every feeling and a juice for every gland; dry up the feelings and you dry up those juices" (Satir, 1971, 1984, personal communication). Do it over enough years and your body begins to suffer the literal consequences of the diminishment of those various juices. Thus, this response is not only ultimately extremely dangerous for the larger society—permitting the behavior of terrorists and all those who believe ends justify means—it is physically dangerous for the person responding super-reasonably.

The premature demise of many great people may be traced to their unawareness that it is *vitally*—and I used the word advisedly—important to find and foster the expression of feelings in ourselves and others. There is mounting evidence that this is literally a life and death issue in terms of physical well-being. At the time of her death, Virginia was still working on the relationship of this stance to cancer (Brothers, 1987a, 1989b, 2000).

Those who are defending themselves via the super-reasonable stance must be brought into emotional touch with their own humanity and that of other human beings. Cognizance of basic worth has to become more than an intellectual concept. Intervention for super-reasonableness includes the expression and "impression" of feelings. The person who has heavily used super-reasonable behavior must reacquaint themselves—not only with anger, sadness, happiness, and fear—but also with body sensate feelings. Body feelings reflect emotional feeling.

Being Irrelevant

Irrelevant responding, though employed less frequently than the other patterns, may be the most difficult with which to deal. The inner dialogue that accompanies this pattern is "I feel so bad about myself that nothing matters at all."

In the presence of someone being irrelevant, one experiences a chaotic feeling that we are not both heading toward the same goal. As soon as I think I know what the other is talking about, she or he is off in another direction. People whose behavior is incongruent in this form are trying to distract attention in a desperate hope that they can escape notice and hide from the other. The extreme of this response is psychosis. The other extreme, toward the creative end of the continuum, is the use of humor. While some humor may be congruent, both the joker/laugher and the hallucinator may be trying, by use of a similar means, to avoid attention to their inner selves.

This behavior is identified by the person frequently changing the subject, particularly when emotion-laden material is introduced into the dialogue.

Summary

Virginia's observation of patterns of communication includes the basic fact of our interdependence and provides a method of bringing into awareness the impact our interactions have on one another. The importance of this work is in its profound implications for healing not only the individual psyche, not only the family system, but potentially *all* human systems—the system of humanity itself.

Since Virginia went around the world looking at thousands of families, when we talk about Virginia's work, we are not talking only about family therapy anymore. If any one of us watch *thousands* of people around the world, we are beginning to talk about patterns of human behavior, not just therapy with families.

We recall again: All human communication both influences and is influenced by self-esteem. Part of looking at an interaction is to consider how one feels *about* how one feels. Virginia studied and taught what she called "Ingredients for an Interaction" (Satir, 1991, 121–129). We will examine those ingredients more closely in chapter 11.

Virginia's deep respect for Beingness, as manifest in the specific person before her, served as a compass point to lead her through that which displays as "pathology." *On the other side of the so-called "pathology," Virginia invariably found a disguised and ineffectual wish to communicate.*

Congruence creates psychological safety in spite of the paradox that it often requires risk. Within a context of congruence, apparent pathology often melts away, replaced by authentic interchange. Being able to distinguish between the life-enhancing nature of congruent communication versus the life-endangering nature of incongruent communication is—literally, over the long haul—as worthwhile a piece of information as being able to distinguish one form of mushroom from another when gathering them in the woods.

Chapter Notes

1. During their mutual tenures at Esalen, along with himself, Fritz Perls accused Virginia, albeit within a warm, complimentary context, of "intellectual systemititis." He characterized them both as not being willing to "settle for mediocrity." He spoke of her "eagerness to learn" and "fantasy for things to come."

2. It is important to note that I have, of course, taken Virginia's notes out of context—and that they are *notes*. Her intent was to write an entire book, which would include this subject. These thoughts, only notes to herself, represent just one piece of her overall thinking about teaching people the skills to become their own decision makers.

3. "Context" is as vital a part of any interaction as is "self" and "other." Virginia's explanation of the importance of context, along with that of Gregory Bateson, can be found in chapters 6 and 12.

4. These celebrations of expression of anger were more prevalent before the advent of managed care; currently, therapy is encouraged to

devolve into manipulation addressed only to symptoms. Buzz words now are "anger management"; encouragement of expression of anger, currently out of vogue, is now being replaced with what might easily become encouragement of super-reasonable behavior.

5. The operative word here is "following"—the "lemming" factor. The leader at the head of the parade does not necessary need to be the last word in evil. They need only set themselves up as having the last word on whatever the subject.

6. Previous wars have proved, over time, to be breeding grounds for future wars:

> Some of the most intractable problems of the modern world have roots in decisions made right after the end of the Great War. Among them one could list the four Balkan wars between 1991 and 1999; the crisis over Iraq (whose present borders resulted from the Franco-British rivalries and casual mapmaking); the continuing quest of the Kurds for self-determination; disputes between Greece and Turkey; and the endless struggle between Arabs and Jews over land that each thought had been promised to them. (MacMillan, 2001, ix)

For each such war, a group of men were rigorously trained in ignoring their own feelings and the humanity of the "enemy" and taught to focus exclusively on the context. Have there ever been any corresponding, sustained, and large scale campaigns to de-program such men? Could a Tim McVeigh have been rehabilitated? We will never know. We used our old familiar domination/submission model and eliminated him instead.

7

THE PATTERNS THAT DISCONNECT: INTRAPERSONAL INCONGRUENCE

Peace Within—Peace Between—Peace Among
—**Virginia Satir**, 1988

It starts with me, it doesn't start with you or me starting with you.
—**Virginia Satir**, 1985

Congruence starts—or does not start—in each person in each specific interaction. The first step will be—or not be—congruence self to self. The questions are "What is going on inside me? Not only what do I *think* but how do I *feel* about what I think? Moreover, how do I feel about how I feel?" The latter is the question that opens the self-worth questions bag.

Many people grow up learning to suppress their feelings into unrecognizable clumps buried deep in their psyches, leaving veritable petri dishes filled with germs of far-reaching social as well as physiological consequences. Virginia Satir's shorthand expression for addressing this systemic sequence was: "Peace Within—Peace Between—Peace Among."[1] The beginning step toward peace among all is dealing with people with those volatile petri dishes, so that they may come to "Peace Within."

"Peace Within" oneself—internal harmony—is the first building block of congruent communication. Expand the "peace betweens" enough, teach and learn those skills, and we ultimately might actually reach "peace among." Here, in these short phrases, Virginia Satir compacted her lifelong examination of the working process of human systems. Here, at least, we do have the formula.

"Peace within" is based on intrapersonal congruence. Congruence always includes awareness and acknowledgement of feelings. Unaware of the dramatic difference it makes, many people, unfortunately and often, lock into denial—the frozen grip on a distorted reality—as in the crucial importance of dealing with feelings.

The dynamic to which Virginia alluded in her theory and observations about cancer, and which is present in other super-reasonable behavior, is known as *denial*. Virginia steered away from using psychoanalytic language partly to avoid triggering old mindsets in her trainees. Instead, Virginia emphasized the essentially *defensive* nature of such mechanisms, reminding therapists of the vulnerability and fear behind them. She preferred to use language that indicated intervention points rather than getting lost in facets of individual behavior taken out of context.

Therapists know denial when they see it: the frozen grip on a distorted reality, the refusal to admit to What Is. Denial is the rigid holding of oneself away from new input, either intellectual or emotional.

Virginia did not focus on denial, per se; she directed her energy toward helping the person feel connected and safe. Denial, as a dynamic, is a feature in the double-level messages about which Virginia did speak, and to which we alluded earlier.

Denial is a defense mechanism learned early in life that comes with high costs later in life. Denial involves an internalized lie that once had an external stimulus. The parent wants a "good" child, which often translates: *quiet* child. The average child around the globe is not carefully taught how to honor her or his feelings and those of others without necessarily acting on all of them. In our own society, a lot of parental energy goes into containing a two-year-old, rather than trying to understand the child's feelings. Instead and all too often, in order to achieve compliance, the parent will say, "You don't really feel that way."

In the process of raising her or him, instilling beliefs considered important, the parent climbs inside the child's being and dwells inside the now grown-up child. Unless this now grown-up person eventually comes to a much fuller understanding of her or his emotional underpinnings, she or he cannot feel good about herself or himself while violating parents' rules—for example, about expression of feeling. The physiological, as well as the psychological price paid for this suppression of feeling can be high.

Honoring, rather than denying, our feelings, whatever their composition, is an essential human task. Simple and reasonable as it sounds, humankind has a history of doing and teaching anything but honoring of feelings. Humankind has waged wars, permitted starvation, promoted slavery, set up Inquisitions, with hosts of variations on that list, behaving as if the feelings of other human beings were without value. Humankind has gritted its teeth and performed these atrocities in the face of its own revulsion at its own acts. Pontius Pilate, who had a gut reaction against allowing that famous crucifixion, pushed back his own humanistic impulse and, as justification for that atrocity, pleaded that the decision was not in his job description.

Mental health and physical health, which cannot be separated from one another, depend on the awareness and acknowledgment, within the self, of joy, pain, fear, sorrow, and rage—either justified or unjustified. Both depend on the awareness that all feelings are valid. Being in indivisible combination, no one aspect can be denied without an impact on the rest. If I am angry and will not acknowledge my anger to myself, my body maintains the nonverbal expression, holding the consequences in my tissue and structure. Giving myself no verbal expression, I remain tight, not permitting the flow of the feeling. Life is about flow. Permitting myself the awareness, acknowledgment and—if appropriate to the context—permission for expression of the feeling gives my body relief of the tension and the corresponding opportunity to go about its normal physiological business. *Not* giving myself this permission, I give myself headaches, or arthritis, or some other choreography which metaphorically represents what is not verbally spoken. Thus, if permission to verbalize, or otherwise honor, the anger is not within my belief system I unwittingly choose the physical manifestation. Denial provides the "unwittingness."

Belief in the essential goodness of humankind must take into account, rather than deny, the shadows and the antithesis, must allow voice to the pain that accompanies that recognition. Evil *unacknowledged* is a far more potent and dangerous adversary. Blindness, ignoring those uncomfortable feelings, arms "evil" in a way that honoring the feelings never could.

After the existence and power of a destructive principle is acknowledged, the individual does become freer to make choices. Actively choosing, in awareness, moves a person into a position for emotional growth. Liberated by intrapersonal congruence, she or he is then able to be open and to allow the free movement of the natural Life process almost as simply as does the growing daisy.

In contrast to daisies, people have to make conscious moment-to-moment choices about emotional growth, which must include the choice of openness to another human being. In this increasingly multifarious, dangerous world, it is my business, as a human being, to be responsible for my role as a life-bearing agent. The daisies, as well as all other living species, are dependent on us. As one of life's most complex organisms, we have a sacred trust—each other and the rest of the planet. We must perpetuate, rather than impede, the flow of Life through what we know of Creation. Connectedness is a time- and space-honored pattern. That flow of life cannot be separated from human relatedness. All the chemical ingredients required to make up a human being are found in a supernova. Our universe is one of relatedness; we are not so separate from the galaxies as our earthbound viewpoint would suggest.

Accepting that the parameters of relatedness and connectedness practically define the design of the human being is fundamental. *Feelings* are an essential part of this matrix. Although that would seem to be obvious, there is a serious temptation, particularly among the more intelligent, to behave as if feelings have no importance in choosing a life-enhancing stance. If I dull my feelings in regard to myself and other people, I place us both in grave danger of the prevailing entropy—death and destruction of the moment. We do not have to call it Evil or Satan to reap the unraveling consequences of ignoring feelings; we have only to sit numbly on our hands. This numb hand-sitting is what permitted the virulent possibility and ensuing reality of Hitler's horrifying, destructive power. The rise of the Third Reich was a result of *super-reasonable* responses on the part of too large a portion of humankind at that time. It is dangerous oversimplification to blame this holocaust only on Hitler.

In some similar way, the world must have turned a blind eye to the raging force that boiled out of the Middle East on September 11, 2001. Otherwise, we would not have been caught by such surprise with the vehemence of that terrorist attack.

That Hitler was allowed to remain in power is a result in the body politic. Terrorist bombings are periodic exclamatory examples punctuating our lives with the consequences of "causes" and *context* valued over human beings. Cancer, as we will see in the next chapter, is one possible result of the numbing of feelings and estrangement from others, the effect on the body of the individual.

Respect for self and other, which includes respect for the *feelings* of self and others, may be the "vaccine" that could help prevent cancer, demonic national leaders, and nuclear war.

Without inner congruence, outer congruence is not possible. One must first acknowledge what is inside before one can present it congruently. As we have said, interconnectedness with others is seriously restricted, if not interrupted altogether, when interactions are incongruent. (See the below figures, portraits of intrapersonal response.)

Portrait of Virginia's Super-Reasonable Intrapersonal Response

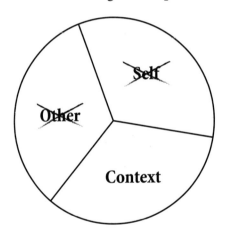

Crossing out the value of one's own humanity: no attention to feelings in the self, blocking awareness of any sense of guilt or responsibility. Crossing out the humanity of others: no concern for the feelings of others, blocking any visceral response to atrocity. Valuing only the task. Regard only for context. No regard for a person's feelings and the implications for those persons. No regard for human beings.

Examples of what people using this response will say: "Hitler is saving the state from inflation and economic ruin," "Allah wants to rid the world of infidels," "As good Christian Bosnians, we want to push those Muslims off our land," "Access to adequate oil supply is essential to the American economy and way of life."

Portrait of a Congruent Intrapersonal Response

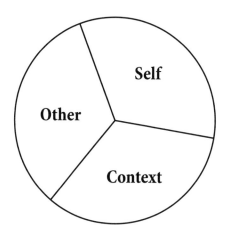

Attending to appropriate internal feelings of horror/response of one's own humanity: "My god, I can't allow this to continue and live with myself." Attending to the feeling/humanity of others: "But these are human beings he is herding around like cattle." Or "We cannot allow whole tribes to starve and suffer."

Contrasting examples of using this response: "The love of wealth prevents the conduct of man. Wherefore the Sage attends to the inner self, and not outward appearances [23]. Wherefore, if a man esteems himself only as much as he esteems the whole world, he will find security therein. If a man loves the world as much as he loves himself, he will find security therein [25] (*Tao Te Ching*, Chen Lin 1969, 78, 80)" and "For what shall it profit a man if he shall gain the whole world and lose his own soul? (Mark 8:38, *King James Version Bible*)

Human connectedness is a conduit for the Possible. Opening of the heart is essential not only to the health of the individual physiological heart and body, but for the healing congruent communication to flow, for life to flow between two individuals and among humanity. The respectful openness, which some religions teach, assumes that each of us, complete with all our feelings, is of value. Our meeting is a cause for celebration because we are magnificent manifestations of Life (Satir, 1986c). Wholeness breeds in that sort of atmosphere. The heart warms, the body relaxes, the physical system is permitted to go about its business of "normal maintenance" undistracted by a need to attend and counter the various physiological implications of stress. The world goes out of attack/defense mode—modus operandi of the domination/submission model—and begins to look to the needs of the suffering. Congruence gives growth a chance, societal as well as individual.

Congruence is relevant on all levels. As we will see in chapter 9, even cancer may possibly serve as a grisly example of the importance of intrapersonal congruence. Authentic honoring of feelings would require the individual to come forth from the "protective" shell, which does *not* protect from the ravages from within, and step out into the sunlight of connection with other human beings—not with a grinning blindness to pain, sorrow, and suffering, but with a receptive step in the direction of belief in the possibility of relationship to another person. Denying feelings blocks growth and connection with others.

Respect for the humanity within each person—including the self— opens the system and allows an entry point, a connecting point between you and me. This entry point can become a growth point. A person can permit himself expression of feeling, make oneself vulnerable to the other, then be available for the level of mutual nurturing that mitigates destruction of the body or of relationships.

Congruent human communication requires the admission of *truth*: that what feels bad, feels bad; that pain hurts. Sorrow is a valid experience and must be allowed its course in the face of true loss, or even of suspected loss. The *feeling* is the same regardless of the fact, and the force is in the feeling. Anger is a valid emotion. It *must be acknowledged* to prevent either its transformation into internalized self-destruction within the body or outside the body of the individual and in the body politic. This magnification into externalized, acted-out destruction could be seen in Hitler's Holocaust, in terrorists slamming planeloads of people into buildings, or turning themselves into human bombs.

Congruent behavior must include an acknowledgment of the existence of whatever dreadful possibilities and/or realities are in the offing, and a grieving appropriate to that condition. After such acknowledgment can come a belief that it does not have to be that way, that the ending to the drama can be rewritten.

Feelings are an integral part of living and aliveness. Denial is a frozenness, an arrest of thought and feeling, isolating the person from his/her own flowing/feeling system and inhibiting genuine contact with the other, with essence of self, with the growth process. One can believe in the possible, an active flowing process that stretches out from the person to embrace all feeling and to connect the whole self with the other and with all the possibility inherent in the Life Force. Faith is believing what can be without denying what is.

Virginia's basic premises included the healing nature of congruent communication. In her words, it "builds bridges rather than walls." As we have seen, it is not so difficult to demonstrate the four behavior stances that represent incongruent communication. That is the kind of communication that goes on between most people most of the time. We are not given to letting each other know when we feel weak or inadequate. We bluster or patronize instead—or lapse into erudition, or change the subject. Virginia put together an effective operational guide to the components of building the bridge.

Virginia's work was about helping people make connection—real and deep—first with self, then with other people.

These four stances—unfortunately by far the most common defensive response to the stress of self-doubt—erode the spirit, soul, and body and erect barriers between us. They are properly called "patterns that disconnect," so profound is their disruptive effect on relationships.

Further Notes on the Importance of Recognizing and Naming Feelings

All four of these patterns of communication are incongruent in that they reflect mismatching of words and bodily expressions with true feelings. To recognize the various patterns of incongruent communication, it is important, as a diagnostic tool, to become aware of one's own feelings. If I start wanting to slap somebody, it probably means that person is placating. If I start wanting to strangle him or her, it probably means the person is being super-reasonable. If I become aware of a queasy feeling in my stomach, it probably means the person is blaming me. If I cannot figure out what the person is talking about, he or she is probably being irrelevant and manifesting distracting behavior.

One's body immediately feels the difference between congruence and incongruence. Muscles relax and tension ebbs. If I say what I really mean—face, body, and words matching feelings—that gives my autoimmune system and physical structure their best chance. It does make a certain kind of obvious sense that if one lines things up, fits things together where they fit, one gets strength and power in that cohesion.

Congruent communication is basically an alignment of the entire system of the individual which creates a magnetic-like pull toward alignment of the system of the other, influencing the system of the other toward also going into alignment. Congruent communication is the structure at the heart of Virginia's "mysteries."

Virginia addressed her own mystique, reiterating that anybody can use the principles and information:

You know people have thought I was remarkable: I had something I was born with that I could go to a place where everybody [would become] different and pretty soon we were all working as people. *It has nothing to do with what I was born with; it has to do with the way we per-ceive and what we understand.* Remember something: I don't know of anyone yet who was taught about communication and worth . . . [We learned about] how we shouldn't be and how we should be, but I don't hear much about how you can really understand communica-tion . . . Many of you must know the relationship between linguistics and health. General semantics [see work of Alfred Korzybski] is based on th[at] principle . . .

Now if you really get that inside of you as a basic human concept— What is "that"? That messages are made of verbal and nonverbal. The nonverbal is the statement of the now and the verbal can come from any other place. (Satir, 1983b, 129–130)

Virginia noted that, while the verbal message may deliver a lie, the nonverbal messages are always here and now statements—which hold the truth. Congruence between the nonverbal and the verbal is what is important.

Virginia observed that when congruence enters, lying exits: "When you are congruent, lying is not part of that . . . And you know what? You cannot fake congruence—that's what's so fascinating" (Satir, 1983b, 129–130).

From Intrapersonal Congruence to Making Connection

Virginia gave a set of principles for moving into intrapersonal congru-ence and then making authentic contact with another which, studies have shown, is essentially a healing process.

Analyzing a demonstration she had given, Virginia described the elements in congruent communication. Basically, Virginia was giving lessons in "how to meet a person."

Perceptual Clearing

Think for a minute of all the people that you meet during our day, who you would meet in the morning and at night and so on. Just think about it. You meet friends, you meet relatives, you meet children, you meet spouses . . . You are a therapist so you meet people that already have names beside their own—names like diagnostic categories, et cetera.

When we meet people, we often do not meet people. We meet our pictures of them or we meet the roles, or we meet their religion, or we meet their skin color, or I don't know what, and we miss the person most of the time that way. You probably never did, but I know that I have. (Satir, 1987a)

Celebrating Uniqueness

Before I ever go into the process of meeting this being, this human being [in the upcoming demonstration], I want to tell you something that I know. I know that she is more like me than different. She is never a total duplicate. [Neither] I or her, [are ever total duplicates], but she is more like me than different. We have something in common. We have sameness and differentness in common and that's where I start. In my mind, I am preparing myself for a celebration, because *to meet another human being is a celebration.* Magic. Many of us do it and we don't even notice the celebration. In my mind then, I am going to meet a being that is both the same and different to me and I am about to have a celebration because, also, she is unique as I am unique. That is really where the cause for celebration comes in. So, I have that in my mind. (Satir, 1987a)

Permission and Clearing the Mind

The next thing that I have in my mind is that I am going to give myself *permission* to meet her. *A lot of people meet people when they haven't given themselves permission to meet people.* But, I am going to give myself *permission* to meet people because I want to get the most out of this wonderful celebration that I can. So, in my mind, I clear my mind of everything except my consciousness of this new being. Whatever it is—whether I paid the bills or if I make a mistake or told my mother this or that or whatever—I put that aside . . . Now . . . with an awareness of this new being, I am taking away anything that could stand between me and her—these old worries or fears or anticipations or whatever. So I clear my mind.

. . . I have said two things. One is that I am giving myself permission and looking at this being as connected with me in sameness and differentness, so I'm not separate from her. It wouldn't matter what she looked like, what language she spoke, what work she did, that would make her separate from me.

The next thing I do is *clear my mind* . . . clear my mind of any awareness except for her [participant in demonstration], so that means that I am meeting her with a clear slate, so to speak. That is all internal. Many of you who are therapists, think what would happen if you were greeting your patients that way. If you are business people, think what would happen if you meet your employees in business that way—or, in your family—that each meeting is a celebration. People know that when others aren't there anymore [have moved away or died], but, you see, I don't want you to wait that long. (Satir, 1987a)

Presence Boundary

Now, the third thing is where I put myself in relation to this being. And, I want to tell you something about what I have learned about people. If I were to put a dowel through this magnificent one's head—or mine, it doesn't matter—and I would come out as far as from her shoulder to where her hand could take mine as in a hello . . . We are approximately a half a meter or a half a yard—eighteen inches—from here to about here. Now, that space between here and there is also the space which shows us where the presence boundary is around a human being. Now, if we were to draw a line that was the same distance from here to here all the way around you, that would be your *presence boundary*. Mine is around me the same way. And what turns out is that in integrated people, the presence boundary is the same. It is the same. You can count on it being the same.

I want to speak about this presence boundary because many people violate that. When they violate the presence boundary, they get into trouble . . . This space between where we connect and with the literal first skin (I sometimes call this the second skin) is sacred space for every human being. Here is the sacred space. We don't violate that space. We don't go there unless we have been invited.

There are many ways to invite you into that space. I don't know if it is apparent, but I don't touch anybody unless I have been invited. I don't always say, "Will you let me touch you?" But I feel these invitations from here. (Satir, 1987a)

Touch

With this hand, right at this moment, I could have a little invitation of going [invitation from participant in demonstration], not much though. I don't know if you [the participant] are aware of that or not, and that is okay, perfectly okay. As we get more in touch with the feeling of touching, then we notice—there was a—it's not there anymore, but it was there—there was a tightness in the thumbs in this muscle right here, so as I held it, it was like with her thumbs she was pushing me to stay where I was and the others were saying, "It is all right." She wanted to be nice about it, but she didn't want me too close. There is nothing wrong with that. Now, this is a new concept to many people, that if the second skin is violated in this space, it makes for trouble. By the time you get to the skin, it is already too late. Much too late. (Satir, 1987a)

Awareness

I have done a lot of work with people who have been out of control in mental hospitals, in mental institutions for criminal behavior and such. One of the first things I began to learn (well, I observed it first, then I learned, too) was what was the difference between when I was here and if I were moving over here. I could feel all kinds of stiffness because I didn't always notice [the differences made by my proximity or distance]. Then I began to watch people and I began to see that there is a difference, even a different energy. We now have instruments to measure the energy that is from here to here as compared with her out here. It is related to how the person is integrated.

. . . Your response to somebody else's energy and find[ing] out your impact on them [is very important]. There are cognitive things we can do to be aware of this...Your connection on this hand will tell you whether you can go further or not go further. This space that must not be violated is important. If I inadvertently violate that space, I will get a message about it. The message may come by a slight movement away. It may be in a turn of the voice. It may be in some other way. Becoming aware of these kinds of responses is going to be a very important thing for you. (Satir, 1987a)

The Delicate Task of Protecting Our Inner Selves

Virginia added the concept of honoring the person's need for psychic safety. Awareness of nonverbal behavior can guide the therapist—or any interacting pair—toward respect for boundaries. Ever mindful of the battering sustained by the core within most people as they were growing up, Virginia was consistently respectful of a person's task of protecting the inner self. Rather than become impatient or label the client "resistant," Virginia might respectfully comment on their ability to protect themselves. Powerful as she was in her own personhood, she was ever mindful of the delicate core within the other. She trod softly on this ground which she considered holy.

If we take the view that we are live beings, which we are, and that *our beingness, at a moment in time reflects our tension—it reflects whether or not we are feeling relaxed and that that [feeling] is all related to how we are trying to protect ourselves in some way.* The most important thing is not to judge it, but to feel it. I won't go to someone that is not ready to go [engage in a therapeutic alliance/interaction]. That does not mean they are bad.

Think of your body as a constant and continual life, responding and sending station, moving all the time. This body is this wonderful sending and receiving instrument. (Satir, 1987a)

Physical Position

[So] the third piece has to do with [physical] position—your and/or my [physical position in relationship to someone] . . . When I started traveling all over the world, people would say, "Well, when you go to the Arab world, stand five feet away. When you go into Italy, go three and a half." You know what I found out? It is all hogwash. Every bit of it. What is important is what happens right here [in the zone between Virginia and participant in demonstration—between therapist and patient] and there are few cultures that do not extend hands in some way. Few . . . What is important is that you have to find your way with each person. [Even] with little babies.

. . . There is no color in this space and there is nothing to alert you about where that space is except your own body. (Satir, 1987a)

Dialogue From Self-Worth Places

Virginia was very aware of the importance of modulating her voice to fit the context. She described how she would intentionally speak from her own core when she wanted contact with the essence of the other. Any serious student of Virginia's work would need to review audio and/or videotapes of her work.

I don't know if I talked to you about voices. My voices come from different places. My *cognitive* voice sounds like this [*demonstrating*]. And my voice that comes from my heart has something more to it. Then, my voice that comes from inside where I'm really connecting is still another voice. So I would be connecting with the voice that would try to reach that little place inside of everyone, which I call the *self-worth* place. And that is the voice that comes from mine [my self-worth place]. So I wouldn't be commanding them, I wouldn't be frightening them, I wouldn't be cajoling them. I would simply come from here and that is a half-meditative voice, too, which would then [also facilitate] get[ting] in touch. And, I don't move until the energies change. When I worked a lot with delinquent boys that were acting out all the time, I could use the same thing. (Satir, 1987a)

Self-Esteem Questions

Virginia made the distinction between the anxiety from sending a message to oneself versus the anxiety from a message sent from someone else. Self-esteem questions rise from the feeling about the feeling, as Virginia often said:

> That poses one question with two parts: [dealing with being] anxious inside. That rolls around in all kind of different ways—the feeling of being sent [a message] from someone and that differing from the anxiety that you get when you send [messages] to yourself. You know: "I'm not doing it right" and "who's going to love me?" and all that kind of stuff. That is usually what that is about . . . your own anxiety. We need to learn to separate what is coming from inside from what is coming from the outside. I can tell the difference in my body between whether or not I am reacting to my own anxiety or responding to something coming from the outside. (Satir, 1987a)

Virginia showed her listeners how to prepare to distinguish between "inside" and "outside." (Note that the "how" is description of an intentional process of internal focus, not a technique.)

This is an example of Virginia's concept of "use of self as change agent." Self-knowledge and self-awareness are paramount. Being able to distinguish between response to outside stimulus versus responding to one's own internal dialogues is also known as recognizing "countertransference." Rather than use such terminology, Virginia preferred to describe the process. She found such description more useful to the trainees.

Projection

When you learn how to center and you can feel your own breathing, then it's like...[the outside message] is acting upon you and you know that is something from the other person. [Later we will show how this feeling relates to styles of communication] . . . a lot of times people are reacting to somebody else when it is actually a projection of their own . . . How many of you have ever had the experience of feeling something and then projecting it onto somebody else and accusing them for your feeling? Our parents did that a lot . . . *to be in touch with what is going on in someone else . . . you need to know what is going on in yourself.* It isn't as hard as it sounds, but when people use so much cognitive stuff without knowing about what else is going on, they make so many mistakes. I watch it. (Satir, 1987a)

Virginia explained the energy of the human spirit as the powerful energy of the force of life itself. It was her observation that *pathology emerges from a perversion or diversion of this life force power.* Behind all corrosive processes is this burgeoning power from the force of the life process.

Personal power comes from the ability to center oneself and restore inner harmony, not in trying to control others. Her centering exercises were designed to reinforce her point about focusing energy and to demonstrate her point about the power garnered from centering oneself.

Virginia's work was the building of bridges—toward and within the self as well as toward the other. The resulting connecting experiences were powerful, healing, and constructive.

She was dedicated to teaching people the best practice skills for being people. Not only is honesty really the best policy, feelings along with respect for self and other matter profoundly. In fact, the fate of the world hangs on it.

Chapter Note

1. Virginia summed up her ideas about peace: "Peace within, peace between, peace among." The quote was published by the Avanta Network on a postcard with a lovely picture of Virginia Satir offering a toast. The photograph was made during the trip to the USSR in 1988 the last May of her life. When that photograph was made, Virginia had just completed a major job of "human gardening," having planted some seeds in Moscow, Russia, in Vilnius, Lithuania, and in Tbilisi, Georgia. From that trip in 1988 evolved the Institute for International Connections, a nonprofit organization that has been returning to Russia and other former Soviet countries in Eastern Europe every year since 1990.

8

THE PATTERNS THAT DISCONNECT: IMPLICATIONS IN THE BODY

The body is trying to say what the mouth can't say.

—**Virginia Satir**, 1972

Physiological Implications of These Stances

Virginia Satir made it clear the body is always "part of the equation" when training, treating, or educating human beings. Virginia considered the specific body-mind-soul of a given person to be one entity, "manifestation of Life" (Satir, 1987a, tape 5), and, by definition, a sacred embodiment. Virginia was about wholeness.

The following explains how and where Virginia got the idea of the specific stances she would instruct people to assume in her sculpted roleplaying about incongruent communication. This innovation was another result of astute clinical observation.

Virginia pointed out that certain, identifiable, physical conditions specific to the four incongruent stances could manifest:

I had a wonderful opportunity at one time. I was with three physicians. This was long ago when I was still in Chicago, so it had to be in the fifties. They knew something about what I was doing and they asked me to see all their patients. At that time, I didn't know about the stances, but I began to watch. I saw patients with all kinds of diseases because one doctor was an internist, one was a gynecologist, and another was a bone person—an orthopedist. I saw all these people, then I began to look at them and watch what happened. And I began to put a voice together, a whiny voice with this kind of humped body with the body kind of being off balance. Then I saw people with stridence in their voices and saw how their muscles were tight. And I began to become aware about the price these people were paying for what was happening to them. But more than that, I could see [what their body positions were saying] and I just exaggerated [the positions] I saw. That is what I created these stances from, then I could understand a whole lot of things. (Satir, 1982)

Virginia wanted her trainees to understand the importance of staying aware of all eight factors in the spiral of the Self Mandala (body, intellect, emotion, senses, nutrition, interaction, context, spirit)—the "universal personal resources." In what follows, she was, however, especially concerned with the function of the body as unerring messenger of what is *really* going on for a person. She was further concerned to show the tragic consequences of *inattention* to the messages that the body continuously offers. Finally, she wanted us to grasp that the body reports with faultless accuracy the activity of senses and emotions.

After discussing the role of the senses, she drew a Self Mandala (see The Universal Human Resources, p. 80) on the blackboard:

Now in the center I want you to make a circle and in that center I want you to write "I." This is all personal, there isn't anything else that isn't personal. Have you ever been aware that there is nothing impersonal in life? Everything is personal; it has to be. So let us forget that non-sense about being personal or impersonal; there isn't any such thing. If I'm doing it, I'm doing it; that's me and that's personal.

That is "I." And I want to write the word on the top: "sacred." And on the bottom I want to write "holy," and on one side I want to write "cosmic joke," and on the other side "cosmic event." (Satir, 1983b, 241–242)

Virginia went through the eight aspects to show her trainees how each aspect is a resource. Full use of our resources make possible both congruence and choice-making. Virginia understood that many persons are—or behave as if they are—unaware of the several factors that make them up and of the necessity of congruence among all those factors. Pointing to the physical aspect on the chart, shown as the first ring, in the center, she said:

Now every "I" . . . sits in a temple. And that temple, a place for the "I" to live, is a body. You can call it anything you want but I call [it] the temple—the body. It houses that "I," that sacred, holy, cosmic event and joke, which you are and I am—different things at different times. So everything physical would be in that, all the things we talk about as physical. (Satir, 1983b, 242)

Virginia elucidated the crucial role played by our sensory apparatus:

The holes that we have we call the senses, but I would like you to see or hear, "sense" and think, "hole"—and when you think "hole," you think something moving back and forth. Something moving out,

143

something moving in. And without these holes we cannot live. We cannot live . . . Each of those holes is capable of putting something out and taking something in. [They are] the literal channels for taking in and giving out. (Satir, 1983b, 244)

Virginia summed up how our culture has compartmentalized, truncated, and/or ignored these eight aspects of the human being:

Historically, we put the spiritual in the hands of religion, permitted only the people in the performing arts to make use of the sensual (learn about their voice, et cetera), behaved as though the contextual did not exist, ignored the implications of the nutritional, only paid attention to the interactional in terms of bad behavior, related the emotional to morality, and left the physical and the intellectual in the hands of physicians and teachers respectively. And none of those people spoke to each other. (Satir, 1983b, 260–261)

This "splitting apart" affects our efforts towards congruence. In what follows, Virginia explained how our various resources can send dissonant messages. She highlighted the distinction between the cognitive message and the affective message, in preparation for pointing to how essential is connecting "mind" and "heart."

The cognitive comes from a totally different place than the affective. The cognitive is that which is made up of the "shoulds," the "oughts," and intellectual output . . . The affective is the body thermometer . . . It is the active manifestation of what is going on in the body. (Satir, 1987a, tape 5)

Profound problems are often created when a given Sam Jones's or Sally Jones's cognitive message doesn't match her/his affective message—when a person is feeling one thing and saying another.

It is possible for these two messages to be split. Cognitive goes this way and the affective goes that way. When we have that, we have what is called an "incongruent message," meaning that the words and the rest don't match (Satir, 1987a, tape 5).

Virginia talked about the impact this will have on the developing child:

> *Affect* is about feeling. *Cognition* is about the intellect. The mother, who cannot herself stand the idea that she is feeling afraid, or guilty, or whatever it is, has to say to the child, "It isn't true, what you see." Everyone of us, with a very few exceptions, got this experience from our parents. The reason for it was not because they wanted to hurt us, but because the cognitive part of what they "should be" didn't match the way they felt . . . You can understand how come you got such crazy messages. You couldn't find out what was going on. (Satir, 1987a, tape 5)

Virginia explained: "The 'should' . . . in your parent would be getting in the way" (Satir, 1987a, tape 5). The parent is so concerned with how he or she "should" appear that he/she defensively presents the child with a double message.

> They couldn't say they were afraid. They couldn't say they felt hurt or whatever it was. They just had to do the defensive reaction.
>
> When you can get no validation cognitively or effectively, two people cannot communicate this way. It's confusing and the kid in us doesn't comprehend and that's where schizophrenia[1] shows itself. I learned that a long time ago. (Satir, 1987a, tape 5)

These words on cognition and affect were preliminary to Virginia's making her explanation of the need for one of her major vehicles—Family

Reconstruction (see chapter 4). She said, "This [parent-child interaction] is where . . . we learned about feeling" (Satir, 1987a, tape 5). After teaching about communication, she would teach this method of going back, through role play, into the previous generations to help the client understand the implication and origins of her or his old learnings. With other participants playing various family members, Virginia would reconstruct important scenes from the "star's" past (Nerin, 1986; Satir, 1991).

Demonstration

Our bodies love the truth.

—**Virginia Satir**, *1987*

Virginia spoke of the power of inhuman system rules, dysfunctional rules taught by parents to children. These rules are often an affront to the person's body, where affective messages are found. She set up an exercise with a volunteer from the participant group to demonstrate the potentially destructive effect of "I must never lie" as a cognitive message:

VIRGINIA SATIR: Alright, Mary, let's have a rule from you: "I must," "I must never"—what is it [your rule]?

MARY: I must never tell a lie and I must never tell the truth about what goes on in this family.

VIRGINIA: Do you notice what she did? She put herself in a double bind right away. She's not supposed to tell a lie and she's not supposed to tell what goes on in the family. So, somebody from out there says, "What is going on in your family?" And she has to lie. Let's take those apart and let's do truth on those. "I must never lie." Another way to put that is "I must always tell the truth." You can [use] either one. Is this one alright for now?

MARY: Yes.

VIRGINIA: I like [this example] because there are a lot of people who categorically think that lying is bad. I think that if you don't know how to lie, and it might be needed once in your life, it should be perfectly developed! Here is the rule "I must never lie." That is the law and we will now go to the first transformation . . . We change "must" to "can" [writing on the chalkboard] and you may read it now: "I can never lie." Can you? Is that true that you can never lie?

MARY: No, that is not true.

VIRGINIA: No! That is a lie if you say it is true. She has to lie and she can't do it. Let's go to "I can sometimes lie." Is that true?

MARY: Yes.

VIRGINIA: And we go to the third one: "I can lie when _____." Let's have three times that you already know when you can lie.

MARY: When I can convince myself that the lie is not a lie. If I feel guilty about things, I can sometimes lie.

VIRGINIA: I just want to know about the truth now. We can take care of the feelings later. I want to know if you have a skill to lie which you can use sometimes.

MARY: Yes.

VIRGINIA: Wonderful! "I can lie _____"—when? When have you noticed that you have been able to lie?

MARY: When I am afraid to tell the truth.

VIRGINIA: "When I am afraid." Alright. That says something to me about when you are afraid of being punished, doesn't it?

MARY: Yes.

VIRGINIA: Let's see another time when you know that you can lie.

MARY: When I think telling the truth is more harmful all around.

VIRGINIA: "When I want to be protected," isn't that what you are saying?

MARY: Or protect somebody else.

VIRGINIA: When I want to protect somebody else. Now, what is the third one?

MARY: When I think the truth is none of your business.

VIRGINIA: Now, Mary, let's have you speak the law, "I must never lie." Feel your body and what is happening in your body?

MARY: Resistance, stubbornness, anger.

VIRGINIA: Your body is undergoing an unbelievable assault. Can you feel that?

MARY: Yes.

VIRGINIA: An unbelievable assault! That comes out. What I am seeing is a picture of you saying with your mouth: "I must never lie" and here is your body all twisted like this and a knife in your hand. Okay? It is an assault to the body, isn't it?

MARY: Yes.

VIRGINIA: I have a picture I am going to share with you for a moment. When you were a little girl, I see you doing lots of penance for when you lied. Is that true? Like sitting in the corner, or doing extra work, or getting beaten, or something of that sort. Does any of that fit?

MARY: It brings memories of absolute confusion and terror.

VIRGINIA: Yes, I know. Feel my hand at this moment, okay? I want you to again allow yourself to say [your] law and this time you are in touch with my hand and just feel what that feels like now, saying "I must never lie."

MARY: I must never lie.
VIRGINIA: What do you feel now?
MARY: Stupid.
(Satir, 1987a, tape 5)

At this point, another aspect of one of the volunteer's old learnings makes an entry. Virginia guided her back toward the physical experience that accompanied her self-effacing thoughts. She was leading the participant toward the evidence available in her own bodily responses.

VIRGINIA: So there is another voice that came in, in a way. But, let us now at this moment take the first transformation and let's see what happens to you . . . [What] I heard from you before is that your muscles tightened up. Now, let's do the first transformation. Read this one [pointing to chalkboard].
MARY: I can never lie.
VIRGINIA: What did your body feel like?
MARY: Nonsense.
VIRGINIA: Okay, but what is a nonsense feeling?
MARY: It's not true.
VIRGINIA: It is an untruth and our bodies love the truth. You will find that out. Let's do the second one: "I can sometimes lie." Okay, what does your body feel like now? First let's ask the truth. We know that is the truth, okay? What did your body feel like?
MARY: Uncomfortable.
VIRGINIA: Okay, this is a different thing from tight.
MARY: Yes.
VIRGINIA: Now let's go to "I can lie when _____."

MARY: I can lie when I am afraid of being punished. I can
   lie when I want to protect someone else or myself. I can lie
   when I think the truth is none of your business.
VIRGINIA: What does your body feel like now?
MARY: Okay.
VIRGINIA: Is the tightness gone?
MARY: Yes.
(Satir, 1987a, tape 5)

Virginia demonstrated the way inhuman rules set up dissonance in
our bodies and in interactions. She has led a demonstration that high-
lights how cognitive messages may diverge from affective messages going
on simultaneously. Virginia was continually working on ways to teach
the principles critical to human communication. Here, she was following
her own guideline outlined in notes made to herself the year before.[2]

Virginia's point was these patterns are all *processes*, not identities. All
the incongruent patterns are unenlightened moves to make the self feel
valued. As *processes*, all are subject to change once an interacting pair can
be made aware of the patterns and of the relationship between these patterns and self-esteem. With *awareness of the incongruence*, the patterns
can be transformed into growth-enhancing responses. Of the five universal patterns, the least familiar one—the congruent response—leads both
self and other, in any given interaction, toward wholeness and integration,
toward Self with a capital "S."

Following this demonstration, which showed the effect of incongruent communication on the body, Virginia instructed the group to
break into triads to practice "transforming your rules." In the process
of the exercise, they should pay close attention to their bodies. She
warned that internal issues will emerge during these triad exercises
as a result of feeling triggered while practicing deliberate incongruent
communication.

She instructed:

Then we look into *what is happening with the body*, so we can get the body feeling of that. Remember, this is not "you should lie or you shouldn't lie." . . . We are not talking, at this moment, about the right or wrong of it. We are talking about the *process of looking at making "what is" very clear* and then moving on to something else. (Satir, 1987a, tape 5)

In making "what is" very clear, she is referring to congruence accurately describing current reality with all the players included.

Using the participants' sensual reaction to the demonstration, Virginia pointed out the way body reacts to thought and feeling and that such reaction is inevitable. Virginia again made the point that physical symptoms are a message from the bodied aspect of the self:

How people convey things back and forth: [that is] the [definition] I give communication. I think that is a relatively easy definition: communication is the giving and receiving of information between two people. That's how it always goes. It is just giving and receiving information. When somebody coughs, what kind of information does the other one receive? Just ask yourself that. If you go beyond words and think about it, when you cross your legs, or you uncross your legs, or lift your head, or say "poof," or your skin color changes, or you get a lump someplace, no matter what, all of that is communication. The giving and receiving of information. (Satir, 1987a, tape 5)

Virginia made clear these conclusions about communication are not theories and ideas she dreamed up one day. They are the results of years of clinical observation. She was reporting what she has witnessed regarding the influence of thought and feeling on body and vice versa.

I watched people, thousands of them. I have told you that I'm fifty-one years in the field this year, so you can imagine how many different interactions I have seen over time. Lots and lots and lots of them. At a certain point . . . one day a grid appeared to me . . . I saw that the communication that was related to dysfunctional behavior was related to people not enjoying their lives and was one of these four forms [placating, blaming, super-reasonable, irrelevant]. (Satir, 1987a, tape 5)

Particularly in the beginning years of Virginia's post graduate professional career, circa 1948, therapy focused on the cognitive almost exclusively. Gestalt therapy and psychodrama became popular much later.[3] As a therapist working in the United States, Virginia predated both; she developed her own teaching modality as a holistic approach, borrowing whatever was useful as she moved along.

Elaborating further on the different kinds of information, she said:

In information, there is (1) cognitive information, there is (2) emotional information, and there is (3) sensual information. What Ernie [Rossi 1986] talks about in his book [on the psychobiology of healing] is that when the information from the endocrine system, the neurological system, and the immune system don't find coding ways to connect with each other, they have to separate. *In the Western world we have given most of our attention to cognitive information.* We read it in a book, we see the words, and the words make the images, but reading it in a book doesn't show how the person is feeling or thinking or how they are gesturing or how they are breathing . . . so it is a totally different thing when we put it into a human context.

I want to give you just enough so that we get a good context for this. If you will remember, when I use information, it is on all levels . . . It is not about just giving words. (Satir, 1987a, tape 5)

Most of our culture is not tuned in, on the aware and intentional levels, to that emotional information Virginia is talking about. And that is the vital difference.

Blocking awareness of emotional information blocks awareness of our nature as whole beings. It also prepares the way for atrocities such as the World Trade Center attacks, the Oklahoma City bombing, the tragedy at Waco at the Branch Davidian compound, the suicide bombers of the Middle East, and on and bloody on. All parties involved were focused on their respective causes, regardless of the literal human beings involved.

This blocking is a major obstacle to serious movement toward peace on any level—individual, family, or world. If I do not care how I feel or how you feel, I can do any sort of thing for a principle. That is where the inhumanity comes in—devotion to the cause above the effect on the human beings. Such blocking paves the way for the threat and reward model Virginia describes. On the other hand, her seed model takes into account all levels and kinds of information.

Virginia had observed (Brothers, 1987a, 1989b) that a body also pays a high price for muting emotional and sensual information. It trains the glands to not perform their normal function simply by continually restraining their output—in Virginia's more colorful words, there being "a juice for every emotion." If the emotions don't flow, the "juices" don't flow.

The cognitive must not be emphasized at the expense of the affective and vice versa. Virginia had this to say about the connections among affect, cognition, and the body:

> To put it into an interactional frame. Here is the cognitive and the affective. That brings out the message. Then, somebody over here is receiving that message. Bear in mind that when somebody's cognitive message and affective message aren't together, they are coming

from two different places. The cognitive comes from a totally different place than the affective. The cognitive is that which is made up of the "shoulds," the "oughts" and intellectual output, so to speak. The brain is very capable of doing all kinds of wonderful things all by itself. *The affective is [accurately registered in] the body [as] thermometer. Remember that the body is the thermometer and it is the active manifestation of what is going on in the body* [body/mind/soul system]. (Satir, 1987a, tape 5)

Virginia observed that our "should" messages are cognitive. Gesturing toward the blackboard, she would write "cognitive" (message) on one side and "affective" on the other. "Thought" would be written under "cognitive" and "feeling" would be written under "affective." Her point would be that problems come when the two do not state the same message. One can verbally say one thing, but the body will be registering the actual affect appropriate to the reality.

One can "do cognitive" however one wants to, but there is always the flow of the affective underneath the verbiage. The body measures and displays feelings. If one is conscious in regard to one's interior processes, the feelings can be verbalized—and one can cry or sweat or blush. If the feelings are not conscious, not in awareness, the body still registers them—still quivers, gurgles, and crackles the chemistry and the electromagnetism. The therapist who has trained herself to watch the body of herself and of the other can see bodily manifestations and help bring them to the awareness of the other.

To spare clients the disrespect of "interpretation," Virginia was meticulously careful to only *describe* what she saw, then *maybe* inquire as to its meaning: "I see your eyebrows knit together right now. Are you aware of that?" Often all that was necessary was for her to just notice the body behavior and draw it to the person's attention. Usually, the person would then become aware of feeling angry or feeling puzzled—or whatever feeling went with the eyebrows.

Double Messages

I have seen the effect on psychotic children and adolescents of receiving double messages from family members. One can watch, on the spot, during the interview, how their speech becomes more confused as their anxiety levels rise. Virginia's intervention would be to give them permission to *verbalize* the anxiety and/or to *comment* on the process. (She credited her work with Gregory Bateson for helping to clarify her own observations in this area.) If the person is able to accept the possibility that he/she is sufficiently valuable as a human being for another person to want to effectively communicate with her/him, they may then move their system toward harmony and alignment by verbally expressing—or acknowledging internally—the feeling that is raging or pouring throughout their body/mind/spirit system. To do so brings congruence. The congruent action includes verbalizing the feeling and commenting on what is perceived—a sanity-making process.

Bringing one's system back into internal harmony means the person would not necessarily have to experience the physiological distress that may accompany the double message. Virginia's theory postulates that cancer comes from giving *oneself* a double-level message. Such a message results in a kind of interior traffic jam: There is no constructive place for the energy to then go.

Many children grow up with double messages. One example is "be strong." In the case of oldest daughters, that can translate as "Take care of yourself and everybody around you." Such a girl, even knowing better on an intellectual level, can grow up with enormous trouble admitting to "weakness" or allowing herself to be emotionally vulnerable . . . all the time being, in fact, quite a sensitive person. Such a person, responding to the parental injunction to *behave as if* she were strong—while receiving the conflicting, overriding, message of fatigue from the body—puts herself in the double-message position by telling herself the lie that she "feels fine."

In growing up, children learn whatever they learn about reality from their parents. If a parent behaves as if you do not need something and you are a very little child, you think that must be fact—even though it flies in the face of your very organism's responses. A parental figure is as much survival mechanism for the very young child as is her/his own physiological instincts.

Here we see a context for emotional factors in the etiology of a variety of human problems.

It is not unreasonable to assume such distorted communication might play a role in the development of a schizophrenic process—if we concede that all human behavior and functioning occurs in the form of process and not static event. Given a somewhat sturdier psyche (for whatever interplay of reasons—genetic, environmental, or interactional), the inner conflict might be stored for a later date and played out in the body. Certainly no thinking therapist would be so simplistic as to suggest that double-messages are the single cause of schizophrenia or cancer. On the other hand, bearing in mind the overriding importance of relatedness and its expression via communication, we see the growing child has what can be a serious dilemma in regard to which message to heed and/or obey.

Babies are not "little vegetables"—they are little humans who have not yet developed the systems to communicate their internal experience. Nonetheless, the experience itself may be as sophisticated as yours or mine. It may not be organized, of course, but there is too much reporting of memories not to believe it is true. One client remembers her mother swearing at her when she stuck herself with a pin from the diaper. Another one remembers events in her household which occurred between the time she was nine months to a year old. One young mother (who happened to be a social worker) related, with appropriate horror, that her three-year-old son had reported sexual abuse by his babysitter. The abuse had occurred when he was eighteen months old—too young to be able to describe it in words. (However, the mother had noticed a sudden, puzzling, and sharp increase in agitation and aggression in the child at the time.) By age three, he had the vocabulary to be able to tell her. He had apparently held the memory in his little mind until enough of the right words entered his world to be able to report the events.

Inhuman Rules

Virginia also talked a lot about the "inhuman rules" we have—those "shoulds" and "oughts" that keep us from clearly stating or even knowing our feelings. She invented the Family Reconstruction tool to take people on tours back in time to help them see where and how their *parents'* (and their parents and their parents . . .) own shoulds and oughts forged those rules. With new information about these "old learnings," a person is in a better position to make choices in reference to these rules.

I remember how startled I was back when I worked in the state mental hospital and mental health system to find myself able to help psychotic people stop their word salad. I simply keyed into what I was guessing their feeling to be and then helped them to identify and comment on the feeling. Simply giving permission to people to openly state how they feel has enormous healing potential.

For Virginia, awareness was the key. The Family Reconstructions were all for the purpose of bringing information into conscious awareness.

Awareness of body response is both an end and a means to the end of "wholing" and learning to live out of wholeness. She would demonstrate how the four incongruent communication stances would feel in the body. After a sequence of having participants sculpt their bodies into one of the four communication stances in the stress ballet, Virginia asked two people to demonstrate the blaming-placating position:

Your body is off-balance and . . . in some way the shoulds and oughts in your life are clashing and old triggers are coming back.

If that [being in the blaming/placating mode] is what we have been doing . . . laws and everything else are into that one [the blaming-placating position]. Here we are, at this seminar becoming more fully human. We are steeped in this, the old, so it's not going to be an easy thing for you to say, "Well, I won't do this anymore." What we need to work on is the *awareness* of this. That's why when you are in your triads and one of you wants to go like that [extending blaming finger], you say, "Bless this for letting me know," instead of saying, "Oh, my god! Look at me. I'm doing the same old thing." This is the idea I would like for you to get into your heads, to be able to substitute "Oh, my god! ain't it awful?" for "Hey, I'm getting to be in touch. What's happening?" That is the part that saves us. (Satir, 1987a, tape 3)

Virginia wanted the participants to understand that the entire month of their training would be devoted to helping them to become aware—of their own insides, of the messages from their colleagues, of the greater context. Neither "nasty" nor "nice" matters. Reality and awareness of reality is what matters.

You can say nice, you can say nasty and even nice or nasty . . . that [blaming-placating] is not a very whole picture. Now, what we're doing this whole month [of this seminar—August 1987] is going to be devoted to becoming aware. *The first thing is to let each of you now become aware of what your body feels like.* Close your eyes, take a breath, and now let your body expand so that it is comfortable and you're on your own feet. When you are on your own feet, you are following your own choice making. (Satir, 1987a, tape 3)

Well aware that she was working with her trainees to go up against human history's eons-long habit of trying to change behavior through threats or rewards, Virginia was striving toward bringing them to the *awarenesses*—that, instead, actually do promote growth and wholeness.

> What we are doing is living through thousands of years of accultura-
> tion about how we [relate to and interact] with one another. Certainly
> western culture. We have been putting our energies into making the
> nasties a little bit not so nasty instead of going where we need to move
> which is a totally new place to being in touch and valuing . . . That's
> what the world needs at this time and that's what peace is about.[4]
> (Satir, 1987a, tape 3)

In this framework, we can understand how the body fits in the picture and how awareness (of one's whole person—body-mind-spirit) can lead to harmony with the self, with a partner, within a family, and on out into the greater community.

Chapter Notes

1. Shortly after one of my monthlong seminars with Virginia, I was employed on the children's service of a mental health center. I elected to see the entire family of one of our psychotic adolescents. The boy, Thomas, from a poor black family, was considered one of the chronic medication patients. His word salad was so consistent that nobody ever considered trying to actively engage him in verbal interaction. Nobody bothered to try to do any kind of therapy with him.

   Fresh from Virginia's seminar, I did. I assembled the whole family, including several brothers and sisters. I asked how Thomas felt about something, fending off the family members who tried to answer for him. To everybody's astonishment, Thomas came back with a clear answer to my question. For a few minutes, we carried on the first coherent exchange his family had ever witnessed him doing in their presence.

Etiology of schizophrenia may be a many-layered phenomenon. Nevertheless, Thomas and I transcended that process for a few minutes that day, proving to me that Virginia was right about there being a relationship between communication and schizophrenic symptomatology.

2. This demonstration follows an outline from Virginia's handwritten, personal notes:

"A Guide for Transforming Rigid Survival Rules into Useful Living Guides"

Rigid (compulsive rule)
State the rule verbally. For example, "I must always work hard."
Change the compulsion into choice.

First Transformation:
Substitute "can" for "must."
Verbalize the new statement: "I can always work hard."
Is that true?
No.
Is it possible for you to "always work hard"?
No, I get tired.

Second Transformation:
Particularize the statement by changing "always" to "sometimes."
Now verbalize new statement: "I can sometimes work hard."

Is it true?

Yes.

Third Transformation:

Make it *specific* by dropping "sometimes" and add "when" to the last
statement and indicate at least three situations in which you see this
as possible now.

Verbalize this transformation.

I can work hard when, for example, I feel the work I am doing is
worthwhile, I feel good, or I get paid well.

Now you have real choices for real situations.

Notice your body feeling as you verbalize each transformation.

Now thank your mother, father or both for giving you the beginning
for a useful guide for yourself.

These survival rules reflect:

    a) The fear of the parent

    b) The internal conflict of the parent or conflict between
       parents

    c) The wish to protect you

    d) Parental ignorance

    e) Parental values

These rules were accepted by you at a time when you needed direction and were too inexperienced and too young to evaluate their usefulness to you.

[In the margin, Virginia wrote, "notes only, not presented."] (Satir, circa 1986)

3. Jacob L. Moreno began psychodrama in Europe in 1923 and Frederick "Fritz" Perls published *Ego Hunger and Aggression* in London in 1947,

but neither modality effectively penetrated the psychoanalytic bubble until the 1960s, well after Virginia's career was underway.

4. "That's what peace is about": becoming aware of one's internal responses, valuing the information, and, as a result, moving into the position of being one's own decision maker. Thus centered, the person is in a place to value the inner experience of the other and to be supportive of the other reaching their own centeredness.

9

INCONGRUENCE AND CANCER

Or you get a lump someplace, no matter what, all of that is communication.

—**Virginia Satir**, 1987

One reason Virginia Satir considered "ability to comment" so important was because of her discovery that "the body says what the mouth does not."(Satir, 1987a, tape 5)

Virginia had scheduled a two-week seminar in March 1972, that happened to fall just three weeks after her father's death. Her mother had died several years before, March of 1964, from cancer. Virginia had been giving considerable thought to the dynamics in her own family of origin. Obviously, cancer was on her mind. The following excerpt is from one of those 1972 lectures following a demonstration of the four incongruent communication responses. All of her listeners have been caught up in the drama of observing how inner stances "sculpt" the body's way of holding itself.

Body Responses

Let's look at the body responses [accompanying the four incongruent stances] . . . My medical friends kind of support me in this.

Let's look at the organs that are most affected.

The organ affected first in placating is your belly—the whole digestive tract, the nausea . . .

You could call this the nauseating response—when I am saying what I don't feel.

Now here [blaming response] what are most affected are the tissues—the linings. [Cites participant with arthritic hands as an example]. The tissues get tight, and there's no flexibility. So explosions and all kinds of things like that are present.

Now here [super-reasonable] we get dryness. There are no juices here. The semen doesn't flow, the milk doesn't flow, the tears don't flow. Just dried up. So the problem here [super-reasonable] is no juice, no flexibility. And up here [placating] no boundaries.

Now we get down here [irrelevant] and what gets affected is the central nervous system—balance, dizziness. If your central nervous system isn't able to give you any kind of balance, all the rest of the parts of your body act accordingly.

What I have done now is to supply a base for psychosomatic medicine. When I said that the body is trying to say what the mouth can't say, in a squeeze, something has to happen.

I have a *theory of cancer*. I've spoken this to some of my friends and once spoke about this at a meeting. If we think about it for a minute, *cancer is wild, uncontrolled growth of a most energetic kind. That's where I start out. This is growth, and it's growth that's killing. What's causing the killing,* I ask myself? It has to be something in the person who won't allow something. What I see with the people that I work *with who have had terminal cancer* and some of those who didn't—none of this may fit anyway[1]—first of all, *such a person has tremendous hopes, tremendous hopes and ambitions. Then somewhere along the line [the person] looks at the reality and says I can't do it. There's no point in hoping. But then the rules of that person are such that he can't allow himself to look like he did that, so now he has to make another rule that says he didn't do what he just did. And then to live as though he hasn't made the first decision.*

First I say to myself I can't do what I want to do. If [only] that, [alone], just happened you just get a depression. That would be like putting one line [metaphorical rope] around your waist and squeezing—separating top and bottom. But then I have to behave as though I am still doing it. So now I have to put one around the neck.

PARTICIPANT: Are you denying the loss of hope or are you denying the hope too?

VIRGINIA: You're denying the hope and the fact that you gave up hope. By this time, you never admitted that you even hoped. You live as though you didn't do either.

If you understand what I am saying, it is like a double level. First of all you tie one [metaphorical line or rope] around here, which says I can't hope anymore. Then you tie one around here that says I didn't have the hope in the first place and I didn't even deny my hope because there wasn't any. I behave as though I'm hopeful and everything is going to be fine.

PARTICIPANT: Which [stress response] does that go with?

ANOTHER PARTICIPANT: Number one.

VIRGINIA: You start out here [number one—placating], then you end up here [number three—super-reasonable]. I watched my mother die of cancer and I knew this all the time. I knew what she was doing. When I was five years old, I knew my mother had tuned herself out of her ambitions—tuned herself completely off sexual joy with my father. I think it has a lot to do with validation in the sexual sphere. I'm now talking male and female, not just genital. I saw her literally behave as though I know she didn't feel. But it is more than just one [level of] lying.

You can just feel depressed. But then if you say to yourself I can't even do that, I have to behave cheery, then you send the body through an absolutely impossible situation. Where is that marvelous growth going to go?

PARTICIPANT (who is an MD): You went through a progression that I missed—one to three.

VIRGINIA: Do you know how many placators are such very hard workers? Just tremendous. At some point, they give up, and it looks like they come over here [to super-reasonable]. But this is more than just a simple thing. After I got onto this and saw this over and over again, I had this couple come in and listened for a while and I heard: This was this woman's second marriage and she didn't see any other place for herself. I heard the things that said to me what I'm just now telling you about. Now it was all right, she was going to live her life this way. You would have to work very hard to hear the depressed part of it. I said to her, "When did you have your last physical?" She told me a few months before. I said, "Listen, I can't tell you why—I did know why, but I wasn't going to tell her because it was a hunch—I want you to go for a physical to a good doctor tomorrow." That was Tuesday. On Friday she had her right breast removed. It was there. You can smell this kind of stuff.

...This is not refined as a mathematical model. But you can begin as you hear this. It's kind of like for me the skeleton and how it gets fleshed in and how it relates. But I do know the physical response that seem to be very obvious in relation to this. (Satir, 1972a, 289)

In her fifty-plus years of experience, Virginia had great opportunity for numerous clinical observations. Although no hard evidence is involved, her theory, if valid, obviously has profound implications for cancer patients and for therapists who work with them.

Virginia's theory of the emotional factors in the etiology is drawn from evidence described in scientific fields as "anecdotal" and not based on methodically conducted research. She, herself, never included it in her own writing for that very reason. Instead, she offered it, from time to time, for her trainees to consider, to make their own observations in their own clinical practices. In that same spirit, I offer it here. If her conclusions do have validity, there are profound implications for psychological as well as physical treatment.

To those who may well take a dim view of the inclusion of material regarding Virginia's theory of emotional factors in the etiology of cancer: (a) These are the emotional factors, which, by no means, rule out possible genetic or environmental factors. (b) What if she had discovered a bona fide underlying principle, which might someday be substantiated by research? Have we all not lost enough friends and relatives to cancer to consider that possibility sufficiently important to take the risk of disquieting the scientific community?

Further Clinical Examples

So in a way we have deluded ourselves to say there is such a thing as safety or security based on keeping the status quo.

It can't happen. That's where I think our cancer comes from. We have got some pretty good evidence for that, about people who are full of wanting to do on all levels down to the cell, but have rules about themselves that they mustn't, so the energy's got to go someplace else.

—Virginia Satir, 1981

Virginia had seen evidence that, in people with passionate ambitions, the creative drive could be said to "go down to the cellular level." However, such people may also have grown up through a maze of constricting, dysfunctional internal rules, which would inhibit their creative drive. All that energy must "go someplace" if diverted from its original productive goal by a misguided attempt to keep a status quo. The person's fear of taking risks would be in serious competition with what such a person wants. This juxtaposition may "create" instead, a path for the development of cancer, which takes the place of the desired goal.

Virginia's work involved making connections between human beings and restoring a fundamental belief in the value of oneself and other selves as an integral part of intimate connecting. Frederick Levenson's (1985, 1987) premise was that people who get cancer have never adequately connected with another human being and that the groundwork for this not connecting was laid in the first three months of their lives when they were having their first experiences with connection on this planet. James Lynch (1977, 1985)[2] has done extensive work on the responses of our literal hearts to the transactions between our figurative ones.

The work of all three suggests there is a life-givingness to intimacy that is not easy to comprehensively describe in words. In addition to the difficulty of trying to contain the concept of Life in sentences and paragraphs, there is the deceptive simplicity that disguises by way of its obviousness. For example, almost any fourteen-year-old knows that the intimacy of sexual intercourse carries the possibility of the subsequent emergence of a new life. We all take that fact so literally that we can't think of it in terms of paradigm. I am suggesting that we do think metaphorically, as well as literally, for a moment. Intimacy has the power to even activate life. Intimacy promotes the context for healing, makes a safe place for growth.

Evidence persuades that, in fact, loving connection with other human beings, with another human being, is a life-or-death matter. Being open to and with others appears to be more than just a nice thing to do. Lost dreams and broken hearts have physiological corollaries and consequences: "independence" is often a snare and a delusion.

Virginia (personal communication 1971, 1972a, 1986c, 1988b) discussed the psychosomatic responses to the four styles of incongruent responses to the stress of low self-worth. Because there was no hard research to back her theory about the etiology of cancer, she was reluctant to be publicly quoted on that subject, so her thinking in this area had not previously appeared in print. However, I was mightily impressed with what I saw as very useful diagnostic information when I first attended her seminars; I returned to my job on the children's service of the public mental health center and found myself being able to pick out women who had surgery for cancer *before* they even told me of having had surgery. I recall checking this out with one woman in a family intake interview and seeing her family members all turn to her in astonishment. Even they had not known about the cancer until that moment. Virginia's theory has a lot to do with false independence and with a compulsive avoidance of intimacy about which Levenson spoke.

Much of the "independence" that forestalls the healing intimacy is a defense against a fear of being unable to separate from another, of being taken over.

Levenson believed the process of cancer is related to the "individual's manner of processing irritation," to whether or not the individual seeks to be with others when depressed or irritated. According to Levenson's thinking, pronounced self-containment, which is anti-intimacy, is also carcinogenic. Levenson (1985) described the individual's pattern for processing irritation as having been laid down in early infancy. In these months, the mother who responds to the infant's hyperirritation with appropriate maternal soothing drains away the irritation much as a spoon in a cup of hot liquid drains off the heat. The mother who responds to the hyperirritation with her own irritation, because of inadequate emotional support, both "trains" her infant to push away from intimacy and may allow for a biochemical reaction on a cellular level. He cited the work of Barbara McClintock regarding translocation of genes in corn cells in response to certain levels of irritation. The insufficiently supported mother does not allow the siphoning off of the biochemical irritants when she brings her own irritation to the hyperirritated infant.

Mothers who respond with irritation instead of soothing often are laying down a template for the same. That person grows up repeating the same process, having learned a pattern of trying to soothe irritation with more irritation. This person would have learned a pattern of addiction to irritation and applies an irritant to the irritant: smoking, alcohol, et cetera.

Levenson went on to explain the psychological/emotional responses of the hyperirritated infant to the hyperirritated mother: if the hyperirritated infant's cries keep drawing to him or her only a hyperirritated mother, the baby will begin to resist the natural bonding process that would normally be occurring in this stage of development.

The parent who is unable to distinguish the needs of the child from her or his own plays a crucial part in setting the child up for psychological and physiological trouble. Blind to the separate personhood of the child, and perhaps consumed by her own unmet needs and harsh rules, such a parent is in no position to appreciate and value the personhood of the new little person. That parent may then be chronically inattentive—or under-attentive—to adequately respond to the infant's needs for soothing. An antibonding pattern is set up in the child; at this point begins the development of a kind of pseudo-independence compatible with Virginia's observation.

"John Wayne" is born. The great American "tough guy," show-no-feelings hero. The persons who resist bonding are self-contained in their emotions. They do not look to other human beings for comfort; they do not have effective ways of discharging irritation. Bonding with another human being is nature's way of discharging the tension and irritation. Here is the deep loneliness of which Virginia spoke—a basic rift in the fabric of that which composes our humanity, the organism deviating from its basic design. A "landmine" (Levenson, 1985, 47) is established in the form of a cell programmed to be unstable in the face of future irritation. Moreover, these individuals grow up seeking irritation to calm their irritations—cigarettes, alcohol, unsatisfying relationships, and so on. Levenson proposed the cancer begins when the cellular landmine, laid in infancy, is sufficiently irritated by a carcinogenic chemical, smoking, or stress of an emotional nature.

The "stress of an emotional nature" was a major point at which Levenson's theory and Virginia's hypothesis interfaced. Virginia's theory also involved the individual's containment of feelings, rather than expression, in a specific configuration. Levenson's "stress of an emotional nature" was further refined, was traced more closely by Virginia—the stress is the person's specific loss and unmourned dream. Virginia's work was based on the relationship among self-esteem, communication, and system rules. She demonstrated the correlation between questioning of self-worth and incongruent communication and the way they affect each other. When issues of self-worth rise, questions rise around what I must do in your presence to feel all right about myself.

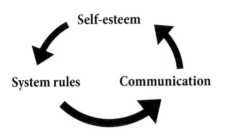

This diagram is a picture of the interlinking relationship among self-esteem, communication, and "system rules" by which a person decides what sort of internal and external communication is permitted.

Self-destructive self-containment, issuing from that need to preserve self-worth, evades the intimacy involved in honest self-sharing. Instead, the person under such duress and self-interrogation will express herself or himself in one of the four incongruent communication styles: (1) Most people placate, silently containing their real pain and behaving as if their own feelings do not matter. (2) Others blame, again containing their self-doubt, and behaving as if the other person's feelings do not matter. (3) The hazard for people with good intelligence is the risk of containing all feeling, behaving as computers, and resolutely relating only to their context. People who react to interactional stress in this way behave as if neither their own feelings nor the feelings of the other matter. (This is the response described as closely fitting the cancer profile). (4) Others become irrelevant to whatever subject is at hand, behaving as if nothing matters—not feelings of the self, not feelings of the other, and not even the context. Even reality does not matter. Pathological self-containment wins out.

In Virginia's observation and personal communication with thousands of families, she saw the individual who succumbs to cancer as responding to self-esteem issues as if his/her feelings don't matter. Her specific hypothesis: The precancerous person has some dream or ambition; something happens so that the dream cannot be realized. The crucial factor is that this person *does not mourn the loss* of the dream. Instead, the person behaves as if the loss is not that important, the dream didn't matter that much anyway. The person who does not mourn the loss provides no direction for her or his growth to go except into the wild, uncontrolled growth of the cells which takes place in cancer.

This dynamic of denial is what constitutes such virulence in the New Age true believers' adamant, and not-really-banal, insistence on "being positive" as opposed to "negative." The mindless acceptance of positive, whatever *that* is, as being inherently and categorically superior to negative, whatever that is, can contribute to therapists' blindness to the devastating destructiveness, on a literal tissue basis, of massive denial. It goes without saying that such blindness exists in the greater culture even without the aid and abetment of the New Age.

This loss of the dream, which—figuring in Virginia's explanation—can serve as "the stress of an emotional nature," to which Levenson referred, serving as a sufficient irritant to set off the land-mine cell. The denial around the importance of the loss discourages the individual from seeking another person for comfort. The individual contains himself or herself, does not look outside the self for soothing. These people have long been led to believe their feelings are nuisances rather than resources. The last thing that would occur to them as useful would be to give in to tears of grief, and certainly not in the presence of another human being.

Some of you, no doubt, have heard the ancient Greek story of the little Spartan who hid a young wolf under his tunic. As the boy sat by the campfire, the hungry wolf began to gnaw the boy's chest where the wolf was concealed under the tunic. The good little Spartan child, taught not to give in to feeling, eventually turned pale and fell over dead, a victim of that which he had been silently hiding. Denying what is "eating at you" can consume you just as effectively in this century as in ancient times.

According to Levenson, the unsatisfactory relationship this individual, who denies his or her loss, experienced around bonding with mother has set him or her up not to be available for bonding with another human being in his or her adult life. Levenson, who accepted for treatment only terminal cancer patients, claimed he has cured them; his method was to allow them to bond with him through psychoanalysis.

What could a therapist do, having this sort of information? Virginia Satir's "points of intervention" (Brothers, 1989b) supply several choices (see figures on following pages).

One would go back to the beginning, the young mother and father. This is always the beginning for us all: that coming together of the two kinds of cells that explode into live presence, immediately beginning to take on the human form and bearing a human name—Sally Jones or Winston Churchill, the beginnings are the same.

This pair, activators of that new life, known as the infant, coming for marital counseling, could learn the difference between incongruent communication and congruent communication, could learn to recognize and sense the difference between defense and authenticity, could learn to be clear about asking for what they want and need. Two people of goodwill can arrange to work toward augmentation (versus mundane argument) of each other's self-esteem, can agree not to engage in the kind of abusive attacks designed to tear at the self-esteem of the other. Anger can be expressed and exchanged in a nontoxic manner. Levenson (1987), in *The Anti-Cancer Marriage*, described the mother's need for support during her pregnancy and the infant's need for support and soothing as she or he goes through the initial experiences with the irritations of life. Here is where the model is laid down for dealing with irritation. Here is where the individual first learns about being soothed and comforted versus not being adequately comforted and soothed.

Intervention Points

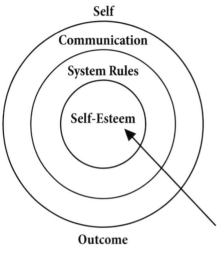

At the Point of Self-Esteem

Self-esteem is balanced on how one feels about whatever feeling one is having. Am I all right as a person if I feel anger, sadness, fear, and so on?

"How do you feel about being sad right now?"

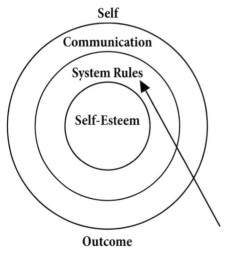

At the Point of System Rules

All too many of us grow up under inhuman rules, then, when grown, visit them upon ourselves.

"What do you think would happen if you allowed yourself to cry right now?"

Intervention Points

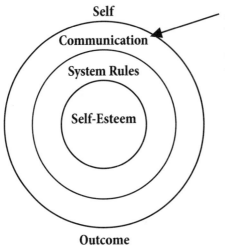

At the Point of Communication
We are not taught to clearly state
our real feelings, facial expressions,
body, words, and tone all matching.

At the Point of Outcome
What happens when one does any
of the following in the presence of
another human being?

    Feels the sadness

    Allows the self the tears

    Clearly states the doubts, fears

    versus

    Numbs the feeling

    Supresses the tears

    Says, "Oh, I'm fine" or makes
      a joke

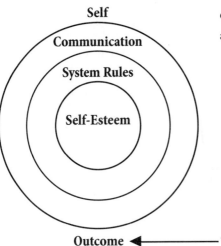

"What happened?"

That infant must experience hunger until somebody decides to bring the breast or bottle, must experience gas pains without benefit of explanation available to the adult mind, must experience the irritation of fatigue without the comfort of knowing that the approaching nap is going to make that bad feeling leave, must experience the dampness of the wet diaper at least until somebody well outside the crib and cradle world can realize that sort of experience may be taking place. This life of the infant is only as easy as his or her caretakers make it. Paying a price for our large-size Homo sapiens brains, we spend our initial years in a state of profound dependency waiting for our physiology to reach the point where autonomy is an option. This small person is utterly dependent on the whim and goodwill of the larger people around him or her.

No wonder so many of us learn such a distaste for "being dependent." Here is the genesis of self-containment in its pathological form. When the small child experiences a certain amount of her or his irritation being met with irritation in the caretaker, he or she begins the development of a pattern of pathological self-containment. The child is launched on the path of looking primarily to the self rather than to others for the meeting of needs, begins that toxic pattern of containment rather than expression.

Two parents who know how to extricate themselves from the anguish of blaming, placating, robot-ness, and irrelevance are free to enjoy the sweetness of genuine exchange of feeling with each other. There is an inherent healing in this exchange; growth can flow like an undammed stream. Reality, acknowledgment of the contents of the heart, holds the healing balm. That acknowledgment has a healing effect on the literal heart, as has been documented by James Lynch (1977) in *The Broken Heart*, and on the entire physiological system; the healing flows out among the constellations of systems which compose a human family— and even on out to and through the other constellations of systems that touch the family and which the family touches. Expression, versus containment, opens hearts, shines light on otherwise mysterious corners, makes possible human connections, for the lack of which our world suffers terribly.

Shining the sharp beam of reality on any given interaction serves to remove the element of toxicity. Differences in points of view do not become breeding grounds for vendetta.

Our young couple, having come to therapy before coming to parenthood, might learn the difference between necessary limits to behavior and the terrible inhuman rules with which so many of us have grown up, "don't cry" perhaps being one of the most malignant.

Examples

In Levenson's workshop, which I attended in Atlanta in 1986, he talked about a man heavily involved in the publishing of his book professing great interest in the contents, having cancer, and yet rejecting all Levenson's suggestions about engaging in therapy.

There is a perniciousness in this buried pain. The fear of this pain exceeds the fear of death itself. The denial, the self-containment, like a grinning death's head guard, ushers the individual out of life while making it possible not to experience that terrible anguish from those early months in infancy, those early years in childhood.

A colleague, musing about these theories, provided another example. Her father, Mr. B., had died of cancer. Throughout her childhood, her father had done a great deal of yelling at her mother. My friend experienced this yelling more as his style than as dangerous or truly violent, but her mother never liked it at all. Not very long before his death, before his diagnosis of cancer, her mother had told him she would leave him if he did not stop the yelling. Although one would think such a pattern would not yield itself to such suggestion, this man did stop the yelling. Then he died. My colleague believed that he could not tolerate the idea of being left and was so frightened that he did contain his behavior in this way. We surmise, within the context of Virginia's hypothesis about cancer, that my colleague's father's yelling could be compared to the infant's wail. As long as the infant is crying, the cry is declaring hope. When the infant falls silent, there is anaclitic depression with terrible potential consequences. With giving up the yelling, this man gave up his hope of being heard, his hope of being understood. His dream of union died, unmourned; and with that dream, his body.

Mr. B. exemplifies Virginia's observation that the intensity of an individual's blaming is proportionate to the intensity of this individual's need to be heard, to be understood. Mr. B's lifetime of yelling reflected his loneliness and his struggle, albeit clumsy, to make that human connection. Mrs. B., with no more skill in achieving intimacy than Mr. B., was no more able to make that bridge than he was. Neither understood these basic principles of human communication, that "communication is to relationship as breath is to the body" (Satir, 1971), and that profound responses in the body are concurrent with incongruent communication.

Responses in the body do attend *all* interactional communication. Some are more profound than others.

Had Mrs. B. even had the information that yelling, onerous as it was to her own sensibilities, might represent a desperate struggle toward love, she might have been able to hear the anguish underneath the noise. A reasonably good marriage counselor, with an understanding of these patterns of communication, might have been able to make the difference between life and death with this couple. Levenson would disagree; he believed the cancer patient and the cancer-prone must experience, in a therapy situation, the bond they did not experience in their infancy. He believed the cancer patient or precancer patient must experience the anaclitic depression within the context of therapy, then fuse with the therapist in the way the mother was not able to allow.

Gerda told me her grandmother said it was weak to cry. She told me that as she clutched her, by then, cancerous stomach, her tears all packed behind the winning smile she had painted on at some point early on in life—freezing all her pain behind a mask of "It's all right," leaving that awful emptiness in the very middle of her. That space now filled with cancer.

Gerda had once been in a large workshop with Virginia. I started the work with her by explaining Virginia's hypothesis about the relationship between unmourned, lost dreams and cancer. In response, Gerda *immediately* told me about a very important recent loss. In this one compact session, we made the leap back to the early loss which the recent one was symbolizing. Then we touched on, all too lightly, that terrible, deep, deep loneliness experienced as hopeless, with no possibility for connection with another human being. That deeply buried, unmet, and hopeless longing is the key factor in the development of cancer. That almost unfathomable pain discovered by an infant as he or she "realizes" in that holistic and kinesthetic style in which an infant "knows" something that she or he is not completely welcome in this world in which he or she is so helplessly now lying. She, in all her vulnerability, with all the freshness of her new humanity, her human body so newly formed, this new hope for life in smooth, pink flesh and blood, is not met. Not met with the heralding that truly is appropriate for the event of new life, new opportunity now made flesh again. Not met. Left in the Emptiness, the all-wrongness, the travesty and injustice is all contained within that small body/soul/mind. The horror of that experience waits for full manifestation and horrible rebirth, bursting carcinomically forth in her lungs or uterus at fifty, in his colon or liver at forty-five.

Gerda said yes, she had experienced a loss. At thirty-five, during the summer, she had miscarried a pregnancy. In her words, she had visualized her uterus as prickly like a cactus and believed she had brought about the miscarriage because she wanted to abort it. Her conflict was around her fear that this might have been her last chance to have a baby and she talked about how important babies were to her.

I had a sense there must be a deeper trail behind this loss. Otherwise, why wouldn't the cancer be in the uterus, the seat of feminine creativity, where it was not? I had seen that development in another patient who justified her existence by having babies. I knew there must be more than this. I also knew that every step Gerda and I took needed to be toward the direction of feeling as opposed to denying of feelings. Rather than pulling away to ask for facts, I asked how she felt and where in her body did she feel it.

According to Virginia's systematology, as well as Gestalt thinking, it is essential to go for the feeling. While I had a sense at this point of "needing more history," it would have been counterproductive to revert to a left-lobe, intellectualizing task- or "problem"-oriented way of asking. Gerda's cancer, the malignance lying hardly inches from my fingers, was a vivid reminder of the potential cost of a misstep.

I was on an odyssey, by then, in search of the wellsprings of the pain which was now manifesting itself in cancer. Doing it without the full enlistment of Gerda would be useless. It would be essential to engage her in a feeling level in the exploration. An intellectual awareness of the dynamics would not have permitted the necessary redecision on the child level (Goulding and Goulding, 1979).

Between flashes of the bright smile she wore for ordinary occasions, the much more appropriate sadness was struggling to break through. When she finally admitted what she was feeling was sadness, I asked her where it was. She motioned over her stomach. That is, in fact, where the cancer was. At this point, I was reaching for the Realm of the Great Patterns, hoping there would be one for this kind of desperate attempt at therapy with these kinds of odds and circumstances. I gently placed my hand on her stomach, so keenly aware of what lay beneath its surface. Her face shifted and looked less troubled. Wanting to be sure what I saw was what I was interpreting it to be and then reinforce it, I asked how she was feeling with my hand there. I had seen the sadness and I had seen her take in some comfort, two major issues for cancer candidates. One of the self-destructive defenses used by the precancer and cancer patient is to pretend the feeling one feels is not there. The congruence among feeling, facial expression, and verbal expression, which I saw in Gerda when she admitted feeling sadness, holds a healing potential. That suspension of this individual's more usual employment of denial left her more available, preparing her to nurture herself as well as allowing the possibility of a human connection. She had taken two steps in the right direction; one was to have achieved that congruence for the moment and the other was to receive the comfort I offered. This bode well. Gerda's face and words were telling me what her insides were feeling. She was allowing me entry and she was allowing the comfort I was offering. The "happy" mask was not in place.

I said, at this point, ever so gently, in touch with her ailing stomach, "Gerda, I think that lost baby might be the one in *you*."

"I was adopted three times" was her simple response.

I felt a chill like a sudden cold north Texas wind blowing across me. Long ago, I had been a child-welfare worker on the windswept plains in North Texas, and an image of the waifs I took from homes and placed in other homes flashed before me. Their images were bright and clear as one of those windswept Texas Panhandle mornings. Their small hands in mine with no option but submission, their little bodies warm in my arms, too young to understand or whence they were borne. Some of them still bear names I gave them. Across the years, I have wondered how they fared.

Here was the loneliness, and here was the loss. I can resonate with deep loneliness, and I know what it feels like to be a minor in a home that is not one's own. I moved in with my uncle after my mother's death, so I know the vulnerability of sleeping in a bed that is not one's own, hanging clothes in a closet not one's own, being where one is through the good graces of the caretaker rather than by birthright. There is the ever-present possibility that one might be as easily dismissed as one was admitted if one became "too much trouble."

And I had been nearly fifteen. How would it have been at five and eighteen months?

Gerda said she was a war orphan from a far northern European country. Her first set of adoptive parents had been killed in an automobile wreck en route to the airport to claim her. Her papers had even been lost in the wreck.

"Gerda, you *must* mourn those multiple losses; you must do something with that pain."

She had filled the void with the cancer. When I asked where it was, she said it was in her stomach and around the region of her heart.

The metaphor in that seemed undeniable to me.

Her face changed again. I was not sure what was going on, but I felt alarmed at whatever I was seeing. Did I sense a retreat, I don't know. But what I asked, in response, was, "Where did you go just now, Gerda?" I asked her.

"Into that place I escape to where nothing makes any difference, so I don't feel so bad."

"Gerda, no, you must come back! That is a deadly trap! You must come back and let out those tears."

She did not come back. She told me, clear as funeral bells, that she could not bear that pain. This lovely woman who had been admitted to one of the most prestigious Ivy League schools at sixteen slipped through my reaching hands, as well as all those bright past opportunities, and died before the year's end.

The babies Gerda had borne were all attempts to fill the void from long ago. The last baby, her last hope for the void-filling, had miscarried. If the void could not be filled with the generative growth of a developing fetus tissue, then it would be filled with the malignant growth of the developing cancerous tissue. Levenson explained:

In every cancer ever studied the genetic structures are unstable. In numerous types of cancers the genes have actually been shown to shift position. Somehow this instability causes the cell to start reproducing much in the way cells reproduce in newborns. Cancer cells reproduce at the same rate as newborn baby cells. Cancer has growth hormones similar or identical to the hormone levels of newborn babies' tissues. (Levenson, 1985, 15)

We may eventually confirm, scientifically, that the high cost of denial and disregarding of feelings is just as toxic as the wastes, the dumping of which we oppose in our rivers. Do we not pollute ourselves with our own inner poisons by not allowing them to flow out of us via congruent bodily and verbal expression?

Chapter Notes

1. "None of this may fit anyway" was Virginia's disclaimer. She never told her trainees, "This is how it is." Instead, her instructions were "These are my observations; go out there, observe, and see what you find."

2. When I spoke with Virginia in 1987 to ask how she would feel about my writing an article on her material regarding the physical implications of incongruent communication, she referred to the work of James Lynch. She was not aware of Dr. Levenson's work, which had not yet been published.

   No attempt will be made here for a current review of the literature on this subject, the focus of this book being the work of Virginia Satir. Lynch is mentioned here because of Virginia's specific reference to his work. Levenson's work is considered because of how well his ideas fit with Virginia's observations.

10

Being Whole—Being Real

I'm not afraid to experiment. I don't know anymore what is right. I only know what is real and whole and if it is congruent or not.

—**Virginia Satir**, 1987

Transforming the Stress Ballet

Virginia Satir's seminars reflected wholeness in structure as well as in content. She understood the value of presenting her material on sensory, cognitive, and affective levels.

It is probably safe to say that she never bored her students. She knew that the whole being of a person had to be involved to maximize learning or therapeutic results.

When I present a concept, I like to have a sight, sound, thought, feeling, and action together with it. A typical picture of what people have given the name "learning"... in the past: somebody stands up and talks, somebody takes that in and writes it down, then writes an exam. That just tests whether you have been listening or not; it doesn't have much to do with learning. For me, learning is change. The ingredients of the two are exactly the same. Reducing to a very precise focus on one level all my writing and work, all that I do, has just one aim: *becoming more fully human.*

Think about when all you use is your left brain. You sit all day, do figures; all you think about is what is rational and analytical. The rest of yourself is paying a high price for that. Another way, a loving way, of talking about that is: all parts of yourself are given a voice and a face. That is really going toward wholeness. (Satir, 1986a, tape 5)

Virginia set up demonstrations of the stress ballet so that trainees would be able to experience the distinct kind of discomfort accompanying each incongruent communication stance. They could then experience and compare the physical relief and emotional difference as they moved into congruence.

This actual physical experience is important. People ordinarily spend most of their time locked into the physiological discomfort of blaming and placating or in the rigid, frozen, and feelingless super-reasonable stance. Unless they viscerally feel the palpable bodied defenses and then get a bodily knowledge of the difference, they can misunderstand and dismiss "congruence" as a cerebral exercise.

Or worse, those who merely read spottily in and about Virginia's work can pick a few sentences out of context and misconstrue Virginia's emphasis on being real as a variation on the encounter group confrontations of the 1960s and 1970s (Brothers, 1996b, 1996c, 123–125, 1996d 127–132; Bula, 1996, 133–141; Waller, 1996, 111–131). In fact, Virginia's work took people to deep levels of resolution within the self and with family members. Mindless confrontation and trite "affirmations" were not part of her repertoire. As noted in chapter 6, even Fritz Perls suggested, during the sixties, that Virginia might be too intellectual (Perls, 1969).[1]

Most people spend their lives trying to move out of misery by shifting among the incongruent stances in attempts to relieve their pain. This shifting from one stance to another is Virginia's reason for referring to this phenomenon as the "stress ballet." In the placating stance, the one who stands at the destructive end of the continuum of that position suffers for the sake of suffering. One's own feelings, one's own inner being, are not sufficiently important to justify one's existence. These people exist in a constant state of wounding out of an inability to celebrate themselves purely for the miraculousness of the manifestation of life which they are in their given time and space. They live in a chronic emotional (and often physical) condition of pain as a result of the steady acid rain of self-blame. Virginia's stress ballet addresses the psychological step the suffering person must make between martyrdom and using one's own pain for empathy, which effects transformation (see pages 126–127 for Portrait of a Super-Reasonable Intrapersonal Response and Portrait of a Congruent Intrapersonal Response).

As we have said earlier, the guilt-ridden patient may well make a detour en route to wholeness: blaming. It is a common therapeutic error not to recognize this as a step rather than an end point. If I recognize it as a part of the process rather than a finished product, my patient and I will be on a far more constructive, productive track. If I forget about the self-esteem factor, my patient may be set up for *more* remorse and self-blame following action taken while in the blaming mode and may relapse into another cycle of blaming and placating.

Standing up for the self in the face of the other is the transformation of the blaming position, but this vital self-care must be aligned with concern for the other included. Further, if a person becomes aware of the implications of all four stances, the transition to self-care can be sustained. Leaders such as Martin Luther King Jr. are examples. His focus was not on what whites were doing to blacks; it was on empowering his people to mobilize their own dignity and resources.

Moving into and remaining in the super-reasonable response can be extremely perilous. On the one hand, if one puts tasks and/or any part of one's greater context before the feelings or value of self or of other human beings, one is releasing the possibility of any sort of horror into the world. On the other hand, super-reasonable transformed—the creative single-minded focus of intelligence—may produce such behavior as exhibited by an Einstein, whose focus on his intelligence did not preclude his humanitarianism.

We have seen the destructive nature of the irrelevant response when used out of awareness, knee-jerk fashion. That style of incongruent communication cuts the person off from authentic, intimate contact and almost guarantees no mutual goal can be accomplished. However, conscious irrelevance is the source of humor. Comedians are examples. Humor is expressed and can be enjoyed when appropriate, according to the context and not simply as a way to divert attention from the self and subject.

These stances occur on a continuum and may range from subtle to blatant.

Interactions Continuum:
Most Dysfunctional to Transformed

Transformations are made by writing back into the picture that which has been crossed out.

Placating

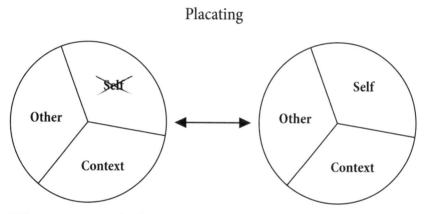

"Whatever you want, dear."
Self is crossed out.
Your needs are important;
mine are not. Ultimate extreme
of crossing out self: suicide.

My needs are important as
yours. All human needs are
important. Implies and requires
authentic concern for others.

Example: Gandhi, Jesus,
Mohammed, Mother Teresa

Blaming

"You can't tell me what to do!"
Other is crossed out. My needs
are important; yours are not.

Extreme: homicide.

Your needs as well as mine are
important, but no more so.
Ability to stand up for oneself.

Example: Martin Luther King Jr.

Super-reasonable

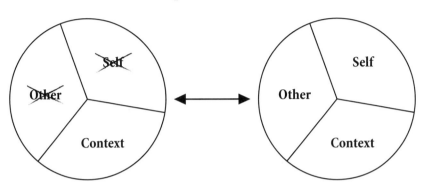

"For goodness sake, don't show any feeling."

Both self and other are crossed out. No human needs are important; only the task matters.

Example: Atrocities like the World Trade Center terrorists.

Human needs are moved to central place. Creative use of intelligence.

Example: Einstein.

Irrelevant

"Now, about the price of tea in China…"

Self, other, and context are crossed out. Nobody's needs are important; no meaning. After all, nothing has meaning anyways.

Example: Insanity, florid psychosis.

Human needs are in a central place and the context taken into consideration. Human beings considered along with the task. Ability to have fun.

Examples: Comedians like Bob Hope.

Virginia's framework is this: the people whose response is usually being super-reasonable are guided to opening up to feeling; those who are placating realize their own value as a unique part of the Great Whole; those given to blaming recognize the value of their fellow travelers; and those taking refuge in irrelevance find meaning as they allow themselves intimate connection with fellow human beings.

Virginia described the "renovation" of the stances in a taped interview from 1974:

> For example, in the family I saw yesterday, I saw the man as making super-reasonable responses. That meant that in my imagination he was standing there very erect, with very little movement, speaking in a rather monotonous way. I saw the woman kneeling before him in a placating position, but at the same time—behind her back—pointing an accusing finger at him. I saw the oldest daughter standing and super-reasonable like her father, looking at neither parent but with one finger barely poking out, pointing at her father. And I saw the next girl very deliberately and in a very obvious way pointing her finger at her mother. The next child was a boy, and I saw him standing very close to his mother and placating her. Then I saw the next child as giving out irrelevant responses by moving all over the place and not being able to fix on anyone. I also saw the youngest child, a five-year-old girl, as being irrelevant.
>
> As I saw these pictures in my mind, it was important to respect them as representing the best ways that these people had developed to cope. Their ways of placating, blaming, and being super-reasonable or irrelevant had formed a kind of system that meant that no one in the family could really approach the personhood of another. They were likely to mishear one another; they were seeing roles rather than real people. So my search and my efforts would be directed to helping these people to *become real* with one another. I looked at this family, and my insides felt them respond to my contact. Full contact, by the way, carries the message of caring—caring in a deep, personal sense—and I regard that contact as a vital basis for developing any changes. There has to be high trust. If people in the family group do not find me trustworthy, I don't think we are going to be able to effect any changes. (Spitzer, 1975, 114–115)

She continued:

The four stances which I expect to see in some combination with all of the people who are experiencing problems in coping . . . all appeared in yesterday's family. Incidentally, one of the things I have become increasingly conscious of is that the American dream about what a person should be really fits my category of the super-reasonable response. This response is, "For goodness sake, don't show any feeling!" This to me is sad, but it is also true.

At this point I will digress a moment and state that the stances are not rigid and unchangeable. *Each of these ways of communicating* can be "renovated." If you are handling your responses by placating, one of the ravages going on within you is that you keep giving yourself messages that you don't count for very much. However, if you know how, you can renovate this ability to be tender and bring it into your awareness instead of just feeling an automatic given that you always have to please everyone.

Renovated blaming becomes your ability to stand up for yourself. Everyone needs to be able to do that, but you must do it realistically rather than automatically.

Renovated super-reasonableness becomes the creative use of your intelligence. Using your intelligence is delightful but if it is used only to protect yourself, it becomes rather boring.

Renovated irrelevancy becomes your ability to be spontaneous and to give yourself direction in awareness and in reality.

In any case, dealing with a super-reasonable person—like the father in yesterday's family—the therapist faces a most difficult problem. Super-reasonable people sit very still and upright; they move their faces very little, their voices are usually in a monotone, and they always talk very reasonably. What you get is this feeling of a kind of drying-up about the person; he is all locked in.

As it happened, the father had been a Fundamentalist minister, and he had strong feelings about what was right and wrong. I noticed that he responded to all my overtures—the handshake, the questions, and the statements I made—in the same way. I felt that he listened, but I wasn't always sure he understood. I did find—and continue to find—with people who organize their responses in this fashion that lots of words are used to say things. It is important for me to try to tune in wherever I can in a way that is going to touch the person. And so when someone is organized by using big words and being reasonable, it is natural for me to come in on that level. Oftentimes therapists get bored by people who talk a lot.[2] However, I need [to listen first] to have them talk enough so that I can understand what they are doing. In the case of this man, he had told me about his repeated efforts to try to do what he wanted to do and how they had failed, Again, this was said in his dry, rather matter-of-fact voice. As I listened to him, I became aware that it sounded as though he had stopped trying. I asked him what had happened to his dreams. It sounded a little to me as if he had given up on his dreams. I began to see a light come into his eyes. The bottom half of his face didn't change particularly, but his eyes became a little wider and there was a little light in them. As I listened to his response, he said it was true that he didn't have any more dreams and that they were dead. So, I use these stances and way of communicating what I hear and see in my mind as my guidelines for the kinds of interventions I make with people. It is a little like tuning in to a place where they can hear me and they can begin to hear themselves. And, of course, if this is done in a trusting, understanding, hearing context, then it happens. By the end of yesterday's interview, the husband's whole face was beginning to respond, not just his eyes. (Spitzer, 1975, 122–123)

Virginia added:

What I really want to emphasize here is that if I hear a person handling his responses in a super-reasonable fashion, my tuning-in is at the level of the intellect but in such a way as to give the person an experience of really being heard and seen. If I shift to a person who—like the wife—is placating, I try to get in touch with what she hoped for herself and lead her to talk about some of her yearnings and loneliness. The wife did this, but it wouldn't have appeared unless I had asked.

In terms of blamers—like the second oldest child—I have to get in touch with the longing to be connected. This was my approach yesterday when, rather than dealing with all the hate feelings, we focused instead on her own feelings about herself. What I found myself doing in each case was trying to help the person stabilize. (Spitzer, 1975, 125)

What had Virginia done? She had *paid attention*, gently and with compassion, with her own "core," to the aching or bruised or burning "core" of each person. Gradually, as each sensed even dimly Virginia's "attunement," that person opened to Virginia in the presence of the now—surprised and unwittingly eagerly-waiting awareness of the others. In that rare open space—and feeling Virginia's deep respect and concern—each was able to lift her or his "eyes" to the others, beginning to really "see" and feel a little what the others felt. The "magic" to which some of Virginia's admirers referred was happening. Heart was beginning to speak—rather *listen*—to heart.

Wholeness

I know when all of these lights are on that the whole world will be lighted in a different way. And I know it is possible . . .
—**Virginia Satir,** *1983*

The description we have just read is one among certainly hundreds, likelier thousands, of such healing and "wholing" incidents. We of the mental health field had among us a person who knew how to consistently help the obviously hurting patients to healthy whole newness and who could and wanted to show us how to become whole ourselves. This was not only for ourselves and our immediate clients but so that they and any among whom we live—the entire human family—might be transformed into real, whole, interconnected vibrant persons. Virginia knew and, with complete confidence, would say: If we can only reach 6 percent of the population, it would begin to happen (Satir, 1992b, 11). Virginia had a dream of wholeness on a vast scale—the entire world. Consciously and deliberately, indefatigably, she worked to shift human behavior across the planet.

This dream of wholeness on a large scale threaded through her process communities, which had evolved from the monthlong seminars she began leading in 1968. The dream had various captions, which also evolved over time: Peoplemaking (Satir, 1977b), The University for Becoming Human, The University for Becoming More Human, The University for Becoming More Fully Human, (Satir, 1977b, 1977c, 1977d, 1981a, 1982, 1983b). The point was to initiate training that would address the *whole person*, to learn the skills which would put the person on the wholeness track. She wanted to see our education as therapists turned around to focus on what makes health, rather than the cataloguing, categorizing, and memorizing of pathology.

We can trace the thread of that dream, finally expressed as University for Being More Fully Human—from a letter written for the purpose of beginning to develop Avanta, the Virginia Satir Network,* which Virginia intended as the faculty of this university:

---

* Avanta is now known as the Virginia Satir Global Network.

I have a dream of developing what I am tentatively calling the University for Being More Human, which is an extension of the month-long training programs I have been doing for the past nine years. I see this [university] as eventually becoming part of the whole Network family. Like all dreams, this one is subject to revision and review. (Satir, 1977b)

Once her "university" was underway, Virginia began the first Process Community Meeting in Crested Butte, Colorado, in 1981. Five years after her first letter, from Process Community Meeting II, August 1982, came this comment:

No maps . . . [when I saw my first family, in 1951], no maps. There are no maps for what we're doing here. We and you, you and us are making those maps as you go through the experience. So I am not thinking in terms of the finished product, because I think we haven't known very much in this world about how and how far we can go. Most of what we know about human beings we got from studying sick people. We don't know much about well people. We don't even know much about how human beings grow and develop. So we are at the beginning of something very exciting and important. (Satir, 1982)

From Process Community III, August 19, 1983, the next year, Virginia spoke about the idea that was forming in her mind for the University for Being More Fully Human:

Now I have had long and wide exposure with almost every professional, educational arm that there is: psychology, nursing, theology, psychiatry, medicine, the arts, management of all sorts of education in the universities. And I was often offered posts to come and stay three months and do this or that. Anyway, the point was that I began, in those earlier years to say to myself, "What's lacking in the university is [the looking] for [and the teaching of] what makes people *human*." I was aware that the instrument that we *are* is what makes us successful or not successful in using the knowledge that we have. None of that was touched and still isn't being touched in many of the university areas . . . if we really understand . . . everybody is unique. That means you cannot deal with [simply] looking [only] at sameness and differentness, you have to look at it in terms of the process. So everyone needs to be in touch with their uniqueness. There is no comparison in uniqueness. All right. So [now] I'm looking at a very different kind of group, evolving . . . By the way, I know that everyone can evolve. And I stretch my neck and my back and my interest and my love and all the rest [of me] in all my seminars to help each person to come to that flowering place. *Because I know when all of these lights are on that the whole world will be lighted in a different way. And I know it is possible, it just depends on how long it will take.* (Satir, 1983b, 741)

Virginia was not the first person interested in creating a "better" world. However, unlike many, her unique stance had nothing to do with "good" versus "bad." Virginia's focus was on *respect for and expression of reality*. Here is where the differences between the threat/reward model and the seed model become glaringly clear. The hierarchy paradigm is about "bad and good"; the seed model is about "real and whole." In the following, Virginia highlighted the difference by describing and commenting on a too common tragedy, pointing out that absence of "whole and real" and not absence of good and presence of "bad" precipitates the chaos. Indeed, she suggested that labeling the situation "bad" will only bring about further tragedy:

I also know deep down that these [domestic atrocities within the home] are outcomes of people whose coping mechanisms are such that this is what [it is about]. Fortunately . . . I've done enough with people like that to know what's underneath. It had nothing to do with love or intention, it is about survival.

As an example, take a parent, a young woman 16 years old, or 17. Having a child before she's ready and her gonads are working so she's got some man around older than herself who is an alcoholic. And she wants very much to hang onto this man; the kid somehow needs her when she wants to do something else someplace else, her needs and the child's need collide. And at a certain point she settles for her needs but at the same time she feels guilty about it, the kid picks up on that and starts to nag. And the nagging, crying gets to her and she wants some shut-up so she can get those places out of her head, and slaps the child in such a way that can hurt the child even then. Then the child cries some more in the same way and that eats on her and pretty soon the child is either seriously hurt or dead.

It has nothing to do with love, and once we get that through our head, I think we will be a lot further ahead. It has to do with wholeness of our-selves. Whole people and people who love themselves do not behave that way. They don't have to.

So, that is why I don't really care much about "good or bad." I think they're both in the same category. What I do [care about and hope to facilitate] is "whole and real"—as much as I know about. When I can develop wholeness . . . people standing on their own feet, that… have their own [inner] radiation and they don't have to ask anybody else to [turn on] the lights. [And] . . . don't have to be nagging peo-ple . . . [hanging desperately on to another perhaps equally "dark" person]. But many of us are far away from that, some of the time, some of us a lot of the time, some of us haven't been there yet . . .

That's one of the reasons why professional education . . . is essen-tial, [in which] . . . we work with our own [bodied selves] before we ever try to fiddle around with anybody's life. (Satir, 1981a, 121)

Virginia was saying, (a) she knew and could teach how to help people develop wholeness; (b) a person developing wholeness is a person aware of his or her own radiance and inner resources; (c) such a person is, therefore, not dependent on others to "turn on the lights"; (d) such a person would not be subject to the kind of desperation that engenders abusive behavior.

In other words, bring the person to full, respectful awareness of their own inner resources, and symptoms become irrelevant and vanish. She knew this worked because she was able to bring it about in patients.

From the same period that gave us the poignant reflection on the sixteen-year-old mother came the following lecture. Virginia was launching her University for Becoming Human and wanted to explicitly reject the threat/reward, domination/submission model. She explained her rationale for the seed model—how and why it provides a framework for the process of "becoming." Helping people augment their humanity is a very different process from hunting down and killing sets of symptoms. The context was Virginia's first monthlong Process Community Meeting at Crested, Butte, Colorado (1981). What follows are Virginia's own words.

I believe that people were meant to be round not flat,[3] and so I can no longer turn my back on the absolute assurance to myself that people were made to be round. True, we have been surrounded for thousands of years by things that have asked us to be flat. You would not be here unless you believed in round people. It is natural for sickness to be with flatness and health to be with roundness, if you follow my metaphor . . . I will be doing everything I can to respect whatever flatness I find, because that is a place that many people begin—and go towards roundness . . . I think there's a definite relationship between how someone sees something and how they proceed. This makes a foundation to my work of trying to help people be round: that means, to help people to be in touch with all their parts.

That also gives you the basis of my ideas about symptomatology. I believe that symptomatology is that which occurs because we are unnourished and unconnected and inharmonious . . . There are many cognitive ways to talk about that, so that if I am going to help somebody with whatever their symptoms are, I am going to go toward helping them to nurture themselves—to nurture themselves, and to get in touch with things that are present but they don't know about, to find access to the things that they have [but] they haven't been able to access; then to help them make connections with themselves in the interest of themselves. And that is an over-simplified way of talking about how to go toward roundness—to move toward growth and wholeness. (Satir, 2000, 5–9)

Making Roundness—Not Treating Symptoms

Virginia continued:

Those who have any training in helping people often have become expert in mental *ill* health. And that means that the focus of where we have come from, most of us, has been looking at the ill-health here, or the symptom. That becomes the center of what we do. Everything else fans out from this. So that what we do and what we've learned for the most part, has been how to take the ill-health aspect and try to do something with *that*.

I don't work that way anymore (i.e. dealing with dis-ease), but I used to. I work on the principle that here is a being that is not yet fully in touch with all the aspects of their health, the resources that they have. And the symptom shows up as a kind of blockage . . . So I start from how to develop health rather than to get rid of ill-health. To me, that is a very important difference. So to put it over-simplified, my goal is how to develop health rather than to get rid of ill-health. Now if I do this, develop health, then there is no need for ill-health. That is an orientation; you can say I am working here about how to make roundness instead of how to stamp something out.

I want to make one other comment about that . . . All the things I have learned about blisters, pain, difficulties, struggles, and all that, I still know, but I use it differently. So this is not an invitation to get rid of everything, no more than it is an invitation when we are an adult to forget all the learnings of our childhood. Because we keep moving and growing in terms of our experience.

Sometimes when I speak like this people say, "Oh, then all the things I learned about _____ don't fit?" No, they fit, but they are used in a different way. Now we are hearing a lot about holistic health and holistic medicine, and what that means really is that we are adding to what we know and using our information differently. The word is "and," not "either/or."

I want to also say that at this point in time all over the world, there are people who have glimpses of what it would be like to be fully functioning people. So one of the challenges is how to take the information that we have and apply it in such a way that it promotes health rather than stamping out illness. So that is the way you will see me operate. *Sometimes when people watch what I do in families, they say it is magic and only I can do it. Not true. It is because of the way that I use what I have* [italics mine]. I will tell you a little story about that. In the early sixties, when I started working like this it was freaking everybody out. I was a nice freak but I was still a freak. And one of the things that happened very early in California through a whole series of funny things, is people wanted me to train them in family therapy, and so I followed the principle that I would show people. I wasn't going to talk about it, I would show. And I would work with people who had been in the hospital eighteen, nineteen, twenty years. Patients in state hospitals. Now at that time, everybody knew, once a chronic, always a chronic. And our hospitals were full of decaying, vegetating people. I said, "I want to work with that population. I want to get somebody who has been in the hospital eighteen or nineteen years who still has a family. And I worked in every state hospital in California, and every one of those people got out of the hospital in ten weeks, after having been there eighteen or twenty years. And then people said, "You know, maybe we made a mistake in diagnosis." I said, "uh-uh." What you noticed led you to that conclusion. I look at different things so I come out in another way." That [series of events] was one of the big elements in starting the movement to change and get rid of those kinds of wards.

So the point of what I am making now is we can focus on anything, and the result of what we focus on is going to show up in what happens. So if I focus on that which is getting you to accent your resources, then you are going to grow. If I focus on that which is all your bad points and try to get rid of them, both of us are engaged in a killing operation. That is the way I see it today.

So how are we going to use the fact that you are too thin, that you are not eating? How are we going to use the fact that you don't see any meaning in life and you call that depression and maybe an invitation to suicide? How are we going to use the fact that at a moment in time you react in such a way that you are blind and deaf and you killed somebody? How are you going to react so that [same] energy can be used[, instead,] in a growth way? Those are some of the challenges that I have given myself and I have seen them pay off all over the world. (Satir, 2000, 5–9)

Where There Is Life, There Is Hope

Virginia wrote about the strength that comes from growth:

If you were to leave this seminar with the idea . . . that *human life and life itself is always capable of growth*, whether in a ninety-four-year-old, a two-day-old, or in forty-year-old. If you come away with the idea that growth is always possible because we are dealing with life and life is capable, always, of growing, that is the nature of it, then you will never have burnout again in your work, never—that I can tell you. You may have pain because the world is full of pain, but you will never have burnout, because you will always know someplace to go. Always have that. And I suppose that that is probably one of the reasons why, for me, I can go anywhere in the world to . . . any kind of difficulty, and know that I can go somewhere [in working with a family or person], because, one, I am working with life, and two, always that possibility is there because there is life. And if you have that, then what to do is to get into a creative place with whomever you work.

. . . *It is not another "should;" it is not that you should, but it is possible*. Do you ever have burn-out? The quickest road to burnout is to figure out that you have got to solve problems and get rid of something. The shortest road to it, because none of us can do it really. I don't know how it is now, but it used to be the way you closed a case was that they either died, moved away or got too old.

So, I surround what I do with life, with hope, knowing absolutely that the human being has that possibility. It may not have been [known] at the time. And it may also be that you at this moment in time feel too afraid or hopeless or whatever to connect with that. There is nothing wrong or right with that, but [nevertheless hope] *is* always possible. (Satir, 2000, 5–9)

To understand Virginia's work, it is critical to understand that she was not trying to develop methods of fixing problems or people. She was teaching a functional way of living life, not offering a magical solution.

Those who dissect her work to find that magic are in danger of missing the essential nature of Wholeness and Wholing. However true the minutiae, one gets a very narrow definition of a rose by separating petal from pistil. If one sat and took the moon apart piece by piece, one would know the geometrical dimensions and chemical composition, but would one know the moon? Without even getting into metaphor or metaphysics, we know such a dissector would have no way of discovering, for example, the moon's influence on the biorhythms of earthly creatures.

To understand Virginia's model, one must understand it is a system of thinking rather than a set of techniques. Virginia, like the rose and the moon, had a strong effect on those on whom she shone—for concrete but difficult-to-measure reasons. Rather than using only theory, she built a very solid system based on keen observation by which she discovered universal principles.

She studied communication theory thoroughly before and during her time on the staff at the Mental Research Institute in Palo Alto, California in the 1960s.

She understood that all things—everything and everybody—have to be seen in a relational context. That was her reason for her emphasis on process rather than content.

Left-brain, linear thinking serves to discipline the intuitive patterns that bob about on the surface of one's consciousness, helping to form the patterns which make the intuitions intelligible and describable. Virginia never denigrated the importance of making categories and never drifted off in fuzzy circles. Anybody who saw her work knows how practical she was as she worked with a given family. She welcomed such explorations of her work. As she said, "I'm not afraid to experiment. I don't know anymore what is right. I only know what is real and whole and if it is congruent or not" (Satir, 1987a, tape 1–6).

Virginia went on to say she concentrated on examining and understanding rather than trying to eradicate. Examining and understanding interaction was always very important in her quest for finding "what is real and whole":

> It reminds me of the days in the '60s with the flower children. I got a lot of criticism because I insisted that I keep my "thinker" available. They said, "Oh, come on. Let all that stuff go. Let's not bother with the thinking, only feel." Well, I could see that I would become a half-wit in another place if I threw away my thinking and only had my feelings. Where we are now is in the integration, in the combining of thinking and feeling. (Satir 1987a, tape 4)

Although she spent an immense amount of time thinking, mentally sorting, and developing methodology, her focus was on the bigger picture: what was this world about and how could she nudge it in a more fulfilling direction?

The apparent magic of Virginia's work was not born out of application of any secret techniques to be found by any clever observer. This "magic" was *in the interaction*, not in something performed on the patients. The inherent result was not from some enlightened form of sorcery; it was from what can happen between two people when body, emotion, words, and facial expression all align in congruence—when people understand the meaning of "whole and real." The reason it seems like magic is because it so rarely happens. By and large, people do not have the courage to admit to self-doubt in the presence of the other—to say what they mean and to mean what they say. Making this admission is remarkably freeing.

Virginia was keenly aware of the risk and courage required in opening oneself to another while, at the same time, protecting that delicate, vulnerable inner self that we all have. This clarity about what lies behind the surface defenses is what guided her toward the gentle, nurturing confrontations for which she became well-known.

Working with exquisite awareness of the nature of systems, Virginia approached the training of therapists from a systemic, "whole and real" point of view. Her training of therapists was always toward their "becoming more fully human." To effectively use the self, that self must function out of "high human"—congruence and compassion. Virginia demonstrated the "how" of this goal partly by personal example, just as we model roles for our patients.

Congruent communication is wholeness in motion and is a health-maintaining process. Virginia's use of this universal fact is a large part of what made her work look like magic.

In these chapters, we have been dealing with the first two of three stages of congruence (Satir, 1991, 68).

The first stage of congruence has to do with awareness, acknowledgment, and ownership of feelings. It is possible to be respectful of self and the other while disagreeing. Expressions of anger can be delivered without involving disrespect of the recipient. All feelings can be honored and acknowledged without necessarily engendering action. The second stage of congruence could be considered an effect of the first stage. Respectfully honoring feelings in self and others leads to wholeness and harmony within the self; the behavior (communicating congruently) is simultaneously self-validating and other-validating. The "third energy" of connectedness emerges and is made possible. In this chapter, we have addressed wholeness. The third stage, having to do with universality and spirituality, is explored in chapter 11. We separate the three stages in order to describe them; but since wholeness is always *becoming*, in practice the "stages" are a fluid unit, a process, which augments at each stage.

Chapter Notes

1. It is not possible to give the page number; Perls deliberately did not number the pages in the book.

2. This interview was conducted while encounter groups were still popular and emphasis on feelings rather than intellect was in vogue. In the climate of the sixties and midseventies, listening was not necessarily a given. Many were trying to model themselves on the rather abrupt style of Fritz Perls. Therapists would tend to interrupt patients engaged in intellectual deliveries to instruct them to get in touch with their feelings. Virginia was pointing out the importance of first listening to the patient.

3. To grasp something of the extensiveness and variety contained in the metaphor, round not flat, you might want to think of a flat, deflated balloon and one merrily rising in the air.

11

THE PATTERN THAT CONNECTS:
CONGRUENCE

Truth is the name given to that which was originally nameless and simple. Though small, the whole world cannot subjugate it. When the rulers abide by it, all animate creation will of their own accord become their servants. Because heaven and earth are one with Truth, they produce rains and dews which benefit all mankind without their asking.

Truth is to the Universe as rivers and seas are to the earth.

—**Lao Tzu**

Virginia sees the goal of her work as one of helping people and families to gain a sense of their wholeness, wholeness being the fundamental charter of the universe.

—**Virginia Satir** and **Michele Baldwin**

Congruence, Truth, Wholeness

What is congruence, why is it so relevant, and why must these questions be asked? In essence, congruence is *truth*. Truth is the basis of wholeness. Wholeness is "the fundamental charter of the universe." Congruence draws the interacting human systems into a state of coherence and resonance. In Virginia's experience, congruent communication, yoked with self-esteem, was the team that pulls the wagon that, for want of a better phrase, we all call mental health. This is prerequisite to what Virginia described as "Peace within [self], peace between [others], and peace among [community]" (Satir, 1987a, tape 1–6).

Pervasive truth provides the solid base for human action and is not available within the context of incongruent interaction. Incongruence requires squandering energy on rigid defense—energy which might otherwise be used for creative purpose. Congruence does not equal passivity and lack of conflict. It equals free expression of individual uniqueness. For Virginia, congruent expression was not material for an esoteric colloquy. Congruent communication is the vitality of the Life Force—real, vibrant exchange between here-and-now human beings.

Virginia Satir was a realistic woman, seriously engaged in practical matters. Her focus on making congruent responses in all her own interchanges was born of her observation that congruence is a functional behavioral necessity, not an idealistic mental concept. She understood congruence to be an enlightened, pragmatic, human choice that could be made rather than an "ideal" or an abstract notion. Having nothing to do with abstract or moralistic sentiments of how people "should" be, this choice to communicate with congruence would deliver a person from the bonds of the misery of self-doubt, self-deprecation, and alienation and into position for intimate connection.

Congruent communication, the life-enhancing pattern of response—the pattern that makes the context for connection between people—is difficult to explain because it is always dynamic. "Describing" a congruent stance is like trying to explain a given ripple in a running brook; before the words have left my mouth, the ripple is in a completely different form and yards downstream. If I take a photograph of the ripple, it is no longer the ripple—it is then a photograph of the ripple. So, no matter how artistic may be my way of explaining ripples, I am always explaining the ripple that was, not the ripple that is. That is one reason definition of congruence is not obvious. Another reason—many times I might be trying to talk of "ripples" to a person who has never seen a stream. The sheer unfamiliarity of the congruent response makes it hard to describe. Virginia's estimate was that people, under the stress of self-doubt, respond congruently only about 4.5 percent of the time.

The possibility of congruence requires practicing *awareness* of our own internal responses to external stimuli, sorting them out, then learning and practicing communication shaped by the intention of truth and coupled with respect. This action is a *skill* that can be learned and taught. For Virginia, learning to monitor one's own "thinking, feeling, and wanting"—internal process—is an integral part of the change process. This is critical to facilitating congruent communication from the therapist and in providing a role model for families. Indeed, Virginia was so keenly cognizant of this deficit in human interaction that her extended training seminars included exercises designed specifically to bring self into such awareness. Exercises always accompanied lectures. Holistic learning was Virginia's mode, engaging body and emotions, including all aspects of the person of the trainee, integrating thinking and feeling. Congruent communication could be explained, learned, taught, and then applied in simple language. The key is *awareness*— so that therapist as well as patient are able to monitor and be guided by internal processes. Through such mindfulness, that which is out of awareness becomes conscious and data for deliberate choice.

Virginia taught therapists to distinguish the body language of a person giving incongruent messages from that of a person who is in a state of congruence. She made clear that what makes all the difference is understanding the implications of the nonverbal message as well as the verbal message:

> [This applies] . . . all over the world. I have [for example] been able to supervise Swedish-speaking therapists with Swedish-speaking families and pick up all the discrepancies, because the language is not all there is . . . In order to give dysfunctional body language, the body is "out of sync." I look at the jaw muscles, I look at the mouth . . . I hope

you will learn how to observe without judging, but just to see. The minute that a self is congruent, everything about that body is relaxed. (Satir, 1987a, tape 5)

Careful observation for clues about deeper and other meaning than the verbal is part of the requisite level of awareness. Virginia's expertise was born of her understanding of her acutely aware *self* as the major instrument for change in the client. Every action was intended to be a move toward authenticity.

The many centering experiences she provided during her training seminars were important tools for helping trainees reach this level of awareness. Through these experiences, which include guided imagery, Virginia brought the participants' concentration, on emotional and kinesthetic levels, to the fact that each one is a particular ball of energy, drawing energy from the physical world "below" and the spiritual world "above"—which is actually all one world. She draws attention to the systemic nature of our beings. Virginia was aware of the implications of the new physics, of Alfred Korzybski's general semantics, of Gregory Bateson's work, and that of Pierre Teilhard de Chardin. All these men recognized the systemic nature of the universe. She was conscious of our existence as—and in—interlapping fields of energy. As noted before, her centering "meditations" were important tools with clear goals: to mobilize the participant to become open to whatever external resources are available to those who are receptive, to focus the participant on his or her inner resources, and/or to make transitions. They were another means to her goal of facilitating congruence in her trainees.

Virginia believed herself and her trainees to be tapping into the Basic Pool of Energy of the Cosmos via her centering processes. In following her instruction, one can feel that grounding energy of the "earth below" and the inspirational energy of the "heavens above." Those words were metaphoric but descriptive of what she believed to be reality—a basic truth regarding our connectedness and our place in the universe. Her exercises were designed to facilitate the participants' experiences of the energy that lies *between*—the energy passing between "heaven" and "earth," the energy between two people who are in congruence with self and other.

Connecting energy is present when communication is congruent, real. If I feel bad, I *say* I feel bad, and my face and posture reflect the words I say as well as reflect my internal experience. "Feel bad" is used here as example rather than "feel good" because more often people have rules against showing pain than showing pleasure. However, with congruent expression, the same connecting energy is mobilized whether the emotion is joy, fear, or sadness.

This concept appears so ordinary that it may easily be dismissed. Being "real," communicating congruently, is as recognizable as well as intrinsically miraculous as sunrises and butterflies—which is one reason it is so difficult to define in just a few sentences. A reasonably intelligent colleague, who had spent only one weekend at one of Virginia's seminars, once asked me, "What is so great about being congruent?

People, so often, are looking for technique in a weekend seminar with a master "craftsman." Virginia was never about technique; she was about essence. The very simplicity of what Virginia was offering could serve to obscure it. A particularly literal-minded person could very well miss the point.

A great many of us are so cut off from our feelings/bodies that we think "congruence" is an idea, rather than a teardrop; a thought, rather than a shiver; a mental construct, rather than a smile. The fact is congruent communication permits any or all of those visceral reactions, given the particular context at a particular time. The essential ingredients are the matching of emotion, thought, words, body, and facial expression, appropriate to the situation.

"Congruence" is no more and no less than being all of who we are with another human being, at a given point in time. It is a committed, active pursuit of clarity of meaning with another person. That pursuit presupposes and includes clarity of one's *self* with oneself. *Intra*personal congruence is essential to *inter*personal congruence in the making of meaning between people.

Congruent communication is a living, dynamic process that can no more be suspended in time than can the growth of caterpillar to butterfly. As soon as one stops the action, one stops the life process. Modern physics has taught us that we cannot even watch a process without influencing it; a "neutral observer" is a figment of imagination that cannot exist in our world. Like Life itself, congruent communication is dynamic, never static. This is the reason Virginia made reference to spirituality—dealing with Life Force energy is a spiritual activity. Congruent communication represents Life in motion: Life stepping from concept into living form in the interaction of two human beings, two "wonderful manifestations of life" as Virginia often said.

Conversely, *in*congruent communication, following an old and rigid pattern, is an old script pulled out of a pocket of past experiences left from childhood—an "old learning" about coping with the stress of threatened self-esteem.

All communication takes place within a given context. Nobody has the ability to step off the planet or outside the known universe and carry on a conversation. The congruent pattern of communication is always appropriate to what is going on *at the time*, within both selves, between both selves, and with the greater context within which the interaction is taking place.

The understanding of this relationship of truth—congruence—to health/growth is an important part of Virginia's legacy.

Quest for Truth

Truth is such a rare thing it is delightful to tell it.
—Emily Dickinson

Ye shall know the truth and the truth will make you free.
—Jesus

Virginia's teaching on the essential relevance of truth to functionality, from the individual through to community, was spoken of centuries ago by Lao Tzu:

> When one's conduct is in accordance with Truth, the inherent qualities become real. When a whole family follows Truth, the inherent qualities become abundant. When a whole village follows Truth, the inherent qualities become enduring. When the whole State follows Truth, the inherent qualities become superabundant. When a whole Empire follows Truth, the inherent qualities become universal. (Chen Lin, 1965, 18)

Virginia, the mother of family therapy, put it concisely: "The family is a microcosm. By knowing how to heal the family I know how to heal the world" (Laign, 1988, 20).

I AM: Progressive Stages of Congruence

The eye in which I see God is the same eye in which God sees me.[1]
—Meister Eckhart

The disciplined and continued practice of congruence will lead the practitioner into the depths of self, where may be found the *heights* of self.

Virginia's opinion of the potential of humankind was quite high because she understood how the process works, the means which would produce the end.

Now all this is relatively new, and we turn to people [like] Lao-Tzu . . . to Buddha, to Christ—because those people knew something about [the potential of human kind]. And I think the world wasn't ready to hear it until now . . .

. . . Now then, what you're having now is a revival come in a new form. It's called *being in touch with yourself*, it's called valuing yourself, it's called understanding how you work—because, "Know yourself," usually meant, in the past, "Know what's bad with you," instead of "How do all these things work?" (Satir, 1983b, 229–230)

Although Virginia did not put it in such terms, an obvious spiritual evolution occurs along the path of persistent commitment to congruence. Earlier (chapter 6), on the communication stances, we dealt primarily with the first stage of congruence.

As expressed in *The Satir Model*:

The first level of congruence focuses primarily on being in touch with our feelings, accepting them, acknowledging them to others, and dealing with them (Satir et al., 1991, 79–80).

When we experience level one, we are aware of our feelings and can acknowledge and accept them. They belong to us. We willingly deal with them, without denial or projection. We are in a state of honesty with our feelings in a nonreactive way. We know they are like double-edged swords: we can use them to bring us more pain or more joy, and we can share them freely with others if we choose.

The Satir Model makes a major contribution to the therapeutic field by showing how to help clients to become more congruent at level one. People can learn to manage their feelings in a wholesome way as well as to enjoy the many positive feelings that are part of our humanness (Satir et al., 1991, 68).

The second level of congruence affects our lives more dramatically. Level two is the state of wholeness, inner centeredness. It focuses on the deeper, inner self. People at this level manifest high self-esteem in harmonious and energetic ways. They are at peace with themselves, with others, and in relation to their context (Satir et al., 1991, 68).

When we speak of the "I am" at the center of the self, we enter the second stage of congruence, which has to do with integrity within the self, and the third stage, which is moving into "harmony with our spiritual essence" (Satir et al., 1991, 81).

Virginia believed this high road to be accessible to everyone, given the right amount of information, embraced deeply and consistently applied. This quality in well-known people who have made major contributions, is, of course, not limited to such people; rather, it could be understood as a defining characteristic. Congruence and integrity are attributes possible for all human beings.

Gandhi spoke to the relationship between truth and people. Here, he and Virginia seem to be on the same track. Virginia's emphasis on there being no "bad people" only "bad processes" was similar to Gandhi's separation of person from deed.

We can see Gandhi's personal integrity leading him to this insight in *Autobiography of a Search for Truth*. Gandhi spoke of "ahimsa," or nonviolence, as being the basis for a search for truth:

Man and his deed are two distinct things . . . "Hate the sin and not the sinner" is a precept which, though easy enough to understand, is rarely practiced, and that is why the poison of hatred spreads in the world . . .

This *ahimsa* is the basis of the search for truth, I am realizing every day that the search is vain unless it is founded on ahimsa as the basis. It is quite proper to resist and attack a system, but to resist and attack its author is tantamount to resisting and attacking oneself. For we are all tarred with the same brush, and are children of one and the same Creator, and as such the divine powers within us are infinite. To slight a single human being is to slight those divine powers, and thus to harm not only that being but with him the whole world. (Gandhi, 1948, 242)

Even though the connection between this search for truth and Gandhi's reflection about hatred is not spelled out here, his suggestion about the importance of mercy is illuminated by Virginia's understanding of the dynamics that go with the blaming response.

Virginia displayed the same conviction of the destructive nature of disrespect of persons, the same level of wisdom and mercy, and the same commitment in nonviolently "attacking" dysfunction in a family member, but never the person himself or herself. In an interview with Virgina's colleague, Sheldon Starr, Virginia states:

Anything . . . that is demeaning, I won't do. Anything that keeps a person from growing, I won't do. Anything that humiliates people, I won't do. I will work every way I can to help people open up. I will deal with their anger and anxieties and all that kind of stuff—but while it is possible to confront in a humiliating way and to confront in a demeaning way—it is also possible to confront in a *real* [congruent] way and most of my confronting is like that. (Starr, 1992d, 13)

In summary, Virginia knew how to put wisdom to work in practical, useable forms. Her commitment to the world was to teach people the steps and methods for bringing wisdom that is truth—reality, joined with respect—to life.

This mentality both informed and formed the background for her monthlong process communities, filled with exercises and demonstrations as well as lectures. She was not just training family therapists. She was teaching people the basic ingredients for accessing their full humanity: congruence in communication, respect for self and other, awareness of context within which an interaction takes place. Her own signature optimism was in her understanding of the importance of the belief in the possibilities resulting from this commitment to truth and respect.

Truth and Use of Language: Words

Existence is beyond the power of words
To define;
Terms may be used
But none of them are absolute.

—Lao Tzu

The truth that may be told is not the everlasting Truth. The name given to a thing is not the everlasting Name.

—Lao Tzu

These two quotations from the Tao serve, in themselves, as examples of the circuitous path words may take toward truth and meaning: they are two quite different translations of the very *same* Chinese text and illustrate the difficulty of stating the truth in *words*. Truth and reality are one. Stating what one gathers about a reality in language is a procedure toward truth. Getting at the truth is a dynamic process and requires careful use of language.

Virginia was well aware that "talking about" a given reality was not identical to producing that reality. In the 1960s, the Mental Research Institute (MRI) in Palo Alto, California, set up a project to study communication, closely examining one family, to explore the way the use of words might contribute to the building or the eroding of "sanity."

Gregory Bateson was aware that Alfred Korzybski had done extensive work on the relationship between thinking patterns and language. Under the directorship of Don Jackson, MD, MRI* received a grant to study this phenomenon in depth. As they observed the family under study, the effects of double-level messages began to become evident.[2]

> That [destructive effect of the double-level message, explained at length in chapter 8] is a piece of information that is strictly from the communication that we developed at MRI [Mental Research Institute] which Gregory [Bateson] was busy with, as was Korzybski. How many of you know about general semantics? Let's see. I advise and recommend strongly that you get material on general semantics because Alfred Korzybski, who lived in the 1920s, wrote a very ponderous book called *Science and Sanity*. He was already aware of how our communication affected our health, our intimacy, our productivity and how we make sense. I was fortunate enough to be introduced to him by Gregory Bateson, who was very much a student of Korzybski and Gregory was also one of my mentors. We were good personal friends as well as professional colleagues. (Satir, 1987a, tape 5)

---

* The Mental Research Institute (MRI) was formed in Palo Alto, California in November of 1958, lead by Don D. Jackson (Jackson, 1968, vi). MRI was created for the purpose of studying the effect of communication within a family.

Confusion engendered by language is addressed in intricate detail in Korzybski's book. In *Science and Sanity*, he went to great lengths (791 pages to be exact) to explain the limitations of human language and its distorting effect on our mental processes. Similar to Lao Tzu's statement that truth is essentially un"know"able, Korzybski held that the "truth" of *any* one word is, in the same sense, unknowable.

Korzybski designated our present limited and distorting language-and-thinking style as "Aristotelian" and his proposed new and more realistic word-and-meaning system as "non-Aristotelian." To prevent possible resistance to Korzybski's insights because of his use of these terms, here is his own explanation:

The system by which the white race lives, suffers, "prospers," starves, and dies today is not in a strict sense an Aristotelian system. Aristotle had far too much of the sense of actualities for that. It represents, however, a system formulated by those who, for nearly two thousand years since Aristotle, have controlled our knowledge and methods of orientations, and who, for purposes of their own, selected what today appears as the worst from Aristotle and the worst from Plato and, with their own additions, imposed this composite system upon us.

In this they were greatly aided by the structure of language and psycho-logical habits, which from the primitive down to this very day have affected all of us consciously or unconsciously, and have introduced serious difficulties even in science and in mathematics . . .

Since our existing systems appear to be in many respects unworkable and involve psychopathological factors owing in the main to certain presuppositions of the Aristotelian system, and also for brevity's sake, I call the whole operating systemic complex "Aristotelian." The outline of a new and modern system built after the rejection of the delusional factors I call "non-Aristotelian." To avoid misunderstandings, I wish to acknowledge explicitly my profound admiration for the extraordinary genius of Aristotle, particularly in consideration of the period in which he lived. Nevertheless, the twisting of his system and the imposed immobility of this twisted system, as enforced for nearly two thousand years by the controlling groups, often under threats of torture and death, have led and can only lead to more disasters. From what we know about Aristotle, there is little doubt that, if alive, he would not tolerate such twisting and artificial immobility of the system ascribed to him (Korzybski, 1933, vi.).

Korzybski meticulously clarified the connection between the serious problems resulting from Aristotelian-thinking styles, which have their origins in our more animal-like evolutionary forebears. He noted that simple, mammalian imitation behavior accounts for this pervasive continued dysfunctional pattern. He asserted that we are imitating more primitive life forms in our behavior, "copying" animals in our thinking because our language structure is based on our prehuman experiences.

An example of this primitive-based style of thought and speech is what Korzybski called the "two-valued 'either-or' type of orientation" that represents an "Aristotelian" style of codification:

"Our relations to the world outside and inside our skins often happen to be, *on the gross level*, two-valued. For instance . . . day or night, land or water, et cetera. On the living level we have life *or* death, our heart beats *or* not. Similar relations occur on higher levels. Thus, we have induction *or* deduction, materialism *or* idealism . . . And on endlessly at all levels.

In living, many issues are not so sharp, and therefore a *system which posits the general sharpness of "either-or," and so objectifies "kind,"* is unduly limited. (Korzybski, 1933, xxxiii)

Korzybski recognized that while no Greek philosopher can be held accountable for this particular development of speech, a way of thinking supplied by a *non*-Aristotelian system is the remedy.

The implication here is that language developed before we had the need to abstract to the extent that would reflect today's world.

The ability to abstract on ever higher levels is a capacity available to modern humankind. Korzybski's presumption: as humans were making the transition from prehuman to human, these prehuman responses got transmitted into our language patterns as early humans developed. Even though we have the capacity for abstraction that lower mammals do not, that capacity does not make the leap into speech patterns.

To illustrate mindless—although conscious—copying behavior, Virginia would tell her trainees about the woman who always cut her roast in half and cooked it in two pans. Her husband questioned this, and the woman said the reason was her mother had always done it this way. The couple made the decision to call the wife's mother to find out why she had always cut her roasts in half. Turns out it was because none of her pans were large enough to hold the entire roast. We may conclude, from this simple illustration, that this sort of copying behavior passes down through generations in many areas on less conscious levels far more important to the psyche than the mechanics of food preparation.

Korzybski discussed conditioned behavior using results of the Pavlovian experiments with dogs to illustrate the difference between animals and humans relative to ability to abstract. Through experimentation with bells, buzzers, and food, it was possible to observe that dogs acquire reactions up to a second order of abstraction: (a) bell equals food, (b) bell equals buzzer, (c) buzzer also equals food. The addition of the buzzer would constitute a secondary acquired reaction, the second order.

In the case of defense reactions, the animals could acquire up to the third order. Korzybski noted that animals' ability to make connections between signals stops at this third order:

This abstracting in indefinitely higher orders no doubt conditions the mechanism of what we call human "mentality." *If we stop this abstracting anywhere, and rest content with it, we copy animals in our nervous processes, involving animalistic s.r.* [semantic reactions]. (Korzybski, 1933, 331–332)

Apparently, the literal-minded, linear thinkers among us are closer to our ape-like evolutionary forebears than are those who have access to both halves of their brain. Using language to try to fit concepts into discreet, separate boxes is the fallacy bred by thought patterns left over from prehistoric times. In point of literal fact, nothing in this universe is a separate object or even a solid object. All things are in constant motion—atoms are all in constant process. Moreover, part of the danger is in the way that misinformation proliferates and travels.

Once an idea does take hold, it takes on a life of its own—and it goes hurtling through the unconscious of anyone who has heard it, changing, twisting perhaps, but subtly influencing behavior. It is as if our ideas behave in the realm of symbol, the way our genes do in the realm of the physical. In our current, complex world in which we are bombarded with "information," we cannot afford to narrowly confine our attention to the consciousness/unconsciousness of the individual or even of group . . . We must be aware of the dynamics of the larger society . . . There is no pure "news" not containing potentially explosive or infectious not-fully-conscious factors. The words we shape, shape *us*. (Brothers, 1985, 94)

Reading Korzybski is worth the concentration required to follow his heavy trains of thought. He was saying that the language patterns of modern humankind have not caught up as we climbed out of our ancient ancestors' primitive world and into the current complexity of our own.

The common [Aristotelian] system and language which we inherited from our primitive ancestors *differ entirely in structure* from the well-known and established [modern] structure of the world, ourselves and our nervous systems included. Such antiquated map-language, by necessity, must lead us to semantic disasters, as it imposes and reflects its *unnatural* structure on the structure of our doctrines and institutions . . . In other words, we read unconsciously into the world the structure of the language we use…It is not the human "mind" and its "finiteness" which is to be blamed, but a primitive language, with a structure foreign to this world, which has wrought havoc with our doctrines and institutions. (Korzybski, 1933, 59–60)

The structure of the world, as we know it today, is far more complex than what the primitive person saw as he sat at the entrance of the cave or even the wiser ancient Greeks sitting around the agora. Quantum physics tells us everything is in process and in relation to everything else. Nothing is just sitting there on its own.

1. Words *are not* the things we are speaking about; and
2. There *is no* such thing as an object in absolute isolation . . .

If words *are not* things, or maps *are not* the actual territory, then, obviously, the only possible link between the objective world and the linguistic world is found in *structure and structure alone.* (Korzybski, 1933, 60–61)

Korzybski's point was that a statement like "This is a pencil" (or apple or shoe, et cetera) is misleading. The word "pencil" is a symbol, not a concrete object. When one says the word "pencil," concrete words don't even fall out of the mouth, let alone actual pencils. Moreover, as we know from quantum physics, a pencil or an apple or a shoe is, in fact, a system of moving objects, constantly in process. This "pencil" only becomes a pencil when a person picks it up and writes. Otherwise, it might as accurately be described as a piece of wood wrapped around a piece of graphite. There is no point at which one can freeze the "is" and refer to any object in isolation from its relationship to its surroundings. One can only artificially impose that freeze by disregarding the facts of modern physics.

This is what Korzybski meant when he said our language does not reflect our modern era or our human capacity for abstraction. One could, with considerable time and effort, teach some gifted gorillas to recognize the symbol for pencil. How long would it take to teach a gorilla about the electrons and protons that make up the more whole reality of that so-called pencil?

Korzybski's contention was that our use of language leads us to behave as if there were such things as objects in isolation.

> If there is *no* such thing as an absolutely isolated object, then, at least, we have two objects, and we shall *always* discover some relation between them . . . Obviously, for a man to speak about anything at all, *always* presupposes *two* objects at least; namely, the object spoken about and the speaker, and so a *relation* between the two is always present. (Korzybski, 1933, 60–61)

Virginia Satir often said, "The map is not the territory" (Satir, 1971, personal communication). She took this thinking deep into the realm of human relations, observing and categorizing communication styles as she observed those relations. Her focus, in her work, was on those *points of relating* going on between people in interaction.

Korzybski went on to explain a third inherent pitfall in our language: our propensity for speaking elementalistically, reducing a reality to a single aspect or element of its wholeness. He was aware that the atom is not composed of ever smaller entities; there is no "basic element." A scientist looking closely at an atom sees a *process*, not a little sack of matter. Picking apart any system and considering the separate parts outside of their relationship to each other is artificial and misleading.

> *Any* organism must be treated as-a-whole; in other words, that the organism is not an algebraic sum, a *linear* function of its elements, but always *more* than that. It is seeming little realized, at present, that this simple and innocent-looking statement involves a full structural revision of our language, because that language, of great prescientific antiquity, is *elementalistic.* and so singularly inadequate to express *nonelementalistic* notions. (Korzybski 1933, 64–65)

Virginia described this nonlinear fact and this concept in her use of bread as an example (see chapter 6). Bread is not a packet of yeast piled on top of a stack of flour and a heap of sugar and salt, wet with milk—the conclusion to which the logic of linear, elementalistic thinking would lead. Plain as is this fact, by and large, people are unaware of this very important dysfunction in thinking and, consequently, in speaking.

> For instance, we see that "emotion" and "intellect" cannot be divided, that this division structurally violates the organism-as-a-whole generalization . . . something similar could be said about the distinction of "body" versus "soul," and other verbal splittings which have hampered sane advance in the understanding of ourselves, and have filled for thousands of years the libraries and tribunes of the world with hollow reverberations. (Korzybski, 1933, 64–65)

An important corollary to the above is this: humans respond to symbols on visceral levels. This means change may be brought about through understanding this response to symbols as if they were reality. An aware person may make deliberate physiological changes in himself or herself by stepping out of the primitive mode of thought.

> Experiments with conditional reflexes and the psychogalvanic experiments which show clearly that the majority of humans *identify* the symbol with actualities, and *secretions very often follow* . . . the *physiological secretion* is uncalled for if the *evaluation would be appropriate* to the situation . . . In a [non-Aristotelian] system of evaluation, which involves on semantic levels the consciousness of abstracting, these exceptional persons . . . with proper evaluation and controlled reactions, *prove the rule* for modern man . . . When he stops the pre-human and primitive identification, [he] will have a much-increased and *conscious control* of his secretions, colloidal states of his nervous system, and so of his reactions and behavior. The above applies to all [semantic responses], "logical" processes included. (Korzybski, 1933, 196)

Quite aware of the interconnectedness of emotion, intellect, and physiology, Virginia described the physical symptoms that might occur with the four incongruent stances. This is what she meant when she said, "There is a gland for emotion and a juice for every gland" (Satir, 1971, personal communication).

Korzybski theorized that our race seems to have developed sound-signs (words) long before there was an apparent need for the use of higher kinds of thought. We have the tools to free ourselves from imitation of antiquated thought patterns. We spent centuries caught in the mold set by language itself, which militated against our doing so.

Korzybski pointed out that our copying primitive humans neglects our powers for higher abstraction. This mindless imitation reflects the structure of our language. Actual reality is "hidden" by the contaminating speech patterns that, entering the deep consciousness of the hearers, affect thinking and one's ideas of the world. This means several things: confusion between word and thing and unawareness of the intrinsic inter-relatedness of all things, of the importance of context, and of the fact that reality never "matches" the "either/or," "black-or-white" mentality within which we seem to make our decisions. This last crippling factor, above all, leads to exaggeration of differences and the creation of tragic divisions. Absolute one or the other leaves no room for gray or any shade of brightness in between often trifling variations.

Virginia understood all these technical semantic elements. She did not attempt to teach semantics as such. Instead, she taught congruent communication in such a way that a person who was committed to becoming more fully human could learn how, in speech, to circumvent the pitfalls and land mines into which we are catapulted by our language structure. In previous chapters, we have seen how Virginia dealt with these language difficulties as she guided participants in demonstrated dialogue.

The Satir Model summarizes Virginia's work regarding the use of language:

> In practicing congruence, Satir considered these components import-
> ant . . . [as part of the process of making meaning]:
>
> Understanding clearly the articulated words
> Understanding intended meaning
> Making the abstract concrete, and the covert overt
> Making the hidden obvious
> Making the general specific and clarifying its relationship to you, me,
>   here, now and the specific situations. (Satir et al., 1991, 83)

Virginia had digested and integrated Korzybski's and Bateson's information and presented it in simple, easy-to-understand sentences and experiential exercises. She paid very close attention to the literal

231

use of language as an essential part of the communication process. "Making meaning" was on her list of important components of congruent communication. She was unswerving in interventions to guide people away from reinforcing their own dysfunctional qualities by using words like "always" and "never." In Virginia's demonstration (see chapter 8), we see her methodically dismantling sentences to get at the volunteer's meaning and to make that person's real meaning match the words. In the demonstration, she led Mary to move from her personal "system rule's" blanket statement ("I must never lie") to state what was true—she could lie under certain circumstances. That she could lie, in good conscience and under the proper circumstances, was her underlying truth. "Making meaning" was included when Virginia was listing the components of congruent communication.

Under the heading "Making Meaning," Virginia integrated aspects of Korzybski's insights about the complexity of identifying feeling with the use of words. To his insight Virginia added, in preparation for these exercises, the fact that "words" swirl in multitudes within a brain. In order to make meaning, each person has the task of selecting what seems to be the most relevant in that moment of interaction. This swirl was another reason that a dyad in dialogue must "check out" presumed meaning, sometimes requiring a series of questions, to learn what the other person means to be saying.

Virginia constructed the "Making Meaning" exercises in which her trainees would practice integrating these various ingredients so that, in the process, meaning would rise to the surface. These exercises address "making meaning" as one of the components necessary for congruence (Schwab et al., 1989, 100).

Korzybski (1933) would bring an apple to an elementary school class and ask the pupils to name everything that could be said about an apple until they could not think of another attribute.

This was his way of making the point that we cannot use our language to describe what an object "is." The "is-es" will string out into infinity. He asserted that true "definition" of an object must mean defining until one reaches the "unspeakable" point.

Understanding this basic ambiguity in the nature of words, so thoroughly spelled out by Korzybski, Virginia counseled against interpretation and labeling of behavior, focusing on observation and description. Additionally, Virginia would set up exercises in dyads where one of the pair was instructed to make a sentence. The other was to ask questions, all of which must begin with "do you mean . . ." until the partner was satisfied the other understood the meaning of her or his original sentence. For example, A makes a short statement about something she or he believes is true. B responds verbally to the statement not by agreeing, disagreeing, or deciding its validity but by trying to understand at least three possible meanings of the statement. Generally, some meanings are those of which A was not aware.

A: I believe that participating in something is more interesting than just observing.

B: Do you mean you'd rather play a musical instrument than listen to someone else?

A: Yes.

B: Do you mean you wanted me to know you play?

A: No.

B: Do you mean you'd like me to ask you to play something now?

A: No.

B: Do you mean you want to know if I play an instrument, too?

A: Yes.

B: Do you mean you wanted to find out what kinds of things we may have in common?

A: Yes. (Schwab et al., 1989, 94–95)

Through exercises like these, Virginia was bringing into awareness that—is important to always be aware that words have no inherent definitions—they are always deeply related to the person using them at any given time. The skill of making meaning between two people requires awareness of the limitation of language.

Chapter Notes

1. I find myself tempted to play in this way with late medieval mystic Eckhart's statement: the eye/I with which I see God is the same eye/I with which God sees me. Since Eckhart was writing in German rather than English, this wordplay cannot be his intent. Nevertheless, it speaks to me of the osmotic "I am-ness" process—the human I am with the Original I Am.

2. Congruence and Cockroaches—Double Messages

In *Supernature*, biologist Lyall Watson describes an extremely interesting example of results of incongruent double-level messages.

Janet Harker's experiment with a pair of cockroaches illustrates Virginia Satir's profound observation concerning the effects of incongruent communication.

> [Harker] . . . .kept one group of cockroaches on a normal schedule and put a second group on a reverse timetable, with lights burning all night and darkness during the day. The second lot soon adapted to this situation and became active during the artificial night, so their rhythms were always out of phase with the control group. A subesophageal ganglion could easily be transplanted from a member of one group to a headless individual in the other, and it would impose its

own rhythm on the recipient, but if the second cockroach kept its own pacemaker as well, there was immediate trouble, the extra ganglion turned out to be a lethal weapon. *Having two time-keepers sending out two completely different signals, the poor insect was thrown into turmoil. Its behavior became completely disorganized, and it soon developed acute stress symptoms, such as malignant tumors in the gut, and died.* (Watson 1973, 15-16)

This experiment conducted by Janet Harker and reported in several scientific journals is tangible evidence of the adverse effect of the double message on a living organism. This is physical evidence that supports Virginia's observation about the physically destructive effects of double-level messages. If there can be such a profoundly destructive effect on even an insect, can we not consider that there may be a universal principle applicable to humans?

12

The Pattern That Connects:
Relationship

[Bateson] declared that relationship should be the basis of all definition and his main aim was to discover the principles of organization in all the phenomena he observed, "the pattern which connects," as he would put it.

—Fritjof Capra

Context

Virginia Satir's work articulated the difference between the Pattern that Connects and the patterns that disconnect. The latter, addressed in previous chapters, always involve double-level communication and are much easier to describe. They are far more familiar.

Virginia worked to bring the natural forces of Life into coherence in the lives of the therapists she trained. This is the result that could be achieved by congruence in communication, an alignment and harmony of energy of the total system. She spoke of her work with Gregory Bateson:

Gregory Bateson probably contributed more to my understanding of human communication than anyone else. He was a loving, caring man, who also was a brilliant researcher and theorist, and I had the good fortune to have known and worked with him. (Satir, 1986b, 279)

Musing on our universal greater context, the whole matrix of the universe, Bateson (1979, 8) uses the phrase, "the pattern which connects" to address the question of "the underlying notion of a dividing line between the world of the living . . . and the world of nonliving billiard balls and galaxies . . ." (Bateson, 1979, 7)

What is the difference between the physical world of pleroma [the nonliving],* where forces and impacts provide sufficient basis of explanation, and the *creatura* [the living], where nothing can be understood until *differences* and *distinctions* are invoked?
. . . What now must be said is difficult, appears to be quite *empty*, and is of very great and deep importance to you and to me. At this historic juncture, I believe it to be important to the survival of the whole biosphere, which you know is threatened.
What is the pattern which connects all living creatures?
. . . My central thesis can now be approached in words: the *pattern which connects is a metapattern*. It is a pattern of patterns. It is that metapattern which defines the vast generalization that, indeed, *it is patterns which connect* . . . We have been trained to think of patterns, with the exception of those of music, as fixed affairs. It is easier and lazier that way, but, of course, all nonsense.
In truth, the right way to begin to think about the pattern which connects is to think of it as *primarily* (whatever that means) a dance of

---

* Bateson was using Jung's words "pleroma" and "creatura" (Bateson, 1979, 7).

interacting parts and only secondarily pegged down by various sorts of physical limits and by those limits which organisms characteristically impose. (Bateson, 1979, 7–8, 11, 13)

Bateson was alluding to the basic stuff of Life. The metapattern, that "pattern which connects" is the universal phenomenon. The *specific* expression occurs within the form of each distinct living entity's own "story":

Thinking in terms of stories does not isolate human beings as something separate from the starfish and the sea anemones, the coconut palms and the primroses. Rather, if the world be connected, if I am at all fundamentally right in what I am saying, then *thinking in terms of stories* must be shared by all mind or minds, whether ours or those of redwood forests and sea anemones. (Bateson, 1979, 13)

Bateson was dealing with the concepts advanced by Korzybski: relationship between objects is the operative factor. Korzybski had pointed out that "there is no such thing as an absolutely isolated object"; therefore, we must look to structure to meaningfully link words with objects. Bateson wrote, "Context and relevance must be characteristic not only of all so-called behavior (those stories which are projected out into 'action'), but also all those internal stories, the sequences of the building up of the sea anemone" (Bateson, 1979, 14).

Echoing Korzybski, Bateson pointed to the essential relationship between context and meaning:

And "context" is linked to another undefined notion called "meaning." Without context, words and actions have no meaning at all. This is true not only of human communication in words but of all communication whatsoever, of all mental process, of all mind, including that which tells the sea anemone how to grow and the amoeba what he should do next. (Bateson, 1979, 15)

Virginia was alluding to the "pattern which connects" with her own metaphor to describe the connection as "a river that goes on all the time." She said:

We began suddenly to be aware that *no human being creates life* . . . No one has been able to create an egg and sperm that can make a human being . . . So what we do is we *activate* life . . . And by a sperm and egg coming together which is the original plan which we had nothing to do with . . . life comes.

You had nothing to do with how you were activated except in maybe an esoteric sense. You get activated and then there's a whole program there for you. You didn't make it. No scientist sat down at the drawing board to figure out a person, that was there.

Now then, we had to face the fact, where do we get created? That's our spiritual base. That is already there and *I look at it as a river that goes on all the time* [italics mine]. That's the basis of ourselves, the spiritual base, that which makes it possible for the egg and sperm to come together. And that can or cannot be religious in my terms. (Brothers, 1999, 4)

Context

Picture of an Interaction

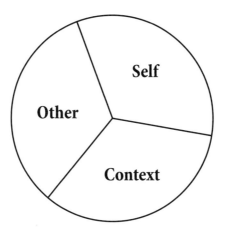

Virginia's diagrams showing elements of an interaction always include "context" in addition to "self" and "other" (Satir 1991, 23). Self and other are easy enough to follow; "context" requires more explanation.

Virginia was one of the first therapists to "put legs" on Bateson's and Korzybski's concept that "without context, words and actions have no meaning at all" (Bateson, 1979, 7). Prior to the invention of family therapy, the analytic therapist behaved as if context did not exist, that therapy occurred in a vacuum. Virginia taught the relevance of awareness of context to effective therapy. Awareness of context is prerequisite to congruence in communication:

> Everything that goes on in anybody at a moment in time in the presence of another person, will have three parts . . . There's me, you and

the context, per se. That means I'm here, you're here, this is a specific time, a specific place, color, whatever it is. The context, the purpose, whenever there are two people together, there are three parts to the whole thing. Me, you, and the context. In a skeletal way, that describes . . . wholeness or an environment of wholeness when two people are present. At anytime, when you are with another person and they are in your presence and you are in their presence, these three things are present [me—you—context]. (Satir, 1987a, tape 5)

Virginia identified the hazards of valuing any given situation—or "context"—over the human beings participating in that situation. Those responding in the super-reasonable fashion are looking *only* at the context—when we "cross out" me and "cross out" you, everything becomes an "it."

She described the super-reasonable, robot-like response, favored by many engineers, college professors, intellectuals[1]—and by our particular society—which erroneously concludes that non-emotion equals "objective," "mature," and/or mental health, accomplishing goals:

Some important thing is missing. We do not live in this world alone so "me" and "you" are very important. We cannot live in this world without connecting with the context, because the context has power and it has information for us. (Satir, 1987a, tape 5)

Virginia synthesized Bateson's attention to the unifying aspect of our larger context, to which he referred as "the pattern which connects" and Korzybski's penetrating exposé of the destruction brought about by mindless imitation of primitive thought patterns (leading to a rigid view of a world built of unconnected boxes). She utilized and made practical their application in her simple and brilliant display of the essentiality of congruent communication to human well-being—to all effective human interaction as well as to effective therapy.

> I can tell you from my experience that 100% of the time when people have any kind of symptoms which are coping difficulties, they will be doing double-level communications. They will be doing it out of the naive idea that they are protecting themselves or somebody else. Their bodies do not reflect that is going on . . .
>
> A lot of times when I move in [to intervene] anywhere, my body tells me: "That person is trying so hard to be brave and they are feeling awful at this point." I don't go around saying, "You're trying hard to be brave." Not that, but I am feeling something. This is where the compassion comes in . . . The effects of double-level communication are terrible, but the compassion is for those who don't know that. People don't know these things. Furthermore, not only do they not know it, but they cannot spot it when it happens. That is one of the reasons why I hope that when you get out of here [from this seminar] you will be clear and very able to spot when you get into double-levels. This is not to say that you are bad, but this is what we have mostly been brought up with. This is what leads to manipulation. (Satir, 1987a, tape 5)

Bateson observed the tragedy of the reductionistic way language arts and sciences are usually presented in classrooms—out of context, showing little relationship to the life the students were living or hoped to live, and without reference to the Whole within which we all float.

> I remember the boredom of analyzing sentences and the boredom later, at Cambridge, of learning comparative anatomy. Both subjects, as taught, were torturously unreal. We *could* have been told something about the pattern which connects: that all communication necessitates

context, that without context, there is no meaning, and that contexts confer meaning because there is classification of contexts.

So we come back to the patterns of connection and the more abstract, more general (and most empty) proposition that, indeed, there is a pattern of patterns of connection. (Bateson, 1979, 17)

Very aware of those limitations, Virginia addressed that issue head-on. Her dream of a university for becoming more fully human embraces Bateson's question about teaching related to the pattern which connects. On a very grounded and down-to-earth level, Virginia was painstakingly teaching the meaning and fundamental factor of *relatedness* between human systems to each other and to the Greater System.

Components of Congruent Communication

As we have indicated in the foregoing section, Virginia, in her indefatigable work of teaching congruent communication, was creating the tools to enable each of us to realize, in our daily interchange with one another, the mystery of that metapattern identified by Bateson and to which Korzybski alluded. Simply as Virginia may have rendered the concepts within her various exercises, she had pulled them from that larger, more complex schema that she had distilled with magnificent practicality into the essential elements of congruent communication: beliefs; physical position of self in relation to other; use of senses; expectations and perceptual clearing; giving feedback; making meaning; sharing and/or taking action. It is important to remember that *each* one of the elements of congruent communication is a point of relatedness; each person in the interchange needs to be aware of how she, herself, is aware of these elements and at the same time to be ready to receive with respect what the other reveals about his or her perhaps very different sense of each element. Let us reflect on the meaning of each these elements.

Beliefs

The first element is a set of beliefs that begins with respect and includes an attitude of reverence toward the Life Process itself; a belief that individual human beings each represent a unique aspect of Life—a belief in the fact that each person is a unique entity and that, as such, each human is a manifestation of the life force. Virginia found compelling evidence of our spiritual dimension in the fact that we cannot produce or create life but may only activate it. A therapist who did not share this deep respect for personhood would be unable to use the Satir Model effectively. Corollary beliefs are:

- That all people have the capacity for personal—psychological and emotional—growth; we are all equipped with inner resources of inestimable value.
- That all people can be intimate; all people can be competent; all people can make sense and meaning; all people can stand on their own two feet; all people can be choosers. (Satir et al., 1991, 83)

Physical Position of Self to Other

Describing where the therapist sits in relation to the patient seems almost too obvious to mention. Nevertheless, in the ordinary course of events, people do not necessarily sit down facing each other, within arm's length, and look each other straight in the eye when their intention is to understand or to be understood by the other.

This vital aspect is among the factors so basic as to be easily missed or dismissed because of its very simplicity. Apparent simplicity or not, the crucial importance is often overlooked. How often do people try to have serious conversations while driving, walking, or continuing—back turned—with household tasks?

Teaching any interacting dyad to look at each other, sitting close enough to see and hear, while intending to communicate clearly must be part of the process.

Use of Senses

Virginia's training included exercises in the use of the senses in which trainer/trainees were taught to consciously, in full awareness, use all five senses. Virginia found that the senses could be sharpened with practice in conscious use. The vehicle for human communication is our senses; the world enters the individual-person-body/mind-emotion-system through eyes, ears, nose, tongue, and skin. In demonstrations, one could see Virginia drawing the participants' attention to specific facial muscle movements that are body messages about interior experience. Deliberate, studied use of our senses is critical to good therapy and critical to all functional communication.

In a demonstration specifically designed to display the elements of congruent communication, Virginia guided interaction between two volunteers:

I just want to do a little sampling. Can I have two people come up here? Any two . . .

All right, hold it just a minute. Somebody tell me what you saw. What did you see? Marie?

"Physically, they are close together."

All right, you noticed something about the space between them, and you said, for you, it is close. I don't know if it would be [close] for someone else or not, but you were attentive to the space between them. So we will put that down [on the blackboard] for a moment. What else . . . ?

"I thought I perceived a change in color in Louise's face, a blush."

All right, marvelous. You are absolutely fantastic. You saw a skin color change. Good. What else did you see? Anybody?

"Sam put his left hand up to his head and swung his body."

All right, we are having a veritable play here, aren't we? Now, anybody else? Yes, Inez?

"I saw Louise, when she went to respond, her left eye contact fluttered—moved—looked away."

All right, now you are touching on another sort of thing that has to do specifically related to the eye movements as you spoke, and the direction the eyes are . . .

All right. Now you have mentioned practically all the elements. (Satir, 1996b, 1–10)

Expectations and Perceptual Clearing

When two people meet, each carries her or his own vast storehouse of previous life experience and her or his own style of making sense of those experiences. Stereotypes and projections form over time as naturally as stalactites in caverns. The key is to have sufficient awareness of one's own projections to be able to slide back the screen of stereotype when meeting a new person.

"With Whom Am I Having the Pleasure?" (Satir et al., 1991, 339–368) is a demonstration and exercise in understanding this particular component of congruence (see Appendix B). Virginia's genius was finding a way to illustrate universal principles and to render them usable by people of all ages and ethnic backgrounds. This exercise is one such gem and is Virginia's way of addressing the ponderous concept of "counter-transference"[2]—not a word Virginia used. She preferred to call the process, instead, "With Whom Am I Having the Pleasure?" and to ask "whose hat" one might be hanging on another person.

> *One of the many things that we have to deal with is how the people we meet are like or unlike our parents.* We have long histories with our parents who are those people who cared for us at a time when we were in a survival state—meaning that we could not do anything for ourselves, and so people around who were in the caretaking position had to do it for us. We attach meaning [to the words and deeds of these caretakers], almost without our knowing it, that becomes a screen through which we look at other people. Following those survival years, [this screen is] almost automatically [incorporated] and can be missed by our thinking it is our personality or [our own thinking] about people. What is important is that we keep [the awareness of that "screen"] in our consciousness. It is like we carry around a cookie cutter . . . [with which to measure people]! We have got our own lenses, and we have already filtered out a lot of things so we do not really see who is there.
>
> With whom am I having the pleasure, with you or my picture of you? (Satir, 1995b, 7)

As we have said, use of terms was important to Virginia; words are major tools that can be used either to nurture or to erode. She preferred not to waste communication opportunities in therapy or training situations with words that did not carry immediate and obvious meaning. Virginia understood that carelessly used words could obfuscate description of interaction and, in her treatment philosophy, clarity is paramount and *process* is the whole story. Conscious choice is not possible without awareness. Virginia's goal was to create a training or therapy context in which the participant would achieve maximum awareness of the antics in her/his inner space.

Rather than use the old psychoanalytic word to deal with "counter-transference," Virginia developed the exercise and experience of "With Whom Am I Having the Pleasure?," providing a simple and efficacious route for obtaining clarity of vision otherwise blocked by stereotyping and projection.

This exercise in perceptual clearing would enable the person—therapist, trainee, or client—to see what is there rather than what he or she "thinks" is there. It is a new way of meeting another person—both the unknown, and, poignantly, the supposedly known. Its value, if deeply assimilated, can become a mode of entering into each event or encounter with new eyes.

"Countertransference"—a factor that affects communication—is meeting whatever angels or devils have taken up residence in one's inner space from the experiences of one's past, along with all the stereotypes and projections that may have accumulated in the interim. The exercise in congruence, "With Whom Am I Having the Pleasure?," offers a means, instead, for meeting the real human being in all her or his uniqueness—the real person, whose essence is never a repetition, whose humanity is not "categorizeable," whose personhood is always a new creation.

Giving Feedback

Letting the other person know what one sees, hears, and perceives is critical to communication. Virginia painstakingly pointed out to her trainees the importance of the choice of description rather than interpretation. Virginia knew that interpretation risks insult and mis-understanding. The difference is simply describing "eyebrows coming together"—and inquiring about awareness of that—rather than, "You are frowning." The important ingredient here is to describe rather than to interpret and to present the feedback as merely one's own perception—not as a statement of objective reality. Often the person in a demonstration would come to a new awareness just from hearing Virginia "give feedback."

Making Meaning

As previously noted, making meaning requires use of language to arrive at understanding. Virginia taught that arriving at understanding is far more important to healing relationships than a goal of reaching agreement. The latter is a circular trap from which the former can deliver a quarreling dyad.

Virginia taught care in the use of language. Questions were to be used only as genuine requests for information; verbal exchanges must be direct. Choice of words and sentence structure make a difference in whether or not people understand each other. Using a question to make a statement or vice versa can confuse meaning. It was important to Virginia to use simple, understandable words that would make clear images in the mind of the other—being understood was her goal.

As she did with the other elements she knew were required for deep understanding, Virginia did not just list the above ingredients in a how-to-be-a-good-therapist recommendation. She also developed specific exercises to teach use of language skill in her seminars. Trainees would break into triads or pairs and practice with structured instructions as took place in the preceding exercise, "With Whom am I Having the Pleasure?"

Sharing and/or Taking Action

The sharing or action taken is the last step in the congruent event: reporting one's own inner space experience to the extent appropriate to the context, being mindful of the impact on one's own self-esteem as well as the self-esteem of the other. Virginia did not necessarily advocate complete revelation of all feelings in all circumstances. She was very respectful of the vulnerability we all carry in regard to our innermost selves. However, all things being equal, it is important to let an interactional partner know how one feels as well as what one thinks.

Taking whatever action would be appropriate to a given situation is a natural component of congruent communication (Satir et al., 1991, 83).

Virginia developed exercises[3] for experiencing all seven of these elements: beliefs, physical position of self in relation to others, use of senses, expectations and perceptual clearing, giving feedback, making meaning, and sharing and/or taking action. These are all factors that make a climate conducive to congruence; by definition, there can be no literal, concrete formula because the essential nature of congruence in communication is dynamic. For purposes of examination and explanation, these components are outlined here, but it must be understood that studying a sample of congruent communication is similar to dipping a bucket into a river; the contents from the first dip would never be identical to the second dip, and so on. "Congruence" can also be described as the process that facilitates growth, in that it is—again, by definition—a bringing into harmony words, feelings, body, and facial expressions. This is how the seed model works.

Virginia had also spent many years talking and thinking with the best psychotherapists of the day. She had a sound and solid base from which she concluded:

Communication is to personal health, satisfactory interpersonal relationships, and productivity as breathing is to life. Effective communication can be both taught and learned. We were not born with the way we communicate. We learned it, most through modeling, in ways no one even knew or intended. (Schwab, 1989, xi)

There is no way to have a sense of the loveliness of the flowing stream that is congruent communication unless you put the components together and *feel* how it works. Here is the definition, including all the components Virginia outlined: Congruent communication is based on the fact that you and I both are unique beings without duplication in this world and on a belief that such uniqueness is of deep value. I will be standing or sitting close enough to see you clearly, close enough to reach out and touch if that becomes appropriate. I am able to make full use of my senses—eyes, ears, touch, smell—to give and receive information. I have cleared my perceptions of preconceived expectations, stereotypes, prejudices, and fantasies about what you might be thinking about me. I have paid attention to the use of language so that I make clear sentences and ask clear questions for the purpose of getting answers. I am aware that what is important is not that we both agree, but that we make mutual meaning. Given all that, I match my facial expressions, body, voice tone, and feelings so they are all congruent; then I tell you how I feel or what I think at any given moment. When I offer you this information, I do so in the most respectful way possible to us both, knowing I have a choice about what I say, how I say it, and how I respond to what you say. Knowing, too, that we both have within us great pools of wisdom and untapped resources.

That incredibly simple performance I just described does not sound like it would stop wars, heal ulcers, reknit broken relationships, and raise happy babies, does it? Strangely enough, it will provide a context for the growth of all of the above. It does not provide a work-every-time guarantee, but it does make a climate in which growth is possible. It is what

Virginia went around doing, that honoring of self and other with her clear, unmistakable reporting of the honoring: creating the atmosphere. It is what four-year-olds will do until or unless they are told by an adult world that they are somehow defective, somehow found wanting.

It looked like magic. If one looked closer, it was simply the essence of a given person having been brought forth and polished to the high sheen that Virginia could see before the polishing. Her demonstrations gave good examples of how she would teach human beings the quite learnable skill of making connections, at depth levels, between themselves.

She was a master architect, designing and constructing bridges that stretched from heart to heart.

Chapter Notes

1. It is important to remember that the super-reasonable response occurs on a continuum. It is not confined to heartless terrorists. Unwitting of the hazard, this response is too often also favored by those with superior intellects who rely heavily on those intellectual capacities for accomplishing goals.

2. This term is being defined here as covering any response, within the therapist to the patient or client, that is characterized by distortion from the therapist's own past.

3. In addition to exercises in *The Satir Approach to Communications* (1989), other exercises can be found in *The New Peoplemaking* (1988), *Virginia Satir Verbatim* (1983), *The Satir Model* (1991), *Training the Trainer: A Process Manual for Successfully Leading Experiential/Cognitive Workshops* (1994), and *Say It Straight* (1990).

13

Gun Power and Seed Power

The difference here is between seed power, which is based on growth and cooperation, and gun power, which is based on threat.

—**Virginia Satir**, 1985

Beyond the Threat/Reward Model: Self-Worth and Real Change

Virginia Satir was clear that, for millennia, in the dynamics of human behavior, humankind has been laboring under a dysfunctional model. We limp along with the same consciousness that predominated in the Middle Ages: if we just punish X hard enough and long enough, then things will get better. The converse is the "bleeding heart" phenomenon: if we nice people stay in (complete!) control and are nice enough, things will get better. These are two faces of the same power coin: threaten

behavior or reward behavior. Both imply hierarchy and somebody calling the shots over others. Both require inequity between two parties.

> Let me take the word hierarchy ... I call this ... the "threat and
> reward model of life"... And this ... [gesturing toward the other
> side of the board] I call the "seed or the yeast model." Have you ever
> looked at seeds, so tiny, and they get great big trees? Do you know how
> big a sperm and egg is? Or a sperm and an ovum? It's very little and
> look at you. Teeny tiny, and it's got so much in it.
>
> Hierarchy within a threat model means a rigid form of rules. If
> you do this, there is a punishment or reward for this. Very, very rigid.
> Hierarchy within the seed or the yeast model merely talks about an
> order of things. An order, that's all ... It is a description of relationship.
>
> Let's take the business about conforming. Conforming in a hier-
> archical model means to the letter and the rul[e]. And within the
> frame of the seed or organic model...your structure works for what
> you want to have happen instead of inhibiting what you want to have
> and [having to fit] the structure instead of having the structure fit
> what you want to do. (Satir, 1981a, 1983b, 1987a)

Virginia explained how the hierarchal model plays out in communities as well as in families. Her understanding of the critically
important differences between the hierarchy and seed models lay behind
her statement: "Peace is not the absence of war" (Satir, 1984, personal
communication).

Enduring peace includes a commitment to work for ongoing *congruence* which would mean ongoing dialogue and concern among all parties
for the welfare and well-being of all parties. Such committed, continuing concern is very much richer and more complex than simply halting
the firing of guns. "War versus peace" is a simplistic, unrealistic concept.
Human interaction always breaks into chaos at various points. Harmony

cannot be a constant phenomenon because change, not homeostasis, is the constant in the basic design of our universe. Maintaining harmony in human interaction is an ongoing process. The more accurate operative terms would be not "war versus peace" but gun power versus seed power.

The continual presence of the threat/reward model is, for Virginia, a symptom of a deeper issue: the necessity of appropriate self-esteem at the core of all persons involved in relationships. Virginia dealt with the issue of self-esteem at the roots of the therapy process—not only in clients but first in their therapists. It was Virginia's policy that "mental health" need not and should not be reserved exclusively for the "mentally ill." She understood there would be no threat/reward model if every person involved in any relationship had appropriate self-esteem.

Centered persons, aware of the importance of respecting self and others, have no need to issue threats, dispense rewards, or manipulate behavior. "Mental health" needs to include education about the importance of being centered—with resultant respect for self and others. Virginia spoke about this at the societal as well as the personal levels:

Societal Level

For real change to take place, [self-worth, awareness of choice . . .] are the ingredients that have to happen . . . Now let me point out something. We have tried to change political systems, we have tried to change rules, we have gotten new laws . . . appearances of change . . . many things in the way that humans are treated . . . need to change. It takes group effort for that. Now I want to get you back to the models I gave: the threat and reward model. Since most of the world is still running on threat and reward model, punishment and reward, our whole society is based upon that, it doesn't matter how long we go. We have no hope of changing that . . . unless we are *changed to a new consciousness of ourselves and to know what change really is*. We have superficially changed by the sword and changed by power, domineering . . . Another kind of change [is necessary]. (Satir, 1983b, 500–501)

Personal Level

95% of the people in the world are following the threat/reward model. That means their self-worth is always subject to somebody else . . . The self worth is always in relation to somebody else . . . An over simplified way of talking about that is, "Without you, I can't live. You are the one who makes me a victim," and all this kind of stuff. Self-worth is in the other's hands. That means every act becomes an act of "Will I live or won't I live?" So that keeps us almost always either a literal or psychological survivor in relation to other people. You look crooked at me and that means you don't like me, and I die. You look happily at me and that means, . . . for the next ten minutes . . . I will live.

The problem with that is that it never gets generalized . . . I have to keep on repeating it. So if I have seventeen marvelous approvals from Suzy in the first hour of our existence together . . . and then the eighteenth one she gives me disapproval, all of that approval is wiped away and [all that's] there is the disapproval. And I "knew" she was lying all the time because she really had all these disapprovals [all along]. It's just [that] the pointing out of things doesn't seem to help much. We have to do something else. (Satir, 1983b, 505–506)

The "something else" is active facilitation of the seed model, hoeing the garden, nurturing the plants. In this lecture, Virginia continued to describe the threat/reward model—in which people are in bondage to roles and dominance/submission behavior.

If a given couple or set of parents—or supervisor, or international leader—sees all relationships mainly in terms of who has the power, such people will behave very differently from a person not locked into a model that features hierarchy. It is not necessary to be Attila the Hun for such attitudes to have destructive consequences; all that is required for a negative impact on human growth and creativity is a preoccupation with and investment in roles as opposed to personhood: me doctor, you nurse; me boss, you worker; me mother, you child.

Virginia spent a lot of energy trying to help family members separate themselves from their roles so they could identify themselves as *persons*:

> Relationship in most people's perceptions is a role definition: father and child, boss and worker, priest and parishioner, teacher and student. Usually role—most of these roles—implies superiority on one level or another, malevolently or benevolently experienced.
>
> . . . Each one is a person. How many times have we used a role to define a person? . . . *The role is not the definition of the person.* (Satir, 1983b, 194–195)

Virginia found that pairing relationships seemed almost invariably to set up in a hierarchy "somebody on the top and somebody on the bottom . . . This whole thing was a form of dominance and submission; the question was whether the nature of it would be malevolent or benevolent" (Satir, 1987a, tape 3).

The net result of benevolent dominance and submission may not produce the immediate and obvious loss of blood and life as will the more malevolent variations; nevertheless, "mother knows best" and "do it because I said so" has condemned many a child to a passive, dependent style of living and to an unfulfilled life, also setting up a "follower" mentality ripe for exploitation by the more malevolent end of the continuum. Benevolent dominance is not necessarily any nearer to mutual respect and parity than is malevolent dominance. In fact, it may simply serve to prepare partners for the latter.

A commitment to Virginia's equation—person equals person—is a rare and beautiful situation in the world. Our survival as a species may well depend on a major shift—worldwide—toward valuing parity over hierarchy in relationship. Virginia's concern was that, far too often, people define themselves in response to their experience in their hierarchal family relationships:

"'Shoulds' are hierarchy from the people who were our survival figures. Whether they meant it or not, that is where it came from: 'What you should be for me to love you'" (Satir, 1983b, 208).

The consequences of trying to be "this" and trying not to be "that" is to render a person unable to focus on his/her *own* essence. Virginia understood that all such demands and corresponding efforts to meet them create illusory comparisons. They were illusory because of the measurable scientific fact that each human being is "one of a kind" and, therefore, incomparable to another. The major aim of her work was to facilitate each person's becoming aware of her or his own uniqueness—that each is a shining jewel in the fabric of the Universe. Such awareness would open the route to self-esteem. Improve self-esteem and chances for growth improve accordingly. People with feelings of high self-worth would then be able to see such value in their children, husbands, and wives, making possible the context for genuine emotional connection with each other.

Virginia believed that the horror of the Holocaust shook the world into an awareness of the importance of looking for some way of preventing the recurrence of such a hideous level of inhumanity, that the human potential movement may have begun to develop, at least partially, in response to that profound shock to the human psyche. The Holocaust had been the most extreme result of the threat/reward model, a mindset that has haunted humankind through the ages.

Virginia, herself, was certainly a part of the wave of newness that swept across the world in the wake of World War II. Concurrent with Murray Bowen, Don Jackson, and Nathan Ackerman, in 1951, she began inventing family therapy. It could be hard for the modern young therapist to understand what a radical step this was in those days. It was, in fact, a violation of the rules of psychotherapy to see family members of a patient in therapy. Up to that point, *all* that had existed in terms of psychotherapy was the psychoanalytic model. All other models were a variation of the threat/reward approach involving institutions still based on the premise that people were "born dirty or sinful."

This premise was visited on us—literally—with a vengeance on September 11, 2001. When planes piloted by terrorists struck the World Trade Center, we were all immediately propelled into a hard game of dominance and submission. The worldview of the perpetrators was that the United States was "sinful" and must be eliminated. Our retaliatory stance: the attacking terrorists were "evil" and must be eliminated. Thus, our Arab brethren raised the stakes exponentially. However much we had developed as an aftermath of World War II, we were suddenly faced with an issue as vital as that of dealing with the Nazi machine and Japanese menace of that time. Today, we have the issue in spades. During World War II, our country had the uncontested, if dubious, luxury of applying nuclear destruction to solve the problem; today, nuclear material is now in *everybody's* back pocket, or in the pocket next door.

Will we be able to pull a higher level of crisis intervention out of all this mayhem? Will we, of the West, eventually be able to work together to help the world to move into awareness of the severe limitations of the threat/reward model and toward the far more functional seed model? The time is short, and the violence already released disheartening.

As long as we continue to function in the domination/submission model, we are nursing a monster that will rise, ever more dangerous, and must be slain again—and again and again.

Virginia went on, in the lecture, to another aspect of her thinking that set her apart from all her contemporaries in the family therapy field: her emphasis on the spiritual essence of a human being. It was

Virginia's own unique contribution to the profession to notice, then begin to persistently, publicly point out, the singular importance of deliberate recognition of the uniqueness of the individual person. She continued in her lecture to show what a profound difference is made by explicit recognition of this uniqueness. She went on to emphasize that this is *fact*, as is the fact that we all, also, have absolute similarities simply by virtue of being born into human bodies. Once anyone accepts these truths as universal, it becomes obvious that persons cannot possibly be "rated" and measured against each other: it is not possible to make comparisons between unique entities. Thus, all people are equal—equally unique.

Virginia went to great lengths to expose the myth that supports parents who believe they own their children because they "created" them. Taking another very obvious fact (Virginia specialized in making profound conclusions from the obvious and apparently simple)—that modern science has never yet solved the riddle of the creation of life— she made the point of our identity, therefore, as spiritual beings. The quest then became one of discovery of all one's own inner resources and the inner resources of the other. This is very different from "falling short of how one should be."

It follows that the definition of a person and definition of relationship can be seen in spiritual terms. This view produces a very different effect than does the dirty > sinful > threat/reward view. The changing of this worldview would make healing changes between couples, family members, and communities. There is much more to say on this subject, but here we will simply reflect on the fundamental reason why the hierarchical model of threat/reward is death-dealing—it violates the nature of persons.

The shift in consciousness from the hierarchical threat/reward model to the seed/growth model would have a crucial effect on relationships in the international community. Not only would this shift be enormously useful in the therapeutic context, it could save us from nuclear destruction if it can be applied in time. The bomb is out there, ready and waiting. We are not nearly so far along in designing interventions based on the seed model.

Empowerment Versus "Power Plays"

Virginia taught that a key element of the seed model is the use of partnership and cooperation rather than competition—endemic in the corporate business world and a major feature of western culture. In teaching about the difference between viewing people and relationships within the domination/submission model versus the seed model, she made clear the contradictions in the presumed benefits in personal competition.

Allowing awareness of the worth of the individual to slip, in the collective mind, to lower priority than "the task" provides a clear road for profoundly destructive consequences, as is evidenced by all manner of fundamentalist risings, from our country's own survivalists, Branch Davidians, Jerry Falwells, and Timothy McVeighs to the Taliban and Al Qaeda. Wholeness, the valuing of *all* aspects of the human being—cognitive, emotional, and sensual—is not a luxury in our modern world, where almost no population is farther away from another than a computer keyboard, and the triggers on everybody's bombs get hairier every year. September 11, 2001 was the grimmest of reminders of the lethal nature of linear thinking and placing tasks and goals before people.

One does not, however, have to be an axe murderer, international terrorist, notorious dictator, or cocky prima donna family therapist to retain a destructive philosophy of self. One may simply be reared with a "good" religious background: Buddhist or Baptist, one can hear among many such folk the fear and loathing of "ego" and "selfishness," as if dispensing with all thought of self would turn the pious toward holiness and away from evil. From the latest popes to the latest maharishis, most of humanity has been taught to confuse authentic self-regard with the attitude of the disdaining narcissist. Consequently, one who aspires to altruism as well as the actual disdaining narcissist are given few guidelines about the healing nature of *connecting* with other human beings as opposed to the manipulation of them.

Narcissism is the *using* of people, with the needs of others being considered secondary—if at all—to the needs of the narcissist. Equal valuing of all "selves" is a very different process and it fosters connection between selves. The mechanism of *connecting* with people both facilitates and results from authentic self-regard. Telling children to set aside their own feelings is toxic advice. Children who are taught to honor feelings are able to honor them in others as well as in themselves. Self-denigration is not a cure for narcissism. Self-nurturing obviates the need for "selfishness" and prepares the way for authentic connection with others.

Attention to self-worth is an antidote to destruction. Knowing the development of self-worth to be an uphill battle against centuries of misinformation, Virginia said:

> There is no question in my mind . . . that everybody has self-worth. But very few people know it. And so letting that self-worth come out is going to make that person whole. *No highly developed self-worth is ever destructive.* When we were kids we were told not to be selfish. Well, you see that would mean we would be selfish *when we didn't have our worth*, and we had to develop all those manipulations in order to live. That's what [incongruent] communication is about. (Satir, 1983b, 85)

Virginia was challenging the parental worry about their children "becoming selfish." She was pointing out that development of self-worth *prevents* rather than *causes* "selfish" behavior. High self-worth is the healing factor. Narcissistic "selfishness" is a kind of desperation based on fear and feelings of not measuring up to others.

Virginia knew that training the family therapist (or, in her words, the "change agent") in awareness of that person's *own* uniqueness would both enrich the therapist and protect the patient from being disempowered. That which builds self-worth is inherently empowering. Real power comes from appropriate self-value.

> There's another word I love very much which is . . . *empowerment.* Empowerment is what we do to eliminate enslavement. We can enslave ourselves with our thoughts: I'm no good. Who wants to have anything to do with me?" We can empower ourselves by saying, "I'm just a fine person and I'm ready to say what isn't so hot about me and so on. It's okay."
>
> . . . I am working toward the empowerment of every human being that I can possibly touch and that includes me. Empowerment comes when we have been able to heal, in our mind, the primary triad [of the family of origin] . . . Until we do that healing, life will always be a divided thing for us. (Satir, 1987a, tape 2)

Virginia envisioned a world in which therapists would have come to understand the old, dysfunctional messages received in their family of origin/primary triad, to understand the inhuman rules which the great majority of us were reared to apply to ourselves, and to be, therefore, in a position to free our patients from the tyranny. Such therapists would serve as models, working cooperatively and in partnership rather than being caught up in the spiraling treadmill of competitive behavior. Life might be experienced in a much more celebratory fashion if it were not perceived as a desperate race to get ahead of the other.

Patients, families, and couples experiencing the therapists who value cooperation more than competition could have, therefore, a model for life as equals rather than a preoccupation with who runs the show. All the destructive "-isms" would atrophy if the competitive "who's got the power" focus could be widely replaced with a model of *mutual* empowerment which follows mutual respect for the uniqueness of each separate self in any dyad.

It was Virginia's belief and experience that this respect naturally follows those encounters between deepest self of the one with deepest self of the other. She based her own training of psychotherapists on that belief.

Virginia was opposed to manipulative therapy which featured techniques performed on patients and strongly objected to any kind of therapy which demeaned or violated a person in any way. She saw the dominance/submission model—however "benevolent"—as a dangerous principle playing out on the world stage. Conversely, the more people who could learn to act from the seed/growth model, the greater hope of avoiding tyrannical governments and nuclear disaster.

Prevention: Changing Our Whole Culture— An Interview

In an interview done by Sheldon Starr in 1985, a colleague who first encountered Virginia when he was a student at the Mental Research Institute in the 1960s, Virginia gave her broad thoughts on the subject of "prevention":

> VIRGINIA: The reason for working with the whole family is that you have the chance to do something much more creative, to heal in a much more effective way. You have the opportunity to intervene so that other family members do not have to continue in some kind of . . .

STARR: It's really doing some kind of preventive work.

VIRGINIA: Absolutely! For me it is *preventive and educational*. After I get to know a family I see a microcosm of the whole world because the family is a microcosm of the whole world.

STARR: Fine, that's great. Suppose we pursue that. How do we use family concepts to avert nuclear disaster? Because that is implied in what we are talking about.

VIRGINIA: . . . I think about this a great deal. The first thing for me is to do and be all that I can to shed light, to help people open up and to enable us to develop the kind of consciousness that makes it possible for us to join and cooperate [= collaborate]. Cooperation is the first thing, *number one*; if we do not do that, nothing else matters. On one level that's a big job. (Satir, 1992b, 8-9)

At this point, the interviewer noted that this joining and cooperating is easier to talk about than to do. Virginia responded with the observation that, yes, cooperation/collaboration is an alien idea in Western civilization and a huge amount of energy is required to deal with it. She replied, nevertheless:

I would predict that if we were able—you and Joan Herrick [mutual friend and also therapist at the Mental Research Institute] and everybody else that we know were able to consciously handle ourselves in such a way as to *reflect the light that we have in our being* and [do so] in our dealings with people, that [alien idea] would [shift]. (Satir, 1992b, 9)

Virginia added that this shift is already in motion. It needs to be increased, which would result in an amplified voice. "The creative energy will change what is going on." Virginia said this change lies "in the *development* of [people's] own consciousness, . . . I see it [happening] because people learn how they can connect with somebody else." Virginia was referring to the power in that third energy that is generated when two persons make authentic, congruent contact.

> STARR: But now you are talking about changing our whole culture.
> VIRGINIA: That's right, and that is what has to happen. (Satir, 1992b, 9)

Virginia clearly said that she made "no apologies" for working to promote major shifts in our world.

The Seed Model

I'm going to give you a definition, my definition of congruence... there could be two definitions: one is a threat/reward definition and the other is a "seed" definition.

A "seed" definition is that what you are feeling you are letting yourself know and are acknowledging it. Whatever it is. Happy, sad, glad, mad, it doesn't matter. That's where I am and I own that. Then, I look at the way I'm feeling, so that I'm not feeling angry and putting on a smile . . . I am feeling what I'm feeling. I'm acknowledging that it belongs to me. I am showing how I'm feeling. I'm saying how I'm feeling. And, then, I'm asking for the help I'm needing . . .

In the threat/reward model, "congruence" is...to be what you're *supposed* to be . . . [for example] "I should always be sweet," so I try that no matter how I'm feeling.

What I would like for you to be in touch with is that when I'm talking about congruence I'm talking about the seed model congruence [dynamic and appropriate to context]. (Satir, 1987a, tape 3)

Explaining the threat/reward model is easy enough. Any child above the age of two has a rudimentary understanding of the domination/submission model and can generally understand even a simple description: There are big people and little people. The big people are better and make rules. The little people must keep the rules. If you keep rules, you are often given nice things. If you break even *one*, you will never get a nice thing—no candy, no cookie, no toy, no dry pants, no dinner!

On the other hand, explaining the implications of viewing the world through the seed model is like the challenge of explaining the concept of congruence. A clear view of the seed model at work in human affairs is such an unfamiliar occurrence that it is difficult to hold the image in mind while considering world events.

What do we do with the September 11 attacks within the seed model? This is an emotional challenge. There is such a temptation to fly into heavy-duty blame mode and desire to just stomp the SOBs to death. (As we witnessed with our own government almost immediately leaping to bombs and invasion.) However, if we pull back long enough to think, we have to remember that this millennia-old response does nothing but breed more such dangerous men who successive generations will feel moved to "stomp to death." This worked as a temporary measure when done with jack boots and rifle butts or stone axes; it is not going to have nearly the same even momentary satisfaction if done with nuclear weapons.

Of course, the United States' invasion of Iraq in 2003 serves as a classic example of the threat/reward model. There is considerable agreement that its consequence also supplies a graphic example in that model's inefficiency. That story will be playing out, in one form or another, for decades.

In the seed model, we would seek to understand Osama bin Laden and all such terrorists in terms of personhood, as human beings. However alien to our understanding of what constitutes "human," nonetheless, Osama bin Laden, Mohamed Atta, Saddam Hussein, Josef Stalin, Ivan the Terrible, and Adolf Hitler were all, at a point in time, vulnerable baby boys in mother's arms. They said first words, took first toddling steps, and thought their cultures' equivalents of teddy-bear and lollipop thoughts that first emerge in a little person's mind as she or he begins to develop language.

Obviously, something went terribly wrong in each one at some point to create such propensities for mayhem. However, there was a point at which the most astute of us would not have been able to pick them out in a nursery, as future threats to civilization. We do not know what intervening experiences—evil, if you will—entered each of these little boys' lives to dim the light with which each infant enters the world. Further, we do not know how any of us might have responded in the face of the same kind of formative early childhood experience.

This is not to say these people should not have been and should not be contained. But containment can be partnered with compassion. Good parents of two-year-olds do it every day. Along with containment in this spirit would be a commitment of equal intensity to the innocents in the line of fire—not an intellectual dismissal as "inevitability of collateral damage." Such a dismissal is the classic super-reasonable response: valuing of task and context over human beings and human feelings.

Rather than brazenly holding Al Qaeda prisoners in cages at the Guantanamo base in Cuba (in spite of protest among many allies as well as enemies), we could have made every effort to determine the legitimacy of their detaining, informed them of their rights, guaranteed humane treatment, and then begun a process of interviewing each one to determine what issues lay behind their participation in a terrorist group—psychological and sociological—or what they needed in order to become whole human beings who do not present such danger to the rest of us. We could gather information about the etiology of this violence and, at the same time, be making a public statement that we are not the monsters Osama bin Laden et al. claim that we are.

This would, of course, suggest a general reform of prison systems from factories for reinforcing antisocial behavior to institutions devoted to humane ways of changing criminal personality structures. This reform is a problem we have long needed to address anyway. Bestial penal systems simply reinforce bestial behavior in inmates (Roberts, 2003).

Any systemic approach to understanding this aspect of what has too often been dismissed as "human nature" would need to be multinational, not so much for political reasons as for making as wide as possible the circle of wisdom and for having the fullest possible view of cultural aspects.

Virginia's seed model image suggests that emotional and psychological hunger is the basis of abusive behavior. If she is correct, then we need to begin massive educational movements and substantially expand current efforts to address those needs.

When we abuse each other what we are doing is saying we are starving to death and we will [engage in] cannibalism in order to live. If I could get this idea over, really over, to the whole world that our abuse of people comes from our own hunger, then when we learn how to feed ourselves . . . And what is that? Learning to love ourselves.

Every morning in the meditations [during the seminars] I do this every single morning. Are you aware of that? I ask you to come in touch with loving yourself. All our parents, on some level, unless they were very, very special, specially trained, or whatever, special in that way—[and] there aren't many—they were hungry. They tried to get their spouses to feed them and they couldn't. And then they asked *us*, their children to feed them and they couldn't get that to work.

Now that is not because they wanted to hurt us. *That is because people never knew [never learned] how to nurture themselves. We have yet to have a society which knew how to do it.* In the good old days, that wasn't happening. People were still eating each other up. But what they did is to develop role definitions. In those role definitions, if you are a woman, you serve and I, the man get it. And I, the woman get the food out of my serving. *What is very important to understand: people are not bad, they are hungry.*

That gives me another chance to say here at a moment in time, I can nurture myself with my own feelings of value and love, of accepting myself, of seeing myself, of hearing myself. And also of allowing myself to involve others in my life by asking whether or not they would like to be there and hearing them if they say no. That nurturing is being in contact, loving, valuing, being able to have each person stand in their own little puddle and connect.

Now the outcome for children in a relationship that has these kinds of things: hungry people that don't know how to get their hunger met. (Satir, 1986a, tape 18)

The seed model is based on the concept that, like plants in a garden, people will grow if obstacles are removed and basic nurturing elements are added. Roses and corn plants do not need an "incentive program" to blossom and ripen. Nor would they respond to beating and cursing— except to wither and die if the former were severe enough to affect their structure.

Basic respect, for self and for other, is essential to emotional growth in human beings. Congruence in communication nurtures growth and healing.

Virginia believed that the human is not only worthy of respect, but deserving of celebration. We are all born of planted seeds and—creatures of spirit, of Life Force—we blossom each into our own unique form, "and then we come up like a fountain . . . and then . . . each one of us become[s] a cocreator after we get here, based upon this spiritual basis" (Satir, 1983b, 229).

14

CULTIVATING, BLOSSOMING, BRIDGING

I believe people are like flowers, and flowers grow because they have sunshine, fertilizer, and water. I have yet to find a plant that would grow by my issuing the edict, "If you don't bloom, I am going to beat you."

—**Virginia Satir**, 1975

Virginia the Gardener

Virginia Satir was not just creating pretty metaphors when she said that "people are like flowers." She understood this as a fact: all living elements share the growth factor inherent in the life force. Virginia did not work from theory; she worked from clinical observations. She took this fact—the nature of growth—into account and incorporated its principles into her work.

In sharp contrast to the poisonous and too usual application of "the rules," which allow and encourage "care" agents to treat human beings as objects to be manipulated, the idea of following the flow of the natural order of life is startlingly refreshing. Virginia spelled out her belief that human beings will blossom and bear fruit if provided the proper human circumstances analogous to sunshine, fertilizer, and water. She used this model as basic in her work and shuddered at the results and evidence of interventions based on the use of force by those in charge of the care of others.

> I also know that a plant sometimes becomes too heavy to bear its own weight, and I then have to put in a stake to help hold it up until it grows strong enough to support itself. *This is my model, and everything I do is related to how I can help the human being open up and blossom.*
>
> What provides nurture for the human being? It is his own ability to ask for what he needs and to be in touch with himself. Then he can work out gratifying interdependent relationships with other human beings—not dependent or independent, but interdependent. Interdependent means two parts functioning together, not two parts merged into one.
>
> The water for our human "plant" consists of the senses.
>
> These are not merely mechanical systems, but dynamic in that they can learn and grow in effectiveness. What is poisonous to us as plants are the inhuman rules we have about how we should be and how we should act. Getting rid of those poisonous rules will help restore health in the person. (Satir, 1975, 166)[1]

Virginia never deviated from that belief—which was based on her personal clinical experience. She points out that "pathology" is problems with coping, that such problems are always associated with the threat/ reward model, which discounts a person's self-worth. She briefly summarized the two models operationally:

I expect anybody who has problems with coping . . . that to me is what a pathology is. I've got something and I can't cope with it: they are always in this *hierarchial* model or the threat and reward model. What can I add to *what is* [the present reality—(see chapters 11 and 12)] to make it possible for people to come over here [gesturing toward "*seed* model" on blackboard]. [This is the] process of transformation. (Satir, 1983b, 232)

Notice that Virginia was not saying she would encourage a person to stop any particular behavior. She was not talking about "eliminating symptoms." She preferred to add what is missing to foster transformation—a changing of the form. Warning that one might lapse back into that same dysfunctional model through linear thinking about *the* one "right way," she went on to explain the keys to transformation: *awareness* of the ability to make choices appropriate to a given situation and the *freedom* to pursue discovery of new paths.

Please don't misunderstand me . . . If we said, "Now that's the *right* way," we're right back there [in the hierarchical model]. Now the choices become more *when* do you want to be linear, *when* are you going to be on top, *when*? and it's done now *by selection* . . . This [seed model] is a process to make good selection and at the same time to nurture yourself. So it's important that it's this [seed model], not that [hierarchal model], because that [hierarchal model] means you have to cut everybody off at the feet and start all over again . . . Instead of a compulsive way of going, we now do it in a selection way.

So there are two words that are very important here, in this one [seed model], and the words are *discovery and choice*. What can I discover and how can I make my choices obvious to me? And over here [in threat and reward model] the two words are "right or wrong"—first of all you judge it. Judge right or wrong. And then whatever the right and wrong is, you enforce it. That is why living in this [seed] model and trying to be good with that [threat/reward] model puts you in a place where you're guaranteed to have difficult problems. (Satir, 1983b, 232)

Virginia presumed we all—as growing live entities on the earth—live in the seed model, whether or not we are aware of the fact. As naturally dynamic creatures, we then block our own life force when we adopt the narrow static "right or wrong" hierarchal model in a wish to "be good." There is inherent power in the life force. Physical as well as emotional problems ensue when the organic movement toward growth distorts en route instead of being permitted its natural course.

Virginia took two familiar notions, love and structure, to illustrate the divergent attitudes of the organic model and hierarchical models. Models are important because behavior follows modeling.

Love

Love—let's take any noun we have. Love within the threat and reward model means, "Listen, I gave birth to you and now you be grateful." It means "I married you and this is what you're supposed to do." It's obligation, it's blackmail. Obligation: "You did this and now this is what you're supposed to do," sometimes called duty . . . Blackmail: "Listen, if you don't do that for me and I will do that for you, and we're going to be very careful how the scale goes."

Now when you put love within—the seed model, because seeds are so tiny and they can come through big mountains—When you have *love within the seed model*, first of all you know that it *comes from a feeling of harmony within yourself, because it's your own harmony that creates the possibility for love.*

It's an outcome of harmony. It is a feeling and it has no obligations. It is free and it forms the context in which intimacy and connectedness can come about. It's a feeling, and we have many different contexts in which we feel love—with a friend, with our parents, with our partners, with our children. *The ingredients of love are all the same, the harmonious flow.* That is why we don't say to somebody—to try to get them to do something—that we won't love them if they don't. No, no. That is not there. What we want to do is negotiate for how to have it happen, because there is no intelligence in love. Love only makes it possible for intelligence to flourish, but love itself has no intelligence whatsoever. (Satir, 1983b, 233–234)

Structure

Now I'll take one other one [example]—I'll take two [examples] just so I won't be in a bind.[2] Let's take "structure." Structure—people are always talking about. Structure in the hierarchial model is something that you make by a group of experts that get together in 1902 about what's right and the others are following that because the experts said it. You squeeze everything into that structure. It's the same as [with] a baby, the baby's twenty-two inches, you measure the baby and build a cradle twenty-two inches. And for the rest of the child's life you squeeze whatever that body does into that twenty-two inches because that's the structure . . . We do it because the structure says so.

The seed model of that—or I've often called it the organic model—you build the baby a crib for it's [sic] bed and then when it gets bigger you extend the crib, it gets bigger, you extend the crib, your structure works for what you want to have happen instead of inhibiting what you want to have and fitting the structure instead of having the structure fit what you want to do. And lots of stuff is going on in little bits and pieces in the world like that. (Satir, 1983b, 234)

Virginia's point: in the hierarchy model, the person is made to fit the structure; in the seed model, the structure is made to fit the person.

Virginia went on in her illustrations of the difference in the two models by pointing out that "discipline" is always punishment in the hierarchical model, whereas, in the organic model, it simply means the ability to appropriately order one's life.

Virginia emphasized that she was describing phenomena that she sees the world as only now discovering. In this era in human history, we have begun to understand the possibilities inherent in a life with awareness of wholeness—people consciously living out of the natural energy that flows through that wholeness. She was the herald for the healing balm of the natural flow of Reality—What Is. Within "What Is"—our comprehensive overall context—flows the Life Force present on our planet. Growth is part of our design and that of all living beings. We share it with houseflies, squirrels, orchids, wide-mouth bass, and towering pines. The energy in wholeness heals and permits the natural form to unfold.

Using the metaphors of "flat" and "round," Virginia made the point about wholeness. She pointed out the hazard in presuming the validity of conventional wisdom. Choice and freedom to *discover* are elements of the organic model. Both were important concepts in Virginia's work.

To illustrate the importance and dynamic of discovery, she wrote:

I want to point out something else. Columbus did not invent the elliptical world, he only discovered it. Like Franklin did not invent electricity, he only discovered it. And what I put to you, this [referring to hierarchical model on blackboard] is a picture of flat people, two dimensional. And what I'm offering you now is a discovery that we are round. I didn't invent it, it's there—and that's really what this seminar is all about. (Satir, 1983b, 238)

Virginia was pointing out that this vibrant world, with all its life-sustaining energy, is a system within which we live. Within that context, *awareness* of our full dimension results from giving ourselves freedom of choice and discovery. If we allow ourselves to be free to consider new possibilities, we are in the process of experiencing our "roundness." Virginia was alluding to the seed model as the natural order when she noted that Columbus, Franklin, and she were *discovering, not inventing.*

Linking operative concepts that are part of the explanation of the organic model, Virginia made the connection between the seed model and spirituality. Seeds and eggs, loaded as they are with the life energy, are concrete and vital evidence of our spiritual base. In making this link, Virginia was showing how humanity fits into the "What Is"—the greater context of the universe—within the Pattern that Connects.

When Virginia spoke about opportunities for psychological/emotional freedom, she was talking about gardens, not wild weed patches:

> The seed model . . . discipline. People always say, "Oh Virginia, you don't believe in discipline." I say, "Yes, I do. I have a great deal of it." Discipline within the hierarchical model is always based on reward and punishment. It has nothing to do with what comes out of it. You do bad in school so they take away your television. What possible relationship is that? You do nice in arithmetic and somebody gives you some money. What in the heck is the relationship between those two things? Nothing. The skill for doing poorly in school is quite different from the skill of looking at television. They're two different things. Now, within the seed model *discipline is becoming connected, related to the thing as it is* and moving and learning from consequences, whatever [they] may be. (Satir, 1983b, 235)

In the seed model, I am not required to squander my energy on somebody else's definition of how I, as a person, "ought" to be. I may exercise my own judgment and make my own choices, freeing myself to move toward that "third birth" Virginia described, in which we become our own choice-makers. Free for self-acceptance, I may embrace my "I am-ness," understand change as a given in the universe, and understand there is never a one-two-three cause or single explanation for any event.

> For a long time people thought that health was the absence of illness. Nothing could be more wrong or that the absence of war is the same as peace. And I think they [those two misconceptions] are the same thing. (Satir, 1986a, tape 3)

"Health" in a body means appropriate nurturing, attention to physical, psychological, and emotional needs, and attention to interactional styles. "Health" in nations means the same thing expanded. We ignore our human need for nurturing at great peril both on an individual basis and on a societal basis.

Importance of Congruence

Acknowledging Feelings

All feelings are honorable. The problem is how we use those feelings. If I am angry, I have many ways to manifest that feeling. I can slug you; I can cry; I can read you a lecture; I can spit; I can faint; I can do all kinds of things as a result of that feeling. In a peculiar way, *I believe we are at the crossroads of a new evolution of man, if we can survive long enough to make it—and I am not at all sure we can. Particularly at this moment it is essential that people be able to be in contact with themselves on the human basis.* I am sure you are well aware that in all the families you deal with, and maybe in your own lives, pain comes from the feeling of being alienated, of feeling not loved, of feeling doubtful about your lovability. Isolation, loneliness, distrust—these are the kinds of words people use. I think that these feelings arise because we ascribe to and allow ourselves to be dominated by some kind of idea of "what is right" that actually is not right.

This is what I mean: How long do you think it takes a child who is told every day not to display his anger, or is slapped every day for showing his anger, to have that feeling go inside and come out some other way? It doesn't take very long. I am not trying to set myself up as the supreme authority, but in my experiences I have studied and dealt with people who have committed all types of monstrous crimes and been involved in every kind of human pain, and underneath every one of these people was a little, lonely child who did not know how to acknowledge and communicate his feelings openly and still survive. This is true of the majority of people in their communication. As a result, there is no chance for a person to feel good about himself because he is too busy trying to keep himself afloat. There is no way for a person to feel the genuineness and the love between himself and another person. There is no way one can fully use his resources on the problem at hand. *The world today is full of many problems; but the one big problem as I see it is that while people try to deal with real problems, they end up dealing not with these problems but with their own feelings of self-worth in an unacknowledged way.* (Satir, 1975, 79–80)

Virginia was describing the terribly destructive effect of unacknowledged feelings of self-doubt. There is an urgent need for human beings to be in contact with themselves, aware of their feelings as well as thoughts, perceptions, and yearnings, all of which include rich inner resources. Virginia knew this self-attendance is (1) critically important and (2) can be taught even to small children.

The concept of systems needs to be applied wherever there are people. Keeping in mind not only that "whatever you see in a person is only a piece of the whole," that person is also a piece of another whole—first their family, then their specific community. Viewing the world in terms of the organic model means staying aware that there are wells of factors behind every interaction in which any human being engages.[3] This view also means awareness that all people are connected to other people in various configurations, influencing and being influenced by the other people with whom they are connected. To simply blame one person for an act, without any consideration of all circumstances, is a very short-sighted, unrealistic view.

Inadvertent Early Childhood Education

So children learn after a while that they must endure all kinds of pain and not comment about it. We have thousands of people in our society who have stopped being in touch with their own pain and are behaving like robots. They will absorb any amount of pain without even recognizing it. The minute you are out of touch with your own pain you become insensitive to the pain of others, because pain does not even register anymore. Our world is full of people like that.

One should not underestimate the importance of what the child learns from these misunderstandings. Every parent wants his child to be all right. Every child would like to feel he can depend upon his parent. Inadvertent learnings . . . become more powerful than any words that can be uttered. (Satir, 1975, 101)

Yesterday's children who have learned by the tens of thousands to stop being in touch with their pain and behave like robots are now among today's terrorists who are making human bombs of themselves. This process is going on as I write, and it is this process which could bring down modern civilization as we have come to know it. These are the people locked into the super-reasonable response to inner pain.

What is the difference in the child who grows up out of touch with his pain and the one who grows up to become, say, an engineer rather than a terrorist? What are the variables? This is part of the work the mental health/sociology community of the world desperately and urgently needs to address.

The need to address this dynamic—the production of toxicity in people who are out of touch with inner pain—has become critical for the continued survival of human life on this planet. Virginia found that teaching basic principles which facilitate human connection is far more valuable than teaching therapists to use any technique.

Techniques in Proper Context

I have rarely had difficulty getting people to take risks, but I do not begin by asking them to do so. You see, just learning a technique can be dangerous and disappointing.

—Virginia Satir, *1975*

Virginia described an event where a nurse came in late in the day on the ninth session of a ten session training program, saw people holding hands, sensed the nurturing atmosphere in the room without observing what led up to it and concluded that "what was helpful was to get people to hold hands." She went back to her adolescent ward at a mental hospital and created an explosive situation by walking into the ward and asking everybody to hold hands. Virginia used this example to point out the danger of learning and using a technique without regard for context.

To be useful any technique must emanate from what is going on at that moment in time because it seems to fit, and it is effective only within a context of trust. I cannot overemphasize that point. *This is why I cannot teach people techniques; I can only teach them some ways in which they can use themselves when certain things happen.* So I could never teach you or anybody "how to do family therapy." As the leader, I teach people by helping them to come to their own awareness and to become familiar with the kinds of interaction phenomena that people are involved in. (Satir, 1975, 136)

Many people came to Virginia hoping they might learn her secrets, copy "her techniques," and go home and "do therapy." Virginia chose, instead, to do her best to teach these people the basic principles of "human beingness," a much broader, deeper subject.

Power in Both Models

Virginia often pointed out the tremendous power in the Life Force—tree roots forcing up concrete slabs, tiny seeds that become elephants and sequoias. She expressed considerable reverence for the process. One might well suggest that the power of her work issued from her awareness and connection to the great creative force of Life itself.

In a presentation at the first Evolution of Psychotherapy conference in 1985, Virginia made the distinction between the partly blind, brutal use of power in the threat and reward model and the clear, solid, healing power in the seed model.

Changes are always connected with chaos and that's what we are seeing right now. The family structure [of the future] will have a much needed facelift when we reshape our attitudes and expectations about the equality and value of human beings.

There also will be a change in how power is used. When people are viewed as equals, power can be used to empower individuals instead of controlling others. The most prevalent use of power among individuals is to control others because of their age, status, relative wealth, sex, or race. The difference here is between *seed power*, which is based on growth and cooperation, and *gun power*, which is based on threat. We have never had a time when the choices of our use of power were as clear and so available. (Satir, 1987c, 60–61)

Outbreaks of Peace

But you can also do something quite different.

—**Virginia Satir**, *1985*

What do outbreaks of wars and outbreaks of peace have to do with family therapy?

Virginia's position was that prevention may be expanded to include the "mental health" of the whole world; her corollary is that change is possible through engagement of the passion of only a small percentage of the population.

A revolutionary concept lies in the segment of the 1985 interview by Sheldon Starr with Virginia. Starr had noted she was talking about changing our whole culture. Indeed, she was. She extended the mental health concept of prevention:

Statistically, if twenty percent of the world is into a new place we've made it . . . Because that is all it takes to get a new thing going. Twenty percent. Six percent to start it off and then another fourteen percent to make it go. Those are the movers and shakers in the world. And if we can get that many we'll have it, we can do it . . . It is also one of the other reasons why, for me, any therapeutic transaction that decreases a person's self-esteem, demeans or humiliates them, defeats the purpose of making this a better world. (Satir, 1985, 11)

I was struck with the echo of Virginia's calculations[4] in the following statement in Hedrick Smith's *The New Russians*, published just *prior* to the attempted coup in the summer of 1991. That was the event that heralded the demise of the Soviet Union.

> "The big surprise for Gorbachev is that there was such a grass-roots upheaval," commented Boris Kurashvili, a scholar at the Institute of State and Law and a daring exponent of reform under Brezhnev. "There will be independent, unmanageable deputies in the new People's Congress—I figure *twenty percent*.
>
> "*Ten percent* is enough to have an opposition that can be heard," Kurashvili emphasized. "There will be enough to form an opposition, an independent bloc" [italics mine]. (Smith, 1990, 451)

And the Soviet Union fell down around Gorbachev's ears in 1991. We saw the power of that 10 to 20 percent.

Virginia was quite consciously proceeding around the world with the goal of sufficiently liberating that "6 percent" of the world's population from self-imposed limitation so that they would have the courage to take the necessary "steps in their own behalf"—and the planet's. This was not simply an idealistic dream; this was Virginia's well-considered plan.

Virginia brought with her as she passed through our world, a vision of possibility that, as she well knew, we sorely need. Seeing effective family therapy and world peace as one entity, she also saw that the essential—as well as eminently practical—point at which to start was the level of self-worth and empowering personhood.

Building Bridges—Not Walls

Only about 5% of the time do families engage in the kind of congruent communication that will build bridges rather than walls.
—Virginia Satir, *1971*

Wars start with alienation between people. Peace starts with the connection of hearts. The former may be seen as issuing from patterns that *dis*connect (see chapter 6) while the latter is part of the basic nature of the Pattern that Connects (see chapter 11). There is a relationship—a correlation—between functional versus dysfunctional communication, peace versus war, and the esteem in which one holds oneself and others. Build bridges, not walls—and reach an open hand across any remaining abyss, struggle to find out what the other is *really* feeling, thinking, and needing underneath whatever defensive wrapping. In the year 1991, we got graphic examples of those walls and bridges.

The first Gulf War "built" a fiery chasm, proving technology now makes it possible to throw up such walls with blinding speed and accuracy. The event in Moscow, which precipitated the crumbling of the Soviet Union, bridged a moat, alive with fifty years worth of snapping, snarling, and waiting nuclear warheads—proving those bridges *can* be built over even the worst of pits.

Now, years later, we have gone on to heavier, harder conflicts. The fiery chasms have grown hotter and higher—threatening huge all-consuming proportions: the bridges are now urgently, desperately needed. We all must reflect on psychohistory as an extension of systems thinking to point to ways human interactions are related, looking into the macrosystems as well as into the microsystems. We all must learn to empower each other to move beyond the archaic defenses learned in childhood; Homo sapiens have a much wider choice in behavior than the narrow "flight or fight" used by mammals with less complex brains.

If we fail to accept our higher heritage, we might find ourselves back with those so-called lesser beings, scrambling among the ruins.

Chapter Notes

1. In this succinct sentence, Virginia summed up the importance of free, full use of senses for growth. The degree of freedom for use of senses is directly related to the degree of self-worth. Freedom to see and hear what others are saying and freedom to use speech to accurately reflect internal experience are vital to congruence. Our senses are our windows and doors to reality. Congruence, based on *what is*, is vital for growth (see chapter 6).

2. Virginia was making an oblique reference to the possibility of choice in all situations and to counter the linear way of thinking: the idea that there is just one way, answer, or explanation. She used two illustrations just to show there *is* always more than one.

3. In *The Satir Model*, the metaphor of an iceberg is used to teach the concept that more goes on "below the surface" of a person than above (Satir, 1991, 172–173).

4. Virginia did not pull those figures out of thin air. Everett Rogers is probabably her source. He is a noted sociologist; professor at Annenberg School of Communications, University of Southern California; fellow of the American Association for the Advancement of Science and the American Sociology Association; and a Fellow and past president of the International Communications Association. In offering a distillation from the tremendous body of research on the diffusion of innovation, he said:

> Once an innovation is accepted by about 15 to 20 percent of the total population involved, such as the total population of the US or the USSR, it cannot be stopped . . . This self-generating quality of the diffusion process has been found in a wide range of conditions, and

for a large number of innovations that have been studied . . . The first adopters of an innovation, called "innovators," are usually perceived as atypical members of their local community, and their example is not immediately followed by others . . . The next category of individuals to adopt the innovation are called "early adopters." They are people who occupy a key position in the local communication network and are seen to embody the norms of the social system...Certain individuals in a social system play an especially important role in the interpersonal diffusion of innovations. They are called "opinion leaders." . . . Once the rate of adoption for an innovation has reached 15 or 20 percent (that is, when the opinion leaders have adopted it), it is usually impossible to prevent further diffusion of the innovation. (Rogers, 1988, 242–243)

The "innovators" and "early adopters" are those "movers and shakers" Virginia described as the "six percent" required "to start it off."

Appreciations

Several friends and colleagues contributed significantly to the creation of *Well-Being Writ Large*.

I deeply appreciate the people, both those living and those now dead, who contributed their own energy to the emergence of this book.

I am in almost daily debt to Virginia Satir (1916–1988). Early on in my professional career, she provided a solid blueprint for the development of my theory of practice, pointing out the essential overlap between an effective professional life and one's own personhood.

Virginia, herself, in 1972, casually suggested to me that I write this book, adding, "Then that's one more I won't have to write."

The other enormous debt is to Sister Fara Impastato, OP, professor emerita at Loyola University in New Orleans. Virginia spent a week with me in New Orleans in 1985, and Sister Fara attended her workshop. One of the following days, the two spent an afternoon together and felt they were kindred souls. Through her editing skills and keen mind, Sister Fara helped me articulate the deep spiritual current in Virginia's message. Later, I found among Virginia's papers in the Virginia Satir Special Collection at the University of California, Santa Barbara, a little personal note: "Met a wonderful nun in New Orleans."

Harvey B. Rifkin, MD, is the psychiatrist who served with me as cotherapist in an ongoing therapy group in New Orleans for over thirty years. I am grateful for his careful reading and comments on the material in the book and his ongoing encouragement.

Jean Houston, who heartily endorsed the first drafts, served as an early receptacle for the concepts. She inspired and helped mobilize my creative energy. The initial framework and impetus for the book emerged through, in large part, my letters written to her, explaining nuances of Virginia's work and how they did or did not fit with those of Jean's work.

I deeply appreciate the opinions offered in the beginning stages by the Reverend W. Craig Gilliam, PhD; Wray Pascoe, PhD; and Judy Bula Wise, PhD. Wray had considerable personal contact as well as training with Virginia, hosting Virginia during her seminars in Canada. Virginia even sat on Judy's doctoral committee. Their advice and encouragement to me were invaluable in those early stages of this book.

I want to offer thanks to the following, who read the manuscript in its final stages: DeWitt Baldwin, MD; Janet Christi-Seely, MD; Laura Dodson, MSW, PhD; Sharon Loeschen, LCSW; and Jean McLendon LCSW, LMFT—all leaders intensely involved in teaching Virginia's work over the years both before and after her death in 1988.

Two people, less intrinsically involved but acquainted to some extent with Virginia's work, served to help me discern the sensibility of the contents for the intelligent reader concerned with making the world a better place: Carolyn Weyland, PhD, psychologist in New Orleans; and Sandra Thomas, PhD, former president of Converse College. In addition to these two, Peggy Dean, MBA, certified trainer in neurolinguistic programming, was most helpful in suggesting the addition of my 1982 interview with Virginia as preface.

Two generous and highly skilled people informally offered professional copyediting and developmental editing: Bea Ferrigno and Suzi

Tucker. I want to thank Steven Young for putting me in touch with Bea Ferrigno and Jeffrey Zeig for introducing my manuscript to Suzi Tucker.

Critical help with the "mechanics" came from the people who made available transcripts of the tapes of Virginia's extended workshops. I believed it was important to base the order of the concepts in this book on the same sequence Virginia, herself, used in her workshops.

Lori H. Gordon, PhD, graciously provided the transcription of the tapes of the two-week residential training she and I attended on Aruba in 1972. Kate Caston shared her copy of the transcription of tapes of the 1981 Satir monthlong workshop. John Banmen published *Virginia Satir Verbatim*, which was the transcription of the 1983 monthlong workshop. Nancy White, PhD, performed the invaluable service of making her own secretary available to transcribe the tapes from Virginia's last monthlong 1987 workshop.

Conversations with my fellow participants in the 1971, 1972, and 1973 residential trainings were also significant contributions to understanding Virginia's work.

I also want to thank my old friends Wray Pascoe and Anne Bell for asking, in virtually every conversation we had over a multiyear period, "How's the book coming?"

Remembering all of you in your contributions to *Well-Being Writ Large* has been a gift itself.

Appendix A
Exercise
Centering

And now begin to let yourself be aware of the miracle: you just wish, you just think, and those beautiful eyelids close. Could it be that you could be in that intimate relationship with the rest of your body?

Now let yourself become aware of your breathing, just aware of it, feeling it coming in, knowing it brings healthy oxygen to your body, feeling all those parts of yourself that were specially designed to give the air a way to get to all your body. And perhaps this morning you can give it some gentle encouragement to move through your body . . .

And if, in the course of the travel of that oxygen through your body you come to some little tight places in yourself, acknowledge them, release them, and bless them especially for letting you know that they had been uncomfortable . . . Parts of you have been uncomfortable in your body, and you, the owner, have now released that discomfort by your breathing and your awareness.

Now, at this moment, feel yourself centered here, your body on the chair, your feet on the floor, your back against the chair . . . and extend the feeling of centeredness to this room, to the outside space of this building, to the [nearby] towns . . . , to the state . . . , [Virginia names the specific towns and state] to the country of the United States, to the North American continent, to the whole Western hemisphere, crossing both oceans and embodying all the countries on the planet, centered here, you in the center of that universe or planet . . .

As you do that, let yourself become aware that we are all, wherever we live, wherever we live, we are all manifestations of the life force.

And perhaps we can, a little bit, get into the shoes of Ed Mitchell, one of our astronauts, who when he was a certain distance from our planet could put the whole planet behind his thumb. As he has said, that was the moment that he knew that all life was the same and all our planet was small, fragile, but it represented the universe. He also knew at that position that he could remember himself being in a certain space, like you are now, aware only of what was immediately around and could easily forget that other position was also there. I call that position which Ed Mitchell talked about, that space from the planet Earth that he could put behind his thumb, the airport control tower position. To be able to view the whole, and at the same time to be able to appreciate the specific and to know that we are all one, only in varying forms . . .

And at this moment, let us now take the energy, our energy, and let us send it to [participant], to her husband, to her father-in-law, to [participant's] mother, to [participant 2], to [participant 3], and to anyone else in your life that you feel would like to have loving energy for healing, for support . . . That could include yourself . . .

[two-minute pause]

And now, being in touch with your own capacity to send energy for healing, can you also now become more fully aware that you have that energy to use for yourself . . . and that it comes from the center of the earth, the energy that moves up through our feet and legs to give yourself grounding? And maybe this morning you can imagine a color that you like of that energy as it moves, flowing, making beautiful circles and movements . . . and be in touch with the energy that comes from the heavens, moving down through your head, bringing with it the energy of inspiration, imagination, the visions of what can be . . . as it moves down into your head and face and neck and arms. And maybe this morning you can imagine a color from that too . . . complementary to the energy of your groundedness.

And as these two energies meet, see them nurturing each other, creating still a *third energy, the energy of your connectedness between yourself and other beings on this earth* [italics mine]. This energy, moving out through your arms and hands when you meet through all of your skin when you hug. And perhaps you could give this a color, vibrant, a color that pleases you. And see the three colors as they move and mingle, shading each other sometimes, adding new dimensions at other times . . . always there, always there for you . . . a fresh supply moment by moment.

And let yourself come in touch with yourself as a miracle, a treasure. *There's no one exactly like you on the face of this earth*, only people who have similarities to you. In the basic ways, we are all alike. Our heads are on the top, our feet are on the bottom, our hearts are somewhere midway in our body. But our specific form is unique to us.

Now go to that place, that place deep within yourself where you keep that miracle, that treasure that is called by your name. And as you approach lovingly, gently, perhaps even excitedly . . . where you *see your resources*; your ability to see, to hear, to touch and taste and smell, to feel and to think, to speak and move and choose . . .

And perhaps at this moment you know that you do that [choosing] also moment by moment . . . And perhaps also you remind yourself that to keep up with [each] moment's needs, you need to exercise your ability to sort, to sort out of all that you have at this time what fits for you now, and to let the other go, again, with your blessings, because it helped you get here where you are now . . . And to look at that which you now have and to look forward to that which you would like to further bring to yourself, through a connection with someone else, through listening to someone talk, to reading, to trying an experiment, to allowing yourself to taste all that comes along, but keeping that wisdom of swallowing only that which fits. And maybe at this time you can give yourself in a most sincere and loving way a message of appreciation for you, for you and all that you have.

And perhaps this morning we can add another dimension, the music of our insides, to think of ourselves not only in color but also in music and sound. Our voices, our breathing, this feeling of harmonious vibrations which can have music also, visualizing ourselves coming in touch with music from the outside, the music of instruments, of other people's voices, of singing, of crying, of laughing . . . and sometimes, too, the music of agony and torment . . . And allowing ourselves to just be in touch also that there is music from the heavens. Some people call it the music of the spheres . . . and when you hear the music just before the meditations, I think some of it does have the music of the spheres.

Now remind yourself at this time that you carry your golden key that is always with you. And you have your wishing stick, your magic wand. Your golden key for continual discoveries, your magic wand for allowing yourself to put your wishes out . . . and to find ways, when you can, of bringing them into actualization.

Now again be in touch with your breathing . . . And at this moment now, perhaps you are even more aware that you have parts of you that are waiting to be discovered by you. And with your willing cooperation, that can happen . . .

And now very gently bring your awareness back to yourself in the chair, in this room, with all of us and with me, at this time in this morning which is called [day of the week] . . . And now find that place in yourself, that special place which opens you up to be able to focus and take in so you can taste . . . to allow yourself in a position of readiness to experiment. And again, allowing yourself to freely take whatever tastes good and fits for you at this point in time . . . And as you hear the music coming on, let yourself slowly come fully to the awareness here, and let any sounds or moves that you want to make come out. (Satir, 1983b, 149–53)

Appendix B

Exercise

With Whom Am I Having the Pleasure?

[Partners have been chosen; exercise begins.]

In the interest of being in a position where you can hear and see each other, I would like to have you each have your body directly across from your partner and each body in comfort.

The name of this exercise is, "With Whom Am I Having the Pleasure? With You or with My Picture of You? . . . " Before we can get started with some of these things we need to know how to clean out our ways of perceiving. All right. So there you are in front of each other.

And what I would like you to do now is close your eyes. Just close your eyes and get comfortable, I would like you, at this moment, to give yourself whatever messages you got from whatever you saw as you looked at your partner in front of you right now. Just be as judgmental as you want, it does not matter. Anything you want, just whatever comes to you. Magnificent . . . beautiful . . . All right. Now just pay attention to that. You know, like you were gathering something for a scrapbook.

Now let yourself into your breathing. At this moment, I would like you to think of your eyes as a camera. You are going to take a picture of your partner; your partner will be taking a picture of you. Open your eyes and take that picture.

So let your eyes gently close. Now you are going into the laboratory of your mind to see what is in that picture you took. And look at the picture you just took. Look at the picture and ask yourself what you see in that picture. While you are looking at that picture, ask yourself what you are feeling inside and what your body is doing, if anything, that you are aware of.

Then let your eyes open gently again, and this time as you look at the person, look for any ways in which they remind you of someone you have ever known before or heard about. Somebody in the funny paper, members of your family in the past, historical figures, figures from the stage—just look and get whatever little or big reminder you have of who your partner reminds you of.

And then let your eyes gently close. And if you have found someone that these people remind you of, let yourself know how you feel about that person that they remind you of . . . and as you are reminding yourself of this and getting into the feelings about that person, or thoughts, ask yourself how you are feeling now. And if your body is giving any messages, just pay attention.

Now this time, as you gently let your eyes open, look at what stands out most about your partner. Does their nose stand out most, their eyes, their hair, their hands, their sex, their age, their I don't know what. What stands out most?

And then let your eyes close. And fill in the picture of that which you picked up. Example, if you noticed glasses, and glasses mean to you that people who wear glasses hide behind them, put that together. If you notice a woman with a certain kind of haircut, and, for you, that means she is studious, put that in. What meaning do you attach—fill it in, your meaning to what you noticed. And, again, be in touch with what is happening in your body as this is going on. What are you feeling and thinking?

Now this time as you open your eyes, let yourself imagine what that other person in front of you has thought, is thinking, has felt, is feeling about you. No matter how torrid or how florid, let yourself have that imagination: what I think my partner is thinking, feeling, seeing, about me.

Then let your eyes close and ask yourself how you are feeling about what you told yourself. Are you scaring yourself to death? Are you making yourself feel juicy? What are you doing with what you told yourself? And, again be in touch with what is going on in your body as you allow yourself into your own dialogue with you.

And, this time, as you let your eyes gently open, let yourself remind you of anything you know about this person through gossip columns, the rumor clinic, if you happen to remember they got the Nobel Prize or suddenly came up with a million dollars—anything you know from a third party source. Anything from a third party source. And if there is something, then let yourself notice it. If there is not, then let it go by. Now ask yourself also if you have any past experience with this person anywhere—ten minutes ago, or yesterday. What past experience have you had? And then ask yourself how did you feel about that past experience then, and how do you feel about it now? Let your eyes close.

Now, at this point, your eyes are closed. You are literally stuffed with information about the other person. All of it, however, is of your own making. As you looked at the person, what did you see? How did you interpret it? Who do they remind you of? How do you feel about that? What did you notice and what conclusions did you put with it? What is your fantasy, imagination, about what that other person is thinking and feeling about you? What is your past experience, if any, and where are you with that now: If you were to leave at this moment, you would go away with what you have got in your head. That is all that you have got. Your approach to the person would be in terms of what you have. People are doing this every day and saying, "I know that person."

What I would like you to do right now is to give yourself permission to share with your partner all that you can or want to about what it was like for you. What you made of it when you looked at them and found out who they reminded you of. What you notice, what your fantasy was, what your third party information was, what your past experience might have been.

Now as I ask you to share, are there little things running through your head that say, "Ooh! Couldn't do that?!" Well, if that is there it is going to be used and may be abused. And maybe if you share it, new lights can come on. So I would like you to be in touch with what kind of barriers you might have or excitement you might have about sharing. Then allow yourself to start off the sharing with telling your partner how you feel about the sharing, and then share all you can or want to . . . [approximately seven-minute intervals].

So let your eyes open and let that happen. [End of first part of exercise.]

Discussion of Exercise

This piece is so fundamental to how we live, so fundamental, that I call it clearing the basis for the foundation of any relationship and of new possibilities for yourself.

When I spoke a little bit before, one of the things I have become aware of is that the basis upon which we make connections with people is some sense of similarity on some level. If it is positive we can go ahead and say, "Mmm!," and if it is negative we say, "Ah-ha—."

It is just marvelous, what happened was that you were focusing on some things that, for instance, we hardly ever focus on: "Oh, I am seeing this; what are they seeing?" Or "What are they seeing" and forget what I am seeing; so we go around half [aware by not asking the whole question] . . . That is what I mean by funny research. We ask and answer our own questions.

Won't it be great when we can all giggle at the fact, "Oh, I mistook you for somebody else!" You know, like people live together, husband and wife, for forty years and only discover each other after that. All this time, they have not been living with who they thought they were living with, they were only living with an image of who they thought they were. And the truth came and it is usually good . . .

One of the things I can underscore again with each pair that has been up here so far: we have these [things]; there is nothing wrong with what we have, but can we check it out? You see when I made the comment that at the end when I asked you to focus and I said [to the volunteers with whom I was demonstrating], "Now you go away," what you go away with is what you have got in your head, and if you do not check it out, you do not get any new information. Maybe one of the most important things I do when I work with families is to get them to get all the checking out done.

But there might be people in the world where if you did not know what you were doing—[for example,] you look at Gary and you say, "Ah, Gary is going to be creative." And then you give him something creative and he falls on his face and you say, "You know what, you betrayed me." That is how it goes.

Completing the Exercise

[Virginia began her customary centering process with which she began and ended each training day. The following is the morning session on Monday, completing this perceptual clearing exercise that she introduced on Friday. The centering exercise helps the trainees to return, emotionally and psychologically, to the process begun before the weekend.]

And as you close your beautiful eyes, be aware of how easily your eyelids responded to just your wish. And perhaps again to entertain the idea that maybe all the rest of our body can do the same thing . . . allow yourself, while centering with your breathing, keeping your body relaxed and yet alert, to again give yourself permission this morning to taste all that comes to you, to swallow only that which fits. And at this moment to bring together the resources that you have for that very important focus that allows you to bring things in for taste so you can see if you want to swallow.

So let your eyes gently open and, without talking, will you find those partners that you had on Friday. You had an experience on Friday where I led you through some things rather rapidly that were related to the kind of trap that we can get into as we come to another person, [making that very important translation] . . . from strangeness into familiarity and doing it in a way that makes it possible for us to really reach the other person and for them to reach us. So this morning, the people that you paired with last time, many of them do not seem like such strangers to you this morning.

So what I would like all of you to do is just to close your eyes and see if you can go back in your mind to when you first sat down with these so-called strangers, before you ever had any talk with them or shared this kind of space. And see if you can remember back to what that picture was. And then advance yourself a little further to where you were at the end of the guided focus I did for you, before you started to talk. And then carry it to where it was when we left each other—in your mind.

And then very gently let your eyes open, and now look at the person in front of you with wherever you are with them and with yourself right now. Just look, taking another camera picture of them now.

And then let your eyes gently close again. And just be aware of this new picture. Is this significantly different or a little different from what the very first picture was that you took of them, which might now seem very long ago. And maybe when you sat down with these people before, having the picture you had then, now having the picture you have now—just let yourself be in touch with any curiosity, things left over from the last time that did not get finished, any new puzzles, as curiosities, as things you want to say, which might in the end raise even more questions and more possibilities. So give yourself permission to take the next five minutes to see now, what are the new possibilities, what are the new questions, what are the curiosities, what are the pieces that were not finished last time. And let that happen and I will come back to you in five minutes.

[Five-minute time lapse—partners share.]

I would like you, at this moment, to just be in touch with what your body is feeling like. Just what it is feeling like. And see if you can hear any messages, from your body, of excitement, of interest, or of questions or whatever. If I stopped you in the middle of something, just be in touch with what your body is doing, going down into your feet and toes if you need to. You are a living organism and your body is constantly responding. And because of all the ways in which most of us were brought up, we only thought of our body as something to keep clean and hidden. But can you hear whatever messages there are right now, whatever they are? Getting in touch with the living messages of you at this moment. And if there are any places of tension go and look and see what the message might be. [Does] it have a little bit in it of, "I am not quite sure what is going on." Is it some little threat, is it some need for some nourishment and letting go, what is it?

And then let yourself be in touch with what you are aware of feeling at this moment about yourself. Your body will be used as the material at which you look, and then how you interpret that in relation to how you are feeling about you. Your loveability, your value for yourself—and then let this go to a further place. It is like our body, being a living organism, is always responding.

Responding to what it was this person reminded you of—I would like you to open your eyes and look at that person now and see if that image of the other person—where that is in relation to the other person right now, to the person in front of you. *I believe we are getting a little closer to who really is in front of you, and who you really are.*

And just let your eyes close again, and for those of you who did find that your partner reminded you of somebody else, could you go back to that place and in a moment, share that again openly about where it was and where it is right now. So let us take about three minutes to do that.

And again, in touch with your breathing, take a little stroll inside you and ask your body, listen to what it is saying at this moment. Let yourself be aware of your feelings and what you are thinking right now. And gently open your eyes . . .

With whom am I having the pleasure, with you or my picture of you? (Satir in Brothers, 1995, 2–7)

REFERENCES

Baldwin, DeWitt C. 1992, March, and 1996, January. Interviews with author.

Bateson, Gregory. 1979. *Mind and Nature.* New York: E. P. Dutton.

Bertalanffy, Ludwig von. 1971. General Systems Theory. *General Systems.* London: Allen Lane.

Bohm, David and David F. Peat. 1987. *Science, Order, and Creativity.* Second edition. New York: Routledge.

Bohm, David. 1989a. Transcription. Meeting. Ojai, California, November 6, 1989.

Bohm, David. 1989b. Transcription. Meeting with Oak Grove Students, Ojai, CA, November 14, 1989.

Bohm, David. 1994. *Thought as a System.* New York: Routledge.

Bohm, David. 1996. *On Dialogue.* New York: Routledge.

Bohm, David and David Peat. 2000. *Science, Order, and Creativity.* Second edition. New York: Routledge.

Briggs, John. 1988. *Fire in the Crucible.* New York: St. Martin's Press.

Brothers, Barbara Jo. 1983. "Virginia Satir: Past to Present." *Voices: The Art and Science of Psychotherapy* 18 (4): 48–56.

Brothers, Barbara Jo. 1985. "Meme-O's." News and Views. *Voices: The Art and Science of Psychotherapy* 21(1): 93–94.

Brothers, Barbara Jo. 1987a. "'Independence' *Avoids* Intimacy: Avoidance of Intimacy Kills." *Voices: The Art and Science of Psychotherapy* 23(1): 10–23.

Brothers, Barbara Jo. 1987b. "Bless Me, Father, For I Have Sinned or: Wake Me Mother, When You Rise . . ." *Voices: The Art and Science of Psychotherapy* 23(3): 12–19.

Brothers, Barbara Jo. 1989a. "Remorse and Regeneration." In *Psychotherapy and the Remorseful Patient*, edited by E. Mark Stern, 47–62. Binghamton, NY: Haworth Press.

Brothers, Barbara Jo. 1989b. "The Cancer Patient Is the Self-Contained Patient." In *The Self-Contained Patient*, edited by E. Mark Stern, 227–241. Binghamton, NY: Haworth Press.

Brothers, Barbara Jo. 1989c. "Virginia Satir and Lao Tzu: New Look at Ancient Wisdom." *Voices: The Art and Science of Psychotherapy* 25(1&2): 105–113.

Brothers, Barbara Jo. 1990a. "Self-Esteem and Congruent Communication: Virginia Satir's Road to Integration." *Advanced Development: A Journal on Adult Giftedness* 2(January): 23–34.

Brothers, Barbara Jo. 1990b. "Healthy Coupling . . . What Makes It?" *Journal of Couples Therapy*, Volume 1 (1): 7–19.

Brothers, Barbara Jo. 1990c. "Intimacy and Autonomy." In *Intimate Autonomy: Autonomous Intimacy*, edited by Barbara Jo Brothers, 1-8. Binghamton, NY: Hawthorn Press.

Brothers, Barbara Jo. 1991a. "Methods for Connectedness: Virginia Satir's Contribution to the Process of Human Communication." In *Virginia Satir: Foundational Ideas*, edited by Barbara Jo Brothers, 11–20. Binghamton, NY: Haworth Press.

Brothers, Barbara Jo. 1991b. "Ask Not for Whom the Siren Wails." In *Coupling—What Makes Permanence?* edited by Barbara Jo Brothers, 11-16. Binghamton, NY: Haworth Press.

Brothers, Barbara Jo. 1992a. "Virginia Satir's Spirituality." In *Spirituality and Couples: Heart and Soul in the Therapy Process*, edited by Barbara Jo Brothers, 9–18. Binghamton, NY: Haworth Press.

Brothers, Barbara Jo. 1992b. "Hope for Healing in Russia: Reflections and Epilogue." In *Couples Therapy, Multiple Perspectives: In Search of Universal Threads*, edited by Barbara Jo Brothers, 145–151. Binghamton, NY: Haworth Press.

Brothers, Barbara Jo. 1994. "From Virginia Satir: Beyond the Threat/ Reward Model; Comment." In *Surpassing Threats and Rewards*, edited by Barbara Jo Brothers, 9–14. Binghamton, NY: Haworth Press.

Brothers, Barbara Jo. 1995. "Countertransference: The Satir Model." In *Couples and Countertransference*, edited by Barbara Jo Brothers, 9–12. Binghamton, NY: Haworth Press.

Brothers, Barbara Jo. 1996a. "Styles of Thinking: Comment on Virginia Satir's 'Ways of Viewing the World.'" In *Couples and Change*, edited by Barbara Jo Brothers, 9–11. Binghamton, NY: Haworth Press.

Brothers, Barbara Jo. 1996b. *Couples and the Tao of Congruence*. Binghamton, NY: Haworth Press.

Brothers, Barbara Jo. 1996c. "Responses to Dr. Waller." In *Couples and the Tao of Congruence*, edited by Barbara Jo Brothers, 123–125. Binghamton, NY: Haworth Press.

Brothers, Barbara Jo. 1996d. "Editor's Comment on 'The Incongruity of Congruence': Congruence as a Viable Model for Intimacy." In *Couples and the Tao of Congruence*, edited by Barbara Jo Brothers, 127–132. Binghamton, NY: Haworth Press.

Brothers, Barbara Jo. 1999. "'We Are Only Activators'—Virginia Satir and the Mystery of Human Life; a Reflection." In *Couples and Pregnancy: Welcome, Unwelcome, and In-Between*, edited by Barbara Jo Brothers, 1–5. Binghamton, NY: Haworth Press.

Brothers, Barbara Jo. 2000. "Virginia Satir." In *Virginia Satir: Her Life and Circle of Influence*, edited by Melvin M. Suhd, Laura Dodson, and Maria Gomori, 1–101. Mountain View, CA: Science and Behavior Books.

Brothers, Robert Lee. 1998. "Sunday . . . the Bells Say." In *Prairie Laureate: Collected Poems of Robert Lee Brothers*, edited by Susan Ford Wiltshire. Austin, TX: Eakin Press.

Bula, Judy. 1996. Commentary on "The Incongruity of Congruence." In *Couples and the Tao of Congruence*, edited by Barbara Jo Brothers, 133–141. Binghamton, NY: Haworth Press.

Bynner, Witter. (Trans.). 1944. *The Way of Life According to Lao Tzu*. New York: Capricorn.

Capra, Fritjof. 1983. *The Tao of Physics*. Boulder, CO: Shambhala Publications.

Capra, Fritjof. 1989. *Uncommon Wisdom*. New York: Bantam Books.

Chen, Lin Kuo. 1969. *Truth and Nature*. Hong Kong: Wan Ku Shu Ten.

Dodson, Laura Sue. 2000. "Dreams Unfold a Life." In *Virginia Satir: Her Life and Circle of Influence*, edited by Melvin M. Suhd, Laura Dodson, and Maria Gomori, 102–159. Mountain View, CA: Science and Behavior Books.

Donne, John. 1624. "Meditation XVII." In *Devotions Upon Emergent Occasions*, reprinted in *The Works of John Donne*, vol III. Henry Alford ed., London: John W. Parker, 1839. 574–5.

Duhl, Bunny S. et al. 1994. *Training the Trainer: Process Manual for Successfully Leading Experiential/Cognitive Workshops*. Available from: The Virginia Satir Global Network, 7301 Indian Rock Road, Wendell, North Carolina 27591.

Duhl, Bunny. 1988, October 27. Virginia Satir Memorial Talk. Presented at the 46th Annual Conference of the American Association of Marriage and Family Therapists in New Orleans, LA. Slightly modified version also published in the *Journal of Marital and Family Therapy* 15(2): 109–110.

Eckhart, Meister. 1986. *Meister Eckhart: Teacher and Preacher*, edited by Bernard McGinn in collaboration with Frank Tobin and Elvira Borgstadt, 270. Translated from DW1, Sermon 12, German text. New York, Mahwah, Toronto: Paulist Press.

Eisler, Rianne. 1987. *The Chalice and the Blade*. San Francisco, CA: Harper and Row.

Englander-Golden, Paul and Virginia Satir. 1990. *Say it Straight*. Palo Alto, CA: Science and Behavior Books.

Engelhardt, H. Tristram. 1996. *The Foundations of Bioethics*, Second Edition. New York: Oxford University Press.

Erickson, Eric. 1969. *Gandhi's Truth*. New York: Norton.

Fromm, Erich. 1976. *To Have or To Be*. New York: Harper & Row.

Fromm, Erich. 1973. *Anatomy of Human Destructiveness*. New York: Holt, Rinehart and Winston.

Frost, Robert. 1958. "The Road Not Taken." In *Immortal Poems*, edited by Oscar Williams, 504. New York: Pocket Books.

Gandhi, Mahatma. 1957. *Gandhi: An Autobiography. The Story of My Experiments with Truth*. Boston: Beacon Paperback Edition.

Goulding, Mary and Robert Goulding. 1979. *Changing Lives Through Redecision Therapy*. New York: Brunner/Mazel.

Harker, Janet E. 1954. "Diurnal Rhythms in *Periplaneta americana* L." *Nature* 173: 689.

Harker, Janet E. 1956. "Factors Controlling the Diurnal Rhythms of Activity in *Periplaneta americana* L." *Journal of Experimental Biology* 33: 224.

Harker, Janet E. 1958. "Diurnal Rhythms in the Animal Kingdom." *Biological Reviews* 33: 1.

House, James S., K. R. Landis, and Debra Umberson. 1988, July 29. "Social Relationships and Health." *Science*: 540–545.

Houston, Jean. 1987. *The Search for the Beloved*. Los Angeles, CA: Jeremy P. Tarcher.

Houston, Jean. 1990, February. "The Mystery of Essence." Lecture. Mystery School—First Weekend Session. Greenkill Conference Center, Huguenot, NY.

Houston, Jean. 1998, December 12. "The Art of Mysticism." Lecture. Mystery School—Last Weekend Session. Greenkill Conference Center, Huguenot, NY.

Jackson, Don D. 1968. *Communication, Family, and Marriage*, Volume I. Palo Alto, CA: Science and Behavior Books.

Jung, Carl G. 1965. *Memories, Dreams, and Reflections*. New York: Vintage Books.

Korzybski, Alfred. 1933. *Science and Sanity*. Lancaster, PA: The Science Press Printing Co.

Kramer, Sheldon. 1995. *Transforming the Inner and Outer Family: Humanistic and Spiritual Approaches to Mind-Body Systems Therapy*. Binghamton, NY: Haworth Press.

Kuhn, Thomas S. 1962. *The Structure of Scientific Revolutions*. Third edition. Chicago: University of Chicago Press.

Laign, Jeffrey. 1988. "Healing Human Spirits, Creating Joy in Living. Interview with Virginia Satir." *Focus on Chemically Dependent Families* 11(Oct./Nov.): 20–21, 28–32.

Levenson, Frederick. 1985. *The Causes and Prevention of Cancer*. New York: Stein & Day.

Levenson, Frederick. 1986. Presentation at American Academy of Psychotherapists Annual Institute and Conference, Atlanta, GA, October 22–26, 1986.

Levenson, Frederick. 1987. *The Anti-Cancer Marriage*. New York: Stein & Day.

Lynch, James. 1977. *The Broken Heart*. New York: Basic Books.

Lynch, James. 1985. *The Language of the Heart*. New York: Basic Books.

MacMillan, Margaret. 2001. *Paris 1919*. New York: Random House.

Mitchell, Stephen. 1988. *Tao Te Ching*. New York: Harper & Row.

Needleman, Jacob. 2002. *The American Soul*. New York: Jeremy P. Tarcher/Putnam.

Nerin, William. 1986. *Long Day's Journey into Light*. New York: W. W. Norton.

Perls, Frederick (Fritz). 1969. *In and Out of the Garbage Pail*. Lafayette, CA: The Real People Press.

Pittman, Frank. 1988. "Remembering Virginia Satir." *The Family Networker* 13(1): 34–35.

Roberts, Robert E. 2003. *My Soul Said to Me*. Deerfield, FL: Health Communications.

Rogers, Everett M. 1988. "Diffusion of the Idea of Beyond War." In *Breakthrough: Emerging New Thinking*, edited by Anatoly Gromyko, Martin Hellman, Craig Barnes, and Alexander Nikitin, 240–248. New York: Walker and Company.

Rossi, Ernest L. 1986. *The Psychobiology of Mind-Body Healing: New Concepts of Therapeutic Hypnosis*. New York: W. W. Norton.

Satir, Virginia. 1967a. *Conjoint Family Therapy*. (Published in 1983 in its third edition; first edition published in 1964.) Palo Alto, CA: Science and Behavior Books.

Satir, Virginia. 1967b. Speaker. Inservice training at Southeast Louisiana Hospital. Virginia Satir Collection. HPA Mss 45. Department of Special Collections, Davidson Library, University of California, Santa Barbara. Box 41:16.

Satir, Virginia. 1968. Presentation at the Annual Conference, Southern Regional Institute. Biloxi, MS, July 12.

Satir, Virginia. 1971. Presentation at monthlong seminar on family therapy. Glenwood Springs, CO.

Satir, Virginia. 1972a. Presentation at a seminar on Aruba, March 12–24, 1972. (Cassette recordings transcript.) Falls Church, VA: Lori Gordon, PAIRS Foundation, 3705 South George Mason Drive, #C35; 22041.

Satir, Virginia. 1972b. *Peoplemaking.* Palo Alto, CA: Science and Behavior Books.

Satir, Virginia. 1975. "You as Change Agent," 37–62; "Intervention for Congruence," 79–104; "Problems and Pitfalls in Working with Families: An Interview with Virginia Satir," 133–160; "A Simulated Family Interview," 163–218. In *Helping Families to Change,"* edited by Virginia Satir, James Stachowiak, and Harvey A. Taschman. New York: Jason Aronson, Inc.

Satir, Virginia, Richard Bandler, and John Grinder. 1976a. *Changing with Families.* Palo Alto, CA: Science and Behavior Books.

Satir, Virginia. 1976. Letter sent October 21, 1976, to fifty selected colleagues and trainees. Virginia Satir Collection. HPA Mss 45. Department of Special Collections, Davidson Library, University of California, Santa Barbara.

Satir, Virginia. 1977a. Personal Notes. Virginia Satir Collection. HPA Mss 45. Department of Special Collections, Davidson Library, University of California, Santa Barbara.

Satir, Virginia. 1977b. Letter. Virginia Satir Collection. HPA Mss 45. Department of Special Collections, Davidson Library, University of California, Santa Barbara. Box 58:9, Box 59:10.

Satir, Virginia. 1977c, January. Draft. Letter to Sponsors. University for Being More Human. Virginia Satir Collection. HPA Mss 45. Department of Special Collections, Davidson Library, University of California, Santa Barbara. Box 58:9, Box 59:10.

Satir, Virginia. 1977d. *What's in the Pot? International Human Learning Resources Network Newsletter 1* (Spring): 2.

Satir, Virginia. 1981a, August. Transcription of Lecture presented at Process Community I, Crested Butte, CO. Virginia Satir Collection. HPA Mss 45. Department of Special Collections, Davidson Library, University of California, Santa Barbara. Box 8:9.

Satir, Virginia. 1981b. Unpublished personal notes. Virginia Satir Collection. HPA Mss 45. Department of Special Collections, Davidson Library, University of California, Santa Barbara. Box 2:4, Box 3:2, Box 3:5.

Satir, Virginia. Early 1980s. Third Birth Notes. Volume I-III. Unpublished personal notes. Virginia Satir Collection. HPA Mss 45. Department of Special Collections, Davidson Library, University of California, Santa Barbara. Box 2:3.

Satir, Virginia. 1982, August. Transcription of lecture presented at Process Community II, Crested Butte, CO. Virginia Satir Collection. HPA Mss 45. Department of Special Collections, Davidson Library, University of California, Santa Barbara. Box 7:9.

Satir, Virginia. 1983a. Third Birth Notes. Volume I. Unpublished personal notes. Virginia Satir Collection. HPA Mss 45. Department of Special Collections, Davidson Library, University of California, Santa Barbara. Box 2:10–12.

Satir, Virginia. 1983b. *Virginia Satir Verbatim 1984*. Transcription of Avanta Process Community III. August 1983. Available from John Banmen, Delta Psychological Associates, Inc. 11213 Canyon Crescent, North Delta, British Columbia, Canada V4E 2R6.

Satir, Virginia. 1984. Conversation with author. January 16, 1984.

Satir, Virginia. 1985. An Interview with Virginia Satir by Sheldon Starr, PhD. Virginia Satir Collection. HPA Mss 45. Department of Special Collections, Davidson Library, University of California, Santa Barbara. Box 6:14.

Satir, Virginia. 1986a. Speaker. Avanta Process Community VI, Module I. August 1986. [Cassette recordings no. 1, 3, 5, 12 & 18]. Crested

Butte, CO: Blue Moon Cassettes. Virginia Satir Collection. HPA Mss 45. Department of Special Collections, Davidson Library, University of California, Santa Barbara.

Satir, Virginia. 1986b. "A Partial Portrait of a Family Therapist in Process." In *Evolving Models for Family Change*, edited by Herman Charles Fishman and Bernice L. Rosman, 278–293. New York: Guilford Press.

Satir, Virginia. 1986c. Presentation at American Academy of Psychotherapists Annual Institute and Conference, Atlanta, GA, October 22–26, 1986.

Satir, Virginia. 1986d. Speaker. "Of Rocks and Flowers." [Video cassette recording VT 104]. Kansas City, MO: Golden Triad Films, Inc.

Satir, Virginia. Circa 1986. Your Third Birth. Unpublished manuscript. Virginia Satir Collection. HPA Mss 45. Department of Special Collections, Davidson Library, University of California, Santa Barbara.

Satir, Virginia. 1987a. Speaker. Avanta Process Community VII, Module I. August 1987. [Cassette recordings no. 1-6]. Crested Butte, CO. Blue Moon Cassettes. Virginia Satir Collection. HPA Mss 45. Department of Special Collections, Davidson Library, University of California, Santa Barbara.

Satir, Virginia. 1987b. "The Therapist Story." In *The Use of Self in Therapy*, edited by Virginia Satir and Michele Baldwin, 24–25. Binghamton, NY: Haworth Press.

Satir, Virginia. 1987c. "Going Behind the Obvious: The Psychotherapeutic Journey." In *The Evolution of Psychotherapy*, edited by Jeffrey Zeig, 68. New York: Brunner/Mazel.

Satir, Virginia. 1987d, October 1987. Speaker. [Videotape]. International Human Learning Resources Network. Hacienda Vista Hermosa, Cuernavaca, Mexico. (Available from Lori Gordon, 3705 George Mason Dr. #C35, Falls Church, VA 22041).

Satir, Virginia. 1988a. *The New Peoplemaking*. Palo Alto, CA: Science and Behavior Books.

Satir, Virginia. 1988b, August 9, 1988. Conversation with author.

Satir, Virginia. 1989. "Benediction: Virginia Satir"; Scranton, Pennsylvania, November 7, 1987. *What's in the Pot? International Human Learning Resources Network Newsletter*. (Available from IHLRN Newsletter, c/o M.A. Bjarkman, 4119 Inglewood Boulevard, Los Angeles, California 90066).

Satir, Virginia, John Banmen, Jane Gerber, and Maria Gomori. 1991. *The Satir Model: Family Therapy and Beyond*. Palo Alto, CA: Science and Behavior Books.

Satir, Virginia. 1994. "From Virginia Satir: Beyond the Threat and Reward Model." In *Surpassing Threats and Rewards*, edited by Barbara Jo Brothers, 1–7. Binghamton, NY: Haworth Press.

Satir, Virginia. 1995a. "Ways of Viewing the World: Beyond the Dominance and Submission Model." In *Power and Partnering*, edited by Barbara Jo Brothers, 1–14. Binghamton, NY: Haworth Press.

Satir, Virginia. 1995b. "'With Whom Am I Having the Pleasure?'" In *Couples and Countertransference*, edited by Barbara Jo Brothers, 1–7. Binghamton, NY: Haworth Press.

Satir, Virginia 1996a. "Ways of Viewing the World; Explanation of Events and Attitude Toward Change." In *Couples and Change*, edited by Barbara Jo Brothers, 1–7. Binghamton, NY: Haworth Press.

Satir, Virginia. 1996b. "Congruent Communication Builds Bridges." In *Couples: Building Bridges*, edited by Barbara Jo Brothers, 1–10. Binghamton, NY: Haworth Press.

Satir, Virginia. 1997. "Ways of Viewing the World: Ways of Putting Things Together to Form the Big Picture: A View of Resistance as a Blessing." In *When One Partner Is Willing and the Other Is Not*, edited by Barbara Jo Brothers, 1–7. Binghamton, NY: Haworth Press.

Satir, Virginia. 1998a "Concepts of Communication—Ways of Perceiving the World: Definition of a Relationship." In *Couples: A Medley of Models*, edited by Barbara Jo Brothers, 1–9. Binghamton, NY: Haworth Press.

Satir, Virginia. 1998b. "Ways of Viewing the World . . . Living Our Lives by Somebody Else's Pattern." In *Couples, Trauma, and Catastrophes*, edited by Barbara Jo Brothers, 1–4. Binghamton, NY: Haworth Press.

Satir, Virginia. 1999. "From Virginia Satir: Models of Perceiving the World—Attitude Toward Change." In *Couples and Managed Care*, edited by Barbara Jo Brothers, 1–5. Binghamton, NY: Haworth Press.

Satir, Virginia. 2000. "Hope, Wholeness, and Helping the Flat to Grow Round." In *Couples Connecting: Prerequisites of Intimacy*, edited by Barbara Jo Brothers, 5–9. Binghamton, NY: Haworth Press.

Satir, Virginia. 2001. "Centered Selves Connecting with Each Other: Elements in Authentic Therapeutic Contact." In *Couples, Intimacy Issues, and Addiction*, edited by Barbara Jo Brothers, 5–16. Binghamton, NY: Haworth Press.

Satir, Virginia and Michele Baldwin. 1983. *Satir Step by Step*. Palo Alto, CA: Science and Behavior Books.

Schwab, Johanna, Michele Baldwin, Jane Gerber, Maria Gomori, and Virginia Satir. 1989. *The Satir Approach to Communication*. Palo Alto, CA: Science and Behavior Books.

Selye, Hans. 1956. *The Stress of Life*. New York: McGraw Hill Books.

Sheldrake, Rupert. 1988. *The Presence of the Past*. New York: Vintage Books.

Smith, Hedrick. 1990. *The New Russians*. New York: Random House.

Spitzer, Robert S. 1975. *Tidings of Comfort and Joy*. Palo Alto, CA: Science and Behavior Books.

Starr, Sheldon. 1991. "An Interview with Virginia Satir." In *Coupling . . . What Makes Permanence?* edited by Barbara Jo Brothers, 5–9. Binghamton, NY: Haworth Press.

Starr, Sheldon. 1992a. "Power Issues in Therapists: An Interview with Virginia Satir." In *Equal Partnering: A Feminine Perspective*, edited by Barbara Jo Brothers, 93–96, Binghamton, NY: Haworth Press.

Starr, Sheldon. 1992b. "Prevention: Changing our Whole Culture—An Interview with Virginia Satir." In *Peace, War, and Mental Health: Couples Therapists Look at the Dynamics*, edited by Barbara Jo Brothers, 7–12. Binghamton, NY: Haworth Press.

Starr, Sheldon. 1992c. "Heart and Soul and Communication: An Interview with Virginia Satir." In *Spirituality and Couples*, edited by Barbara Jo Brothers, 1–8. Binghamton, NY: Haworth Press.

Starr, Sheldon. 1992d. "'All Good Therapy Has the Same Ingredients': An Interview with Virginia Satir, Part IV." In *Couples Therapy, Multiple Perspectives: In Search of Universal Threads*, edited by Barbara Jo Brothers, 7–14. Binghamton, NY: Haworth Press.

Tarnas, Richard. 1991. *The Passion of the Western Mind: Understanding the Ideas that Have Shaped Our World View*. New York: Ballentine Books.

Teilhard de Chardin, Pierre. 1963. *Activation of Energy*. St. James Place, London: Collins.

Teilhard de Chardin, Pierre. 1965. *The Phenomenon of Man*. New York: Harper & Row. (originally published in French as *Le Phenomene Humain*, Copyright 1955 by Editions du Seuil, Paris).

Vygotsky, Lev. 1986. Internet (1) *Thought and Language*. Cambridge, Massachusetts: The MIT Press.

Vygotsky, Lev. 1962. Internet (2) "Chapter 1, The Problem and the Approach." *Thinking and Speaking*.

Waller, Margaret. 1996. "The Incongruity of Congruence." In *Couples and the Tao of Congruence*, edited by Barbara Jo Brothers, 111–121. Binghamton, NY: Haworth Press.

Walters, James W. 1997. *What Is a Person?* Urbana: University of Illinois Press.

Watson, Lyall. 1973. *Supernature*. Garden City, NY: Anchor Press/ Doubleday.

White, John. (1972). *Highest States of Consciousness*. New York: Doubleday.

Wilhelm, Richard. (Trans.). 1985. *Tao Te Ching; The Book of Meaning and Life*. New York: Arkana. (Original work published 1925).

Wolfson, Richard. 2000. "Wave or Particle." *Einstein's Relativity and the Quantum Revolution: Modern Physics for Non-Scientists, Part II*, Audiotape Lecture 18. Course #152. Middlebury College, VT. Chantilly, VA: The Teaching Company, 4151 Lafayette Center Drive, Suite 100.

Zukav, Gary. 1979. *The Dancing Wu Li Masters*. New York: Bantam Books.

INDEX

stress ballet, 108, 113, 187. *See also*
    being whole/being real
    transforming, 185–188
stress of emotional nature, 171, 173
super-reasonable, 191. *See also* selves,
    full and centered
    behavior, 62, 72
    being, 106–107, 114–117
    blaming to, 109–110
    intrapersonal response, 126
    person, 116
    renovated, 194
    response, 242, 253
support, need for, 174–177
symbols, humans response to,
    229–230
symptomatology, 201–202
systems theory, 102. *See also*
    Bertalanffy's systems theory

Tarnas, Richard, 20
technique, 49
Teilhard de Chardin, Pierre, 17, 22, 214
theory of cancer, 164–165
theory of emotional factors, 167
therapist's personhood, involvement
    of, 77
therapist's use of self, 48, 76, 138
third birth, 78–79. *See also*
    personhood
third energy, 12, 33, 208, 299
    centering, 49
    centering exercises, 37–39
    communication sequence, 51–52
    connecting two persons, 37
    demonstrating essence meeting
        essence, 48–49
    examination of connecting process,
        41–47

generating, 39–41
mutual understanding, 36
preparing to connect, 37–39
principles in connecting, 48
real communication as learnable
    skill, 50–51
therapist's use of self, 48, 76, 138
truth, 52
"vehicle" vs. "technique", 49
Third Reich, rise of, 125
threat/reward model, 255–257, 269.
    See also seed model; shift toward
    parity over hierarchy
beyond, 255–257
congruence, 268
dominance/submission
    behavior, 258
hierarchy within threat model, 256
Holocaust, 260
impacts of, 22, 261
vs. seed model, 199
United States' invasion of
    Iraq, 269
thwarted growth process, 8–9
touch, 134–135
transformations, 189
transgressions, 68
transmission through nonverbal
    behavior, 44–45
triad exercises, 150
true lover of self, 29
true partnering, 27, 30–31
truth, 52, 211. *See also* congruence;
    third energy
and people, 219–220
pervasive, 212
quest for, 217
and use of language, 221–234
and wholeness, 211–216

two-valued 'either-or' type of
orientation, 224–225. *See also*
congruence

unconscious, 24
understanding, mutual, 36
understanding nonverbal
message, 213
uniqueness, celebrating, 132
permission and clearing the
mind, 133
Universal Human Resources, 80
universal personal resources, 142
University for Being More Fully
Human, 197–198, 244
unwittingness, 124
use of self, 48, 76, 138
as change agent, 138
use of senses, 246–247. *See also*
congruent communication
components
freedom for, 276, 290
use of terms, 248

"vehicle" vs. "technique", 49
verbal splittings, 229
Virginia Satir Global Network. *See*
Avanta
Virginia's model, 275–278
vulnerability, feeling of, 111

wars, 116, 120
war vs. peace, 256–257, 289. *See
also* shift toward parity over
hierarchy

what is, 5–6, 8, 30, 101, 122, 280–281
whole culture, changing, 266–268
wholeness, 103, 128, 185, 196–202,
211, 263. *See also* being whole/
being real; congruence
bad and good, 199–201
dream of, 196–198
rationale for seed model, 201
symptomatology, 201–202
threat/reward model vs. Seed
model, 199
truth and, 211–216
University for Being More Fully
Human, 197–198, 244
"wholing", 64, 157, 197, 206
With Whom Am I Having the
Pleasure?, 247, 303
completing the exercise, 307–310
discussion of exercise, 306–307
steps, 303–306
women therapists, 27
work
alignment with living force, 5
multidimensional, 11
simplicity in, 4
working habit, 3–4
writing style and intended
audience, 12